THINK LIKE A MONK

TRAIN YOUR MIND for PEACE and PURPOSE EVERY DAY

JAY SHETTY

SIMON & SCHUSTER

NEW YORK LONDON TORONTO SYDNEY NEW DELHI

Simon & Schuster, Inc.
1230 Avenue of the Americas
New York, NY 10020

First Simon & Schuster hardcover edition April 2020

Interior design by Ruth Lee-Mui

Manufactured in the United States of America

15 17 19 20 18 16 14

Library of Congress Cataloging-in-Publication Data

Names: Shetty, Jay, author.
Title: Think like a monk : train your mind for peace and purpose every day / Jay Shetty.
Description: New York : Simon & Schuster, [2020] | Includes index. |
Summary: "Jay Shetty, social media superstar and host of the #1 podcast On Purpose, distills the timeless wisdom he learned as a monk into practical steps anyone can take every day to live a less anxious, more meaningful life"—Provided by publisher.
Identifiers: LCCN 2020000011 (print) | LCCN 2020000012 (ebook) |
ISBN 9781982134488 (hardcover) |ISBN 9781982149819 (paperback) |
ISBN 9781982134501 (ebook)
Subjects: LCSH: Self-realization. | Meaning (Psychology) | Conduct of life. |
Hindu monastic and religious life.
Classification: LCC BF637.S4 S526 2020 (print) | LCC BF637.S4 (ebook) |
DDC 158.1—dc23 LC record available at https://lccn.loc.gov/2020000011
LC ebook record available at https://lccn.loc.gov/2020000012

ISBN 978-1-9821-3448-8
ISBN 978-1-9821-3450-1 (ebook)

For my wife,
who is more monk
than I will ever be

Contents

PART TWO
GROW

PART THREE
GIVE

Introduction

If you want a new idea, read an old book.
—attributed to Ivan Pavlov (among others)

When I was eighteen years old, in my first year of college, at Cass Business School in London, one of my friends asked me to go with him to hear a monk give a talk.

I resisted. "Why would I want to go hear some monk?"

I often went to see CEOs, celebrities, and other successful people lecture on campus, but I had zero interest in a monk. I preferred to hear speakers who'd actually *accomplished* things in life.

My friend persisted, and finally I said, "As long as we go to a bar afterward, I'm in." "Falling in love" is an expression used almost exclusively to describe romantic relationships. But that night, as I listened to the monk talk about his experience, I fell in love. The figure on stage was a thirty-something Indian man. His head was shaved and he wore a saffron robe. He was intelligent, eloquent, and charismatic. He spoke about the principle of "selfless sacrifice." When he said that we should plant trees under whose shade we did not plan to sit, I felt an unfamiliar thrill run through my body.

I was especially impressed when I found out that he'd been a student at IIT Bombay, which is the MIT of India and, like MIT, nearly impossible to get into. He'd traded that opportunity to become a monk, walking away from everything that my friends and I were chasing. Either he was crazy or he was onto something.

My whole life I'd been fascinated by people who'd gone from nothing to something—rags-to-riches stories. Now, for the first time, I was in the presence of someone who'd deliberately done the opposite. He'd given up the life the world had told me we should *all* want. But instead of being an embittered failure, he appeared joyous, confident, and at peace. In fact, he seemed happier than anyone I'd ever met. At the age of eighteen, I had encountered a lot of people who were rich. I'd listened to a lot of people who were famous, strong, good-looking, or all three. But I don't think I'd met anyone who was truly happy.

Afterward, I pushed my way through the crowds to tell him how amazing he was, and how much he'd inspired me. "How can I spend more time with you?" I heard myself asking. I felt the urge to be around people who had the values I wanted, not the things I wanted.

The monk told me that he was traveling and speaking in the UK all that week, and I was welcome to come to the rest of his events. And so I did.

My first impression of the monk, whose name was Gauranga Das, was that he was doing something right, and later I would discover that science backs that up. In 2002, a Tibetan monk named Yongey Mingyur Rinpoche traveled from an area just outside Kathmandu, Nepal, to the University of Wisconsin–Madison so that researchers could watch his brain activity while he meditated. The scientists covered the monk's head with a shower cap–like device (an EEG) that had more than 250 tiny wires sticking out of it, each with a sensor that a lab tech attached to his scalp. At the time of the study, the monk had accumulated sixty-two thousand hours of lifetime meditation practice.

As a team of scientists, some of them seasoned meditators themselves, watched from a control room, the monk began the meditation protocol the researchers had designed—alternating between one minute of meditating on compassion and a thirty-second rest period. He quickly cycled through this pattern four times in a row, cued by a translator. The researchers watched in awe; at almost the exact moment the monk began his meditation, the EEG registered a sudden and massive spike in activity. The scientists assumed that with such a large, quick bump, the monk must have changed positions or otherwise moved, yet to the observing eye, he remained perfectly still.

What was remarkable was not just the consistency of the monk's brain activity—turning "off" and "on" repeatedly from activity to rest period—but also the fact that he needed no "warm-up" period. If you're a meditator, or have at least tried to calm your brain, you know that typically it takes some time to quiet the parade of distracting thoughts that marches through your mind. Rinpoche seemed to need no such transition period. Indeed, he seemed to be able to come in and out of a powerful meditative state as easily as flipping a switch. More than ten years after these initial studies, scans of the forty-one-year-old monk's brain showed fewer signs of aging than his peers'. The researchers said he had the brain of someone ten years younger.

Researchers who scanned Buddhist monk Matthieu Ricard's brain subsequently labeled him "the World's Happiest Man" after they found the highest level of gamma waves—those associated with attention, memory, learning, and happiness—*ever recorded by science*. One monk who's off the charts may seem like an anomaly, but Ricard isn't alone. Twenty-one other monks who had their brains scanned during a variety of meditation practices also showed gamma wave levels that spiked higher and lasted longer (even during sleep) than non-meditators.

Why should we think like monks? If you wanted to know how to dominate the basketball court, you might turn to Michael Jordan; if you wanted to innovate, you might investigate Elon Musk; you might study Beyoncé to learn how to perform. If you want to train your mind to find peace, calm, and purpose? Monks are the experts. Brother David Steindl-Rast, a Benedictine monk who cofounded gratefulness.org, writes, "A layperson who is consciously aiming to be continuously alive in the Now is a monk."

Monks can withstand temptations, refrain from criticizing, deal with pain and anxiety, quiet the ego, and build lives that brim with purpose and meaning. Why shouldn't we learn from the calmest, happiest, most purposeful people on earth? Maybe you're thinking it's easy for monks to be calm, serene, and relaxed. They're hidden away in tranquil settings where they don't have to deal with jobs and romantic partners and, well, rush hour traffic. Maybe you're wondering, *How could thinking like a monk help me here in the modern world?*

First of all, monks weren't born monks. They're people from all sorts of backgrounds who've chosen to transform themselves. Matthieu Ricard, "the World's Happiest Man," was a biologist in his former life; Andy Puddicombe, cofounder of the meditation app Headspace, trained to be in the circus; I know monks who were in finance and in rock bands. They grow up in schools, towns, and cities just like you. You don't need to light candles in your home, walk around barefoot, or post photos of yourself doing tree pose on a mountaintop. Becoming a monk is a mindset that anyone can adopt.

Like most monks today, I didn't grow up in an ashram. I spent most of my childhood doing un-monk-like things. Until the age of fourteen, I was an obedient kid. I grew up in north London with my parents and my younger sister. I'm from a middle-class Indian family. Like a lot of parents, mine were committed to my education and to giving me a shot at a good future. I stayed out of trouble, did well in school, and tried my best to make everybody happy.

But when I started secondary school, I took a left turn. I'd been heavy as a child, and bullied for it, but now I lost that weight and began playing soccer and rugby. I turned to subjects that traditional Indian parents don't generally favor, like art, design, and philosophy. All this would have been fine, but I also started mixing with the wrong crowd. I became involved in a bunch of bad stuff. Experimenting with drugs. Fighting. Drinking too much. It did not go well. In high school I was suspended three times. Finally, the school asked me to leave.

"I'll change," I promised. "If you let me stay, I'll change." The school let me stay, and I cleaned up my act.

Finally, in college, I started to notice the value of hard work, sacrifice, discipline, persistence in pursuit of one's goals. The problem was that at the time, I didn't have any goals apart from getting a good job, getting married one day, maybe having a family—the usual. I suspected there was something deeper, but I didn't know what it was.

By the time Gauranga Das came to speak at my school, I was primed to explore new ideas, a new model of living, a path that veered from the one everyone (including myself) assumed I would take. I wanted to grow as a person. I didn't want to know humility or compassion and empathy only as abstract concepts, I wanted to live them. I didn't want discipline, character, and integrity to just be things I read about. I wanted to live them.

For the next four years, I juggled two worlds, going from bars and steakhouses to meditation and sleeping on the floor. In London, I studied management with an emphasis on behavioral science and interned at a large consulting firm and spent time with my friends and family. And at an ashram in Mumbai I read and studied ancient texts, spending most of my Christmas and summer holidays living with monks. My values gradually shifted. I found myself wanting to be *around* monks. In fact, I wanted to *immerse* myself in the monk mindset. More and more, the work I was doing in the corporate world seemed to lack meaning. What was the point if it had no positive impact on anyone?

When I graduated from college, I traded my suits for robes and joined the ashram, where we slept on the floor and lived out of gym lockers. I lived and traveled across India, the UK, and Europe. I meditated for hours every day and studied ancient scriptures. I had the opportunity to serve with my fellow monks, helping with the ongoing work of transforming an ashram in a village outside Mumbai into an eco-friendly spiritual retreat (the Govardhan Ecovillage) and volunteering with a food program that distributes over a million meals a day (Annamrita).

If I can learn to think like a monk, anyone can.

The Hindu monks I studied with use the Vedas as their foundational texts. (The title is from the Sanskrit word *veda*, meaning knowledge. Sanskrit is an ancient language that's the precursor of most of the languages spoken in South Asia today.) You could argue that philosophy began with this ancient collection of scriptures, which originated in the area that now covers parts of Pakistan and northwest India at least three thousand years ago; they form the basis of Hinduism.

Like Homer's epic poems, the Vedas were first transmitted orally, then eventually written down, but because of the fragility of the materials (palm leaves and birch bark!) most of the surviving documents we have are at most a few hundred years old. The Vedas include hymns, historical stories, poems, prayers, chants, ceremonial rituals, and advice for daily life.

In my life and in this book, I frequently refer to the Bhagavad Gita (which means "Song of God"). This is loosely based on the Upanishads, writings from around 800–400 BCE. The Bhagavad Gita is considered a kind of universal and timeless life manual. The tale isn't told about a monk or meant for a spiritual context. It's spoken to a married man who happens to be a talented archer. It wasn't intended to apply only to one religion or region—it's for all humanity. Eknath Easwaran, spiritual author and professor who has translated many of India's sacred texts, including the Bhagavad Gita, calls it "India's most important gift to the world." In his 1845 journal, Ralph Waldo Emerson wrote, "I owed—my friend and I owed—a magnificent day to the Bhagavat Geeta [*sic*]. It was the first of books; it was as if an empire spoke to us, nothing small or unworthy, but large, serene, consistent, the voice of an old intelligence which in another age and climate had pondered and thus disposed of the same questions which exercise us." It's said that there have been more commentaries written about the Gita than any other scripture.

In this book one of my goals is to help you connect with its timeless wisdom, along other ancient teachings that were the basis of my education as a monk—and that have significant relevance to the challenges we all face today.

What struck me most when I studied monk philosophy is that in the last three thousand years, humans haven't really changed. Sure, we're taller and on average we live longer, but I was surprised and impressed to find that the monk teachings talk about forgiveness, energy, intentions, living with purpose, and other topics in ways that are as resonant today as they must have been when they were written.

Even more impressively, monk wisdom can largely be supported by science, as we'll see throughout this book. For millennia, monks have believed that meditation and mindfulness are beneficial, that gratitude is good for you, that service makes you happier, and more that you will learn in this book. They developed practices around these ideas long before modern science could show or validate them.

Albert Einstein said, "If you can't explain something simply, you don't understand it well enough." When I saw how relevant the lessons I was learning were to the modern world, I wanted to dive deeper into them so that I could share them with other people.

Three years after I moved to Mumbai, my teacher, Gauranga Das, told me he believed I would be of greater value and service if I left the ashram and shared what I'd learned with the world. My three years as a monk were like a school of life. It was hard to become a monk, and even harder to leave. But applying the wisdom to life outside the ashram—the hardest part—felt like the final exam. Every day I am finding that the monk mindset works—that ancient wisdom is shockingly relevant today. That is why I'm sharing it.

These days I still consider myself a monk, though I usually refer to myself as a "former" monk, since I'm married, and monks aren't permitted to marry. I live in Los Angeles, which people tell me is one of the world capitals of materialism, facade, fantasy, and overall dodginess. But why live in a place that's already enlightened? Now, in the world and in this book, I share my takeaways from the life I've lived and what I've learned. This book is completely nonsectarian. It's not some sneaky conversion strategy. I swear! I can also promise that if you engage with and practice the material I present, you will find real meaning, passion, and purpose in your life.

Never before have so many people been so dissatisfied—or so preoccupied with chasing "happiness." Our culture and media feed us images and concepts about who and what we should be, while holding up models of accomplishment and success. Fame, money, glamour, sex—in the end none of these things can satisfy us. We'll simply seek more and more, a circuit that leads to frustration, disillusion, dissatisfaction, unhappiness, and exhaustion.

I like to draw a contrast between the monk mindset and what is often referred to as the monkey mind. Our minds can either elevate us or pull us down. Today we all struggle with overthinking, procrastination, and anxiety as a result of indulging the monkey mind. The monkey mind switches aimlessly from thought to thought, challenge to challenge, without really solving anything. But we can elevate to the monk mindset by digging down to the root of what we want and creating actionable steps for growth. The monk mindset lifts us out of confusion and distraction and helps us find clarity, meaning, and direction.

MONKEY MIND	MONK MIND
Overwhelmed by multiple branches	Focused on the root of the issue
Coasts in the passenger seat	Lives intentionally and consciously
Complains, compares, criticizes	Compassionate, caring, collaborative
Overthinks and procrastinates	Analyzes and articulates
Distracted by small things	Disciplined
Short-term gratification	Long-term gain
Demanding and entitled	Enthusiastic, determined, patient
Changes on a whim	Commits to a mission, vision, or goal

Amplifies negatives and fears	Works on breaking down negatives and fears
Self-centered and obsessed	Self-care for service
Multitasking	Single-tasking
Controlled by anger, worry, and fear	Controls and engages energy wisely
Does whatever feels good	Seeks self-control and mastery
Looks for pleasure	Looks for meaning
Looks for temporary fixes	Looks for genuine solutions

"Thinking like a monk" posits another way of viewing and approaching life. A way of rebellion, detachment, rediscovery, purpose, focus, discipline—and service. The goal of monk thinking is a life free of ego, envy, lust, anxiety, anger, bitterness, baggage. To my mind, adopting the monk mindset isn't just possible—it's *necessary*. We have no other choice. We need to find calm, stillness, and peace.

I vividly remember my first day of monk school. I had just shaved my head but I wasn't wearing robes yet, and I still looked like I was from London. I noticed a child monk—he can't have been more than ten years old—teaching a group of five-year-olds. He had a great aura about him, the poise and confidence of an adult.

"What are you doing?" I asked.

"We just taught their first class ever," he said, then asked me, "What did *you* learn in *your* first day of school?"

"I started to learn the alphabet and numbers. What did *they* learn?"

"The first thing we teach them is how to breathe."

"Why?" I asked.

"Because the only thing that stays with you from the moment you're born until the moment you die is your breath. All your friends, your family, the country you live in, all of that can change. The one thing that stays with you is your breath."

This ten-year-old monk added, "When you get stressed—what changes? Your breath. When you get angry—what changes? Your breath.

We experience every emotion with the change of the breath. When you learn to navigate and manage your breath, you can navigate any situation in life."

Already I was being taught the most important lesson: to focus on the root of things, not the leaf of the tree or symptoms of the problem. And I was learning, through direct observation, that anybody can be a monk, even if they're only five or ten years old.

When we're born, the first thing we must do is breathe. But just as life gets more complicated for that newborn baby, sitting still and breathing can be very challenging. What I hope to do in this book is to show you the monk way—we go to the root of things, go deep into self-examination. It is only through this curiosity, thought, effort, and revelation that we find our way to peace, calm, and purpose. Using the wisdom I was given by my teachers in the ashram, I hope to guide you there.

In the pages ahead, I will walk you through three stages of adapting to the monk mindset. First, we will let go, stripping ourselves from the external influences, internal obstacles, and fears that hold us back. You can think of this as a cleansing that will make space for growth. Second, we will grow. I will help you reshape your life so that you can make decisions with intention, purpose, and confidence. Finally, we will give, looking to the world beyond ourselves, expanding and sharing our sense of gratitude, and deepening our relationships. We will share our gifts and love with others and discover the true joy and surprising benefits of service.

Along the way, I will introduce you to three very different types of meditation that I recommend including in your practice: breathwork, visualization, and sound. All three have benefits, but the simplest way to differentiate them is to know that you do breathwork for the physical benefits—to find stillness and balance, to calm yourself; visualization for the psychological benefits—to heal the past and prepare for the future; and chanting for the psychic benefits—to connect with your deepest self and the universe, for real purification.

You don't have to meditate to benefit from this book, but if you do, the tools I give you will be sharper. I would go so far as to say that this entire book is a meditation—a reflection on our beliefs and values and intentions, how we see ourselves, how we make decisions, how to train our minds, and our ways of choosing and interacting with people. Achieving such deep self-awareness is the purpose and reward of meditation.

How would a monk think about this? That may not be a question you ask yourself right now—probably isn't close at all—but it will be by the end of the book.

PART ONE

LET GO

ONE

IDENTITY

I Am What I Think I Am

It is better to live your own destiny imperfectly than to live an imitation of somebody else's life with perfection.

—Bhagavad Gita 3.35

In 1902, the sociologist Charles Horton Cooley wrote: "I am not what I think I am, and I am not what you think I am. I am what I think you think I am."

Let that blow your mind for a moment.

Our identity is wrapped up in what others think of us—or, more accurately, what we *think* others think of us.

Not only is our self-image tied up in how we think others see us, but most of our efforts at self-improvement are really just us trying to meet that imagined ideal. If we think someone we admire sees wealth as success, then we chase wealth to impress that person. If we imagine that a friend is judging our looks, we tailor our appearance in response. In *West Side Story*, Maria meets a boy who's into her. What's her very next song? "I Feel Pretty."

As of this writing, the world's only triple Best Actor Oscar winner, Daniel Day-Lewis, has acted in just six films since 1998. He prepares for each role extensively, immersing himself completely in his character. For the role of Bill the Butcher in Martin Scorsese's *Gangs of New York*, he trained as a butcher, spoke with a thick Irish accent on and off the set, and hired circus performers to teach him how to throw knives. And that's only the beginning. He wore only authentic nineteenth-century clothing and walked around Rome in character, starting arguments and fights with strangers. Perhaps thanks to that clothing, he caught pneumonia.

Day-Lewis was employing a technique called method acting, which requires the actor to live as much like his character as possible in order to *become* the role he's playing. This is an incredible skill and art, but often method actors become so absorbed in their character that the role takes on a life beyond the stage or screen. "I will admit that I went mad, totally mad," Day-Lewis said to the *Independent* years later, admitting the role was "not so good for my physical or mental health."

Unconsciously, we're all method acting to some degree. We have personas we play online, at work, with friends, and at home. These different personas have their benefits. They enable us to make the money that pays our bills, they help us function in a workplace where we don't always feel comfortable, they let us maintain relationships with people we don't really like but need to interact with. But often our identity has so many layers that we lose sight of the real us, if we ever knew who or what that was in the first place. We bring our work role home with us, and we take the role we play with our friends into our romantic life, without any conscious control or intention. However successfully we play our roles, we end up feeling dissatisfied, depressed, unworthy, and unhappy. The "I" and "me," small and vulnerable to begin with, get distorted.

We try to live up to what we think others think of us, even at the expense of our values.

Rarely, if ever, do we consciously, intentionally, create our own values. We make life choices using this twice-reflected image of who we *might* be, without really thinking it through. Cooley called this phenomenon the "Looking-Glass Self."

We live in a perception of a perception of ourselves, and we've lost our real selves as a result. How can we recognize who we are and what makes us happy when we're chasing the distorted reflection of someone else's dreams?

You might think that the hard part about becoming a monk is letting go of the fun stuff: partying, sex, watching TV, owning things, sleeping in an actual bed (okay, the bed part was pretty rough). But before I took that step there was a bigger hurdle I had to overcome: breaking my "career" choice to my parents.

By the time I was wrapping up my final year of college, I had decided what path I wanted to take. I told my parents I would be turning down the job offers that had come my way. I always joke that as far as my parents were concerned, I had three career options: doctor, lawyer, or failure. There's no better way to tell your parents that everything they did for you was a waste than to become a monk.

Like all parents, mine had dreams for me, but at least I had eased them into the idea that I might become a monk: Every year since I was eighteen I'd spent part of the summer interning at a finance job in London and part of the year training at the ashram in Mumbai. By the time I made my decision, my mother's first concern was the same as any mother's: my well-being. Would I have health care? Was "seeking enlightenment" just a fancy way of saying "sitting around all day"?

Even more challenging for my mother was that we were surrounded by friends and family who shared the doctor-lawyer-failure definition of success. Word spread that I was making this radical move, and her friends started saying "But you've invested so much in his education" and "He's been brainwashed" and "He's going to waste his life." My friends too thought I was failing at life. I heard "You're never going to get a job again" and "You're throwing away any hope of earning a living."

When you try to live your most authentic life, some of your relation-

ships will be put in jeopardy. Losing them is a risk worth bearing; finding a way to keep them in your life is a challenge worth taking on.

Luckily, to my developing monk mind, the voices of my parents and their friends were not the most important guidelines I used when making this decision. Instead I relied on my own experience. Every year since I was eighteen I had tested both lives. I didn't come home from my summer finance jobs feeling anything but hungry for dinner. But every time I left the ashram I thought, *That was amazing. I just had the best time of my life.* Experimenting with these widely diverse experiences, values, and belief systems helped me understand my own.

The reactions to my choice to become a monk are examples of the external pressures we all face throughout our lives. Our families, our friends, society, media—we are surrounded by images and voices telling us who we should be and what we should do.

They clamor with opinions and expectations and obligations. Go straight from high school to the best college, find a lucrative job, get married, buy a home, have children, get promoted. Cultural norms exist for a reason—there is nothing wrong with a society that offers models of what a fulfilling life might look like. But if we take on these goals without reflection, we'll never understand why we don't own a home or we're not happy where we live, why our job feels hollow, whether we even want a spouse or any of the goals we're striving for.

My decision to join the ashram turned up the volume of opinions and concerns around me, but, conveniently, my experiences in the ashram had also given me the tools I needed to filter out that noise. The cause and the solution were the same. I was less vulnerable to the noises around me, telling me what was normal, safe, practical, best. I didn't shut out the people who loved me—I cared about them and didn't want them to worry—but neither did I let their definitions of success and happiness dictate my choices. It was—at the time—the hardest decision I'd ever made, and it was the right one.

The voices of parents, friends, education, and media all crowd a young person's mind, seeding beliefs and values. Society's definition of a happy

life is everybody's and nobody's. The only way to build a meaningful life is to filter out that noise and look within. This is the first step to building your monk mind.

We will start this journey the way monks do, by clearing away distractions. First, we'll look at the external forces that shape us and distract us from our values. Then we will take stock of the values that currently shape our lives and reflect on whether they're in line with who we want to be and how we want to live.

IS THIS DUST OR IS IT ME?

Gauranga Das offered me a beautiful metaphor to illustrate the external influences that obscure our true selves.

We are in a storeroom, lined with unused books and boxes full of artifacts. Unlike the rest of the ashram, which is always tidy and well swept, this place is dusty and draped in cobwebs. The senior monk leads me up to a mirror and says, "What can you see?"

Through the thick layer of dust, I can't even see my reflection. I say as much, and the monk nods. Then he wipes the arm of his robe across the glass. A cloud of dust puffs into my face, stinging my eyes and filling my throat.

He says, "Your identity is a mirror covered with dust. When you first look in the mirror, the truth of who you are and what you value is obscured. Clearing it may not be pleasant, but only when that dust is gone can you see your true reflection."

This was a practical demonstration of the words of Chaitanya, a sixteenth-century Bengali Hindu saint. Chaitanya called this state of affairs *ceto-darpaṇa-mārjanam*, or clearance of the impure mirror of the mind.

The foundation of virtually all monastic traditions is removing distractions that prevent us from focusing on what matters most—finding meaning in life by mastering physical and mental desires. Some traditions give up speaking, some give up sex, some give up worldly possessions, and some give up all three. In the ashram, we lived with just what we needed and nothing more. I experienced firsthand the enlightenment of letting go. When we are buried in nonessentials, we lose track of what is truly significant. I'm not asking you to give up any of these things, but I want to help you recognize and filter out the noise of external influences. This is how we clear the dust and see if those values truly reflect you.

Guiding values are the principles that are most important to us and that we feel should guide us: who we want to be, how we treat ourselves and others. Values tend to be single-word concepts like freedom, equality, compassion, honesty. That might sound rather abstract and idealistic, but values are really practical. They're a kind of ethical GPS we can use to navigate through life. If you know your values, you have directions that point you toward the people and actions and habits that are best for you. Just as when we drive through a new area, we wander aimlessly without values; we take wrong turns, we get lost, we're trapped by indecision. Values make it easier for you to surround yourself with the right people, make tough career choices, use your time more wisely, and focus your attention where it matters. Without them we are swept away by distractions.

WHERE VALUES COME FROM

Our values don't come to us in our sleep. We don't think them through consciously. Rarely do we even put them into words. But they exist nonetheless. Everyone is born into a certain set of circumstances, and our values are defined by what we experience. Were we born into hardship or luxury? Where did we receive praise? Parents and caregivers are often our loudest fans and critics. Though we might rebel in our teenage years, we are generally compelled to please and imitate those authority figures. Looking back, think about how your time with your parents was spent. Playing, enjoying conversation, working on projects together? What did they tell you was most important, and did it match what mattered most to them? Who did they want you to be? What did they want you to accomplish? How did they expect you to behave? Did you absorb these ideals, and have they worked for you?

From the start, our educations are another powerful influence. The subjects that are taught. The cultural angle from which they are taught. The way we are expected to learn. A fact-driven curriculum doesn't encourage creativity, a narrow cultural approach doesn't foster tolerance for people from different backgrounds and places, and there are few opportunities to immerse ourselves in our passions, even if we know them from an early age. This is not to say that school doesn't prepare us for life—and there are many different educational models out there, some of which are less restrictive—but it is worth taking a step back to consider whether the values you carried from school feel right to you.

THE MEDIA MIND GAME

As a monk, I learned early on that our values are influenced by whatever absorbs our minds. We are not our minds, but the mind is the vehicle by which we decide what is important in our hearts. The movies we watch, the music we hear, the books we read, the TV shows we binge, the people we follow online and offline. What's on your news feed is feeding your mind. The more we are absorbed in celebrity gossip, images of success, violent video games, and troubling news, the more our values are tainted with envy, judgment, competition, and discontent.

Observing and evaluating are key to thinking like a monk, and they begin with space and stillness. For monks, the first step in filtering the noise of external influences is a material letting go. I had three stints visiting the ashram, graduated college, then officially became a monk. After a couple months of training at the Bhaktivedanta Manor, a temple in the

TRY THIS: **WHERE DID YOUR VALUES COME FROM?**

It can be hard to perceive the effect these casual influences have on us. Values are abstract, elusive, and the world we live in constantly pushes blatant and subliminal suggestions as to what we should want, and how we should live, and how we form our ideas of who we are.

Write down some of the values that shape your life. Next to each, write the origin. Put a checkmark next to each value that you truly share.

Example:

VALUE	ORIGIN	IS IT TRUE TO ME?
Kindness	Parent	✓
Appearance	Media	Not in the same way
Wealth	Parent	No
Good grades	School	Interfered with real learning
Knowledge	School	✓
Family	Tradition	Family: yes, but not traditional

countryside north of London, I headed to India, arriving at the village ashram in the beginning of September 2010. I exchanged my relatively stylish clothes for two robes (one to wear and one to wash). I forfeited my fairly slick haircut for . . . no hair; our heads were shaved. And I was deprived of almost all opportunities to check myself out—the ashram contained no mirrors except the one I would later be shown in the storeroom. So we monks were prevented from obsessing over our appearance, ate a simple diet that rarely varied, slept on thin mats laid on the floor, and the only music we heard was the chants and bells that punctuated our meditations and rituals. We didn't watch movies or TV shows, and we received limited news and email on shared desktop computers in a communal area.

Nothing took the place of these distractions except space, stillness, and silence. **When we tune out the opinions, expectations, and obligations of the world around us, we begin to hear ourselves.** In that silence I began to recognize the difference between outside noise and my own voice. I could clear away the dust of others to see my core beliefs.

I promised you I wouldn't ask you to shave your head and don robes, but how, in the modern world, can we give ourselves the space, silence, and stillness to build awareness? Most of us don't sit down and think about our values. We don't like to be alone with our own thoughts. Our inclination is to avoid silence, to try to fill our heads, to keep moving. In a series of studies, researchers from the University of Virginia and Harvard asked participants to spend just six to fifteen minutes alone in a room with no smartphone, no writing instruments, and nothing to read. The researchers then let them listen to music or use their phones. Participants not only preferred their phones and music, many of them even chose to *zap themselves with an electric shock* rather than be alone with their thoughts. If you go to a networking event every day and have to tell people what you do for a living, it's hard to step away from that reduction of who you are. If you watch *Real Housewives* every night, you start to think that throwing glasses of wine in your friends' faces is routine behavior. When we fill up our lives and leave ourselves no room to reflect, those distractions become our values by default.

We can't address our thoughts and explore our minds when we're preoccupied. Nor does just sitting in your home teach you anything. There are three ways I suggest you actively create space for reflection. First, on a daily basis I recommend you sit down to reflect on how the day went and what emotions you're feeling. Second, once a month you can approximate the change that I found at the ashram by going someplace you've never been before to explore yourself in a different environment. This can be anything from visiting a park or library you've never been to before to taking a trip. Finally, get involved in something that's meaningful to you—a hobby, a charity, a political cause.

Another way to create space is to take stock of how we are filling the space that we have and whether those choices reflect our true values.

AUDIT YOUR LIFE

No matter what you *think* your values are, your actions tell the real story. What we do with our spare time shows what we value. For instance, you might put spending time with your family at the top of your list of values, but if you spend all your free time playing golf, your actions don't match your values, and you need to do some self-examination.

Time

First, let's assess how you spend the time when you're not sleeping or working. Researchers have found that by the end of our lives, on average, each of us will spend thirty-three years in bed (seven years of which will be spent trying to sleep), a year and four months exercising, and more than three years on vacation. If you're a woman, you'll spend 136 days getting ready. If you're a man this number drops to 46 days. These are just estimates of course, but our daily choices add up.

TRY THIS: AUDIT YOUR TIME

Spend a week tracking how much time you devote to the following: family, friends, health, and self. (Note that we're leaving out sleeping, eating, and working. Work, in all its forms, can sprawl without boundaries. If this is the case for you, then set your own definition of when you are "officially" at work and make "extra work" one of your categories.) The areas where you spend the most time should match what you value the most. Say the amount of time that your job requires exceeds how important it is to you. That's a sign that you need to look very closely at that decision. You're deciding to spend time on something that doesn't feel important to you. What are the values behind that decision? Are your earnings from your job ultimately serving your values?

Media

When you did your audit, no doubt a significant amount of your time was spent reading or viewing media. Researchers estimate that, on average, each of us will spend more than eleven years of our lives looking at TV and social media! Perhaps your media choices feel casual, but time reflects values.

There are many forms of media, but most of us aren't overdoing it on movies, TV, or magazines. It's all about devices. Conveniently, your iPhone will tell you exactly how you're using it. Under Settings, look at the screen time report for the last week and you'll see how much time you spend on social media, games, mail, and browsing the Web. If you don't like what you see, you can even set limits for yourself. On Android, you can look at your battery usage under Settings, then, from the menu, choose "Show full device usage." Or you can download an app like Social Fever or MyAddictometer.

Money

Like time, you can look at the money you spend to see the values by which you live. Exclude necessities like home, dependents, car, bills, food, and debt. Now look at your discretionary spending. What was your biggest investment this month? Which discretionary areas are costing you the most? Does your spending correspond to what matters most to you? We often have an odd perspective on what's "worth it" that doesn't quite make sense if you look at all your expenditures at once. I was advising someone who complained that the family was overspending on afterschool classes for the kids . . . until she realized that she spent more on her shoes than on their music lessons.

Seeing posts on social media that compared spending and our priorities got me thinking about how the ways we spend our time and money reveal what we value.

A 60-minute TV show ("Flew by!")
A 60-minute lunch with family ("Will it ever end!")
Everyday coffee habit ($4/day, almost $1,500/year) ("Need it!")
Fresh healthy food choices (an extra 1.50/day, about $550/year) ("Not worth it!")
15 minutes scrolling social media ("Me time!")
15 minutes of meditation ("No time!")

It's all in how you see it. When you look at a month of expenses, think about whether discretionary purchases were long- or short-term investments—a great dinner out or a dance class? Were they for entertainment or enlightenment, for yourself or someone else? If you have a gym membership, but only went once this month and spent more on wine, you have some rethinking to do.

CURATE YOUR VALUES

Doing a self-audit tells you the values that have crept into your life by default. The next step is to decide what your values are and whether your choices are in alignment with them. Contemplating monk values may help you identify your own. Our teachers at the ashram explained that there are higher and lower values. Higher values propel and elevate us toward happiness, fulfillment, and meaning. Lower values demote us toward anxiety, depression, and suffering. According to the Gita, these are the higher values and qualities: fearlessness, purity of mind, gratitude, service and charity, acceptance, performing sacrifice, deep study, austerity, straightforwardness, nonviolence, truthfulness, absence of anger, renunciation, perspective, restraint from fault finding, compassion toward all living beings, satisfaction, gentleness/kindness, integrity, determination.

(Notice that happiness and success are not among these values. These are not values, they are rewards—the end game—and we will address them further in Chapter Four.)

The six lower values are greed, lust, anger, ego, illusion, and envy. The downside of the lower values is that they so readily take us over when we give them space to do so, but the upside is that there are a lot fewer of them. Or, as my teacher Gauranga Das reminded us, there are always more ways to be pulled up than to be pulled down.

We can't pull a set of values out of thin air and make sweeping changes overnight. Instead, we want to let go of the false values that fill the space in our lives. The ashram gave us monks the opportunity to observe nature, and our teachers called our attention to the cycles of all living things. Leaves sprout, transform, and drop. Reptiles, birds, and mammals shed their skins, feathers, fur. Letting go is a big part of the rhythm of nature, as is rebirth. We humans cling to stuff—people, ideas, material possessions, copies of Marie Kondo's book—thinking it's unnatural to purge, but letting go is a direct route to space (literally) and stillness. We separate ourselves—emotionally if not physically—from the people and ideas who fill up our lives, and then we take time to observe the natural inclinations that compel us.

Choices come along every day, and we can begin to weave values into them. Whenever we make a choice, whether it's as big as getting married or as small as an argument with a friend, we are driven by our values, whether they are high or low. If these choices work out well for us, then our values are in alignment with our actions. But when things don't work out, it's worth revisiting what drove the decision you made.

TRY THIS: PAST VALUES

Reflect on the three best and three worst choices you've ever made. Why did you make them? What have you learned? How would you have done it differently?

Take a close look at your answers to the Try This above—buried in them are your values. Why did you make a choice? You may have been with the right or wrong person for the same reason: because you value love. Or maybe you moved across the country because you wanted a change. The underlying value may be adventure. Now do the same thing for the future. Look at your biggest goals to see if they're driven by other people, tradition, or media-driven ideas of how we should live.

TRY THIS: VALUE-DRIVEN DECISIONS

For the next week, whenever you spend money on a nonnecessity or make a plan for how you will spend your free time, pause, and think: What is the value behind this choice? It only takes a second, a flash of consideration. Ideally, this momentary pause becomes instinctive, so that you are making conscious choices about what matters to you and how much energy you devote to it.

FILTER OEOS, DON'T BLOCK THEM

Once you filter out the noise of opinions, expectations, and obligations (OEOs), you will see the world through different eyes. The next step is inviting the world back in. When I ask you to strip away outside influences, I don't want you to tune out the whole world indefinitely. Your monk mind can and must learn from other people. The challenge is to do so consciously by asking ourselves simple questions: What qualities do I look for/admire in family, friends, or colleagues? Are they trust, confidence, determination, honesty? Whatever they may be, these qualities are, in fact, our own values—the very landmarks we should use to guide ourselves through our own lives.

When you are not alone, surround yourself with people who fit well with your values. It helps to find a community that reflects who you want to be. A community that looks like the future you want. Remember how hard it was for me to start living like a monk during my final year of college? And now, it's hard for me to live in London. Surrounded by the people I grew up with and their ways of living, I'm tempted to sleep in, gossip, judge others. A new culture helped me redefine myself, and another new culture helped me continue on my path.

Every time you move homes or take a different job or embark on a new relationship, you have a golden opportunity to reinvent yourself. Multiple studies show that the way we relate to the world around us is contagious. A twenty-year study of people living in a Massachusetts town showed that both happiness and depression spread within social circles. If a friend who lives within a mile of you becomes happier, then the chance that you are also happy increases by 25 percent. The effect jumps higher with next-door neighbors.

Who you surround yourself with helps you stick to your values and achieve your goals. You grow together. If you want to run a 2:45 marathon, you don't train with people who run a 4:45. If you want to be more spiritual, expand your practice with other spiritual people. If you want to grow your business, join a local chamber of commerce or an online group of business owners who are similarly driven toward that kind of success. If you're an overworked parent who wants to make your kids your priority, cultivate relationships with other parents who prioritize their kids, so you can exchange support and advice. Better yet, where possible, cross groups: Foster relationships with family-oriented spiritual entrepreneurs who run marathons. Okay, I'm kidding, yet in today's world where we have more ways to connect than ever, platforms like LinkedIn and Meetup and tools like Facebook groups make it easier than ever to find your tribe. If you're looking for love, look in places that are value-driven, like service opportunities, fitness or sports activities, a series of lectures on a topic that interests you.

If you're not sure where others fit in relation to your values, ask yourself a question: When I spend time with this person or group, do I feel like I'm getting closer to or further away from who I want to be? The answer could be clear-cut; it's obvious if you're spending four hours at a time playing FIFA soccer on PS2 (not that I've ever done that) versus engaging in meaningful interaction that improves the quality of your life.

Or the answer could be more vague—a feeling like irritability or mental fuzziness after you spend time with them. It feels good to be around people who are good for us; it doesn't feel good to be around people who don't support us or bring out our bad habits.

TRY THIS: COMPANION AUDIT

Over the course of a week, make a list of the people with whom you spend the most time. List the values that you share next to each person. Are you giving the most time to the people who align most closely with your values?

Who you talk to, what you watch, what you do with your time: all of these sources push values and beliefs. If you're just going from one day to the next without questioning your values, you'll be swayed by what everyone else—from your family to hordes of marketing professionals—wants you to think. I remind myself of the moment in the storeroom all the time. A thought comes into my mind and I ask myself, *Does this fit my chosen values or those that others have selected for me? Is this dust or is it me?*

When you give yourself space and stillness, you can clear the dust and see yourself, not through others' eyes, but from within. Identifying your values and letting them guide you will help you filter external influences. In the next chapter these skills will help you filter out unwanted attitudes and emotions.

TWO

NEGATIVITY

The Evil King Goes Hungry

It is impossible to build one's own happiness on the unhappiness of others.
—Daisaku Ikeda

It is the summer after my third year of college. I have returned from spending a month at the ashram and am now interning for a finance firm. I'm at lunch with a couple of my colleagues—we've grabbed sandwiches and brought them to the concrete courtyard in front of the building, where low walls crisscross the hardscaping and young people in suits eat speedy lunches, defrosting in the summer sun before returning to the hyper-air-conditioned building. I am a monk out of water.

"Did you hear about Gabe?" one of my friends says in a loud whisper. "The partners tore apart his presentation."

"That dude," another friend says, shaking his head. "He's sinking fast."

I flash back to a class Gauranga Das taught called "Cancers of the Mind: Comparing, Complaining, Criticizing." In the class, we talked about negative thought habits, including gossip. One of the exercises we did was keeping a tally of every criticism we spoke or thought. For each one, we had to write down ten good things about the person.

It was hard. We were living together, in close quarters. Issues came up, most of them petty. The average time for a monk's shower was four minutes. When there was a line at the showers, we would take bets on who was taking too long. (This was the only betting we did. Because: monks.) And though the snorers were relegated to their own room, sometimes new practitioners emerged, and we rated their snores on a scale of motorcycles: this monk's a Vespa; that one's a Harley-Davidson.

I went through the exercise, dutifully noting every criticism I let slip. Next to each, I jotted down ten positive qualities. The point of the exercise wasn't hard to figure out—every person was more good than bad—but seeing it on the page made the ratio sink in. This helped me see my own weaknesses differently. I tended to focus on my mistakes without balancing them against my strengths. When I found myself being self-critical, I reminded myself that I too had positive qualities. Putting my negative qualities in context helped me recognize the same ratio in myself, that I am more good than bad. We talked about this feedback loop in class: When we criticize others, we can't help but notice the bad in ourselves. But when we look for the good in others, we start to see the best in ourselves too.

The guy sitting next to me on the wall nudges me out of my reverie. "So you think he'll last?"

I've lost track of what we're talking about. "Who?" I ask.

"Gabe—he shouldn't have been hired in the first place, right?"

"Oh, I don't know," I say.

Once I'd spent time in the ashram, I became very sensitive to gossip. I'd gotten used to conversations with primarily positive energy. When I first arrived back in the world, I was awkwardly silent. I didn't want to be the morality police, but I also didn't want to participate. As the Buddha advised, "Do not give your attention to what others do or fail to do; give it to what you do or fail to do." I quickly figured out to say things like "Oh, I'm not sure . . ." or "I haven't heard anything." Then I'd shift the conversation to something more positive. "Did you hear they've asked Max to stay on? I'm psyched for him." Gossip has value in some situations: It helps society regulate what is acceptable behavior, and we often use it to see if others agree with our judgments about other people's behavior and therefore our values. But there are kinder ways to negotiate these questions. More often, we use gossip to put others down, which can make us feel superior to them and/or bolster our status in a group.

Some of my friends and colleagues stopped trying to gossip with me altogether; we had real conversations instead. Some trusted me more, realizing that since I didn't gossip with them, I wouldn't gossip about them. If there were people who thought I was just plain boring, well, I have nothing bad to say about them.

NEGATIVITY IS EVERYWHERE

You wake up. Your hair looks terrible. Your partner complains that you're out of coffee. On the way to work some driver who's texting makes you miss the light. The news on the radio is worse than yesterday. Your coworker whispers to you that Candace is pretending to be sick again. . . . Every day we are assaulted by negativity. No wonder we can't help but dish it out as well as receive it. We report the aches and pains of the day rather than the small joys. We compare ourselves to our neighbors, complain about our partners, say things about our friends behind their backs that we would never say to their faces, criticize people on social media, argue, deceive, even explode into anger.

This negative chatter even takes place throughout what we might consider to be a "good day," and it's not part of anyone's plan. In my experience, nobody wakes up and thinks, *How can I be mean to or about other people today?* or *How can I make myself feel better by making others feel worse today?* Still, negativity often comes from within. We have three core emotional needs, which I like to think of as peace, love, and understanding (thanks Nick Lowe and Elvis Costello). Negativity—in conversation, emotions, and actions—often springs from a threat to one of the three needs: a fear that bad things are going to happen (loss of peace), a fear of not being loved (loss of love), or a fear of being disrespected (loss of understanding). From these fears stem all sorts of other emotions—feeling overwhelmed, insecure, hurt, competitive, needy, and so on. These negative feelings spring out of us as complaints, comparisons, and criticisms and other negative behaviors. Think of the trolls who dive onto social media, dumping ill will on their targets. Perhaps their fear is that they aren't respected, and they turn to trolling to feel significant. Or perhaps their political beliefs are generating the fear that their world is unsafe. (Or maybe they're just trying to build a following—fear certainly doesn't motivate every troll in the world.)

For another example, we all have friends who turn a catch-up phone call into an interminable vent session describing their job, their partner, their family—what's wrong, what's unfair, what's never going to change. For these people, nothing ever seems to go right. This person may be expressing their fear that bad things are going to happen—their core need for peace and security is threatened.

Bad things *do* happen. In our lives, we're all victims at some point—whether we're being racially profiled or being cut off in traffic. But if we adopt a victim mentality, we're more likely to take on a sense of entitlement and to behave selfishly. Stanford psychologists took 104 subjects and assigned them to one of two groups—one told to write a short essay about a time they were bored, and the other to write about a time when life seemed unfair or when they felt "wronged or slighted by someone." Afterward, the participants were asked if they wanted to help the researchers with an easy task. Those who'd written about a time they'd been wronged were 26 percent less likely to help the researchers. In a similar study, participants who identified with a victim mindset were not only more likely to express selfish attitudes afterward, they were also more likely to leave behind trash and even take the experimenters' pens!

NEGATIVITY IS CONTAGIOUS

We're social creatures who get most of what we want in life—peace, love, and understanding—from the group we gather around us. Our brains adjust automatically to both harmony and disagreement. We've already talked about how we unconsciously try to please others. Well, we also want to agree with others. Research has proven that most humans value social conformity so much that they'll change their own responses—even their perceptions—to align with the group, even when the group is blatantly wrong.

In the 1950s Solomon Asch gathered groups of college students and told them they were doing a vision test. The catch was that in each group, everyone was an actor except one person: the subject of the test.

Asch showed participants an image of a "target" line first, then of a series of three lines: one shorter, one longer, and one that was clearly the same length as the target line. The students were asked which line matched the length of the target line. Sometimes the actors gave correct answers, and sometimes they purposefully gave incorrect answers. In each case, the real study participant answered last. The correct answer should have been obvious. But, influenced by the actors, about 75 percent of the subjects followed the crowd to give an incorrect response at least once. This phenomenon has been called *groupthink bias*.

We're wired to conform. Your brain would rather not deal with conflict and debate. It would much prefer to lounge in the comfort of like-mindedness. That's not a bad thing if we're surrounded by, say, monks. But if we're surrounded by gossip, conflict, and negativity, we start to see the world in those terms, just like the people who went against their own eyes in Asch's line experiment.

The instinct for agreement has a huge impact on our lives. It is one of the reasons why, in a culture of complaint, we join the fray.

And the more negativity that surrounds us, the more negative we become. We think that complaining will help us process our anger, but research confirms that even people who report feeling better after venting

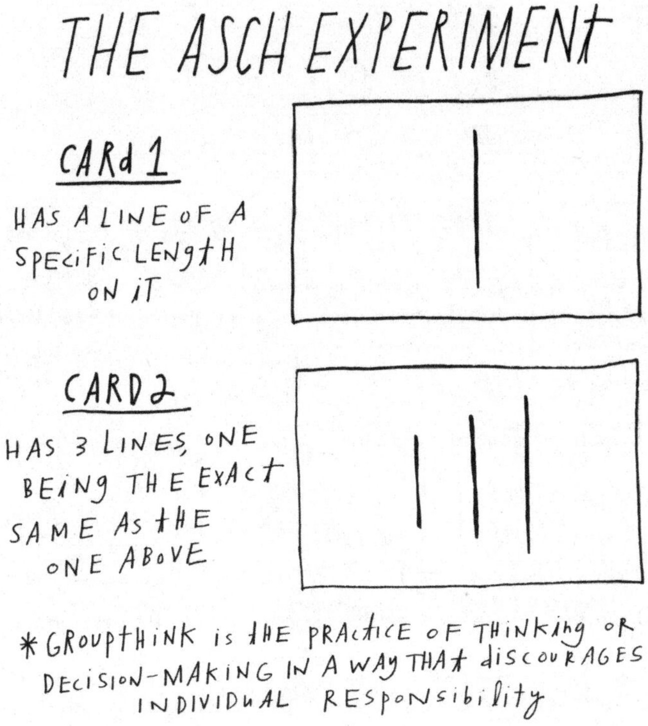

are still more aggressive post-gripe than people who did not engage in venting.

At the Bhaktivedanta Manor, the temple's London outpost, there was one monk who drove me crazy. If I asked him how he was in the morning, he'd tell me about how badly he'd slept and whose fault it was. He complained that the food was bad, and yet there was never enough. It was relentless verbal diarrhea, so negative that I never wanted to be around him.

Then I found myself complaining about him to the other monks. And so I became exactly what I was criticizing. Complaining is contagious, and he'd passed it on to me.

Studies show that negativity like mine can increase aggression toward random, uninvolved people, and that the more negative your attitude, the more likely you are to have a negative attitude in the future. Studies also show that long-term stress, like that generated by complaining, actually shrinks your hippocampus—that's the region of your brain that affects

reasoning and memory. Cortisol, the same stress hormone that takes a toll on the hippocampus, also impairs your immune system (and has loads of other harmful effects). I'm not blaming every illness on negativity, but if remaining positive can prevent even one of my winter colds, I'm all for it.

TYPES OF NEGATIVE PEOPLE

Negative behaviors surround us so constantly that we grow accustomed to them. Think about whether you have any of the following in your life:

- Complainers, like the friend on the phone, who complain endlessly without looking for solutions. Life is a problem that will be hard if not impossible to solve.
- Cancellers, who take a compliment and spin it: "You look good today" becomes "You mean I looked bad yesterday?"
- Casualties, who think the world is against them and blame their problems on others.

- Critics, who judge others for either having a different opinion or not having one, for any choices they've made that are different from what the critic would have done.
- Commanders, who realize their own limits but pressure others to succeed. They'll say, "You never have time for me," even though they're busy as well.
- Competitors, who compare themselves to others, controlling and manipulating to make themselves or their choices look better. They are in so much pain that they want to bring others down. Often we have to play down our successes around these people because we know they can't appreciate them.
- Controllers, who monitor and try to direct how their friends or partners spend time, and with whom, and what choices they make.

You can have fun with this list, seeing if you can think of someone to fit each type. But the real point of it is to help you notice and frame these behaviors when they come at you. If you put everyone into the same box of negativity ("They're so annoying!"), you aren't any closer to deciding how to manage each relationship.

On the day I moved to the ashram with six other new monks traveling from England, they told us to think of our new home as a hospital, where we were all patients. Becoming a monk, detaching from material life, was not seen as an achievement in and of itself. It simply meant that we were ready to be admitted to a place of healing where we could work to overcome the illnesses of the soul that infected us and weakened us.

In a hospital, as we all know, even the doctors get sick. Nobody is immune. The senior monks reminded us that everyone had different sicknesses, everyone was still learning, and that, just as we would not judge anyone else's health problems, we shouldn't judge someone who sinned differently. Gauranga Das repeated this advice in brief metaphorical form that we often used to remind ourselves not to harbor negative thoughts toward others: *Don't judge someone with a different disease. Don't expect anyone to be perfect. Don't think you are perfect.*

Instead of judging negative behavior, we try to neutralize the charge, or even reverse it to positive. Once you recognize a complainer isn't looking for solutions, you realize you don't have to provide them. If a commander says, "You're too busy for me," you can say, "Should we find a time that works for both of us?"

REVERSE EXTERNAL NEGATIVITY

The categories above help us step away from the negative person in order to make clearheaded decisions about our role in the situation. The monk way is to dig to the root, diagnose, and clarify a situation so you can explain it simply to yourself. Let's use this approach to define strategies for dealing with negative people.

Become an Objective Observer

Monks lead with awareness. We approach negativity—any type of conflict, really—by taking a step back to remove ourselves from the emotional charge of the moment. Catholic monk Father Thomas Keating said, "There is no commandment that says we have to be upset by the way other people treat us. The reason we are upset is because we have an emotional program that says, 'If someone is nasty to me, I cannot be happy or feel good about myself.' . . . Instead of reacting compulsively and retaliating, we could enjoy our freedom as human beings and refuse to be upset." We step away, not literally but emotionally, and look at the situation as if we are not in the middle of it. We will talk more about this distance, which is called detachment, in the next chapter. For now, I'll say that it helps us find understanding without judgment. Negativity is a trait, not someone's identity. A person's true nature can be obscured by clouds, but, like the sun, it is always there. And clouds can overcome any of us. We have to understand this when we deal with people who exude negative energy. Just like we wouldn't want someone to judge us by our worst moments, we must be careful not to do that to others. When someone hurts you, it's because they're hurt. Their hurt is simply spilling over. They need help. And as the Dalai Lama says, "If you can, help others; if you cannot do that, at least do not harm them."

Back Slowly Away

From a position of understanding, we are better equipped to address negative energy. The simplest response is to back slowly away. Just as in the last chapter we let go of the influences that interfered with our values, we want to cleanse ourselves of the negative attitudes that cloud our outlook. In *The Heart of the Buddha's Teaching*, Thich Nhat Hanh, a Buddhist monk who has been called the Father of Mindfulness, writes, "Letting go gives us freedom, and freedom is the only condition for happiness. If, in our heart, we still cling to anything—anger, anxiety, or possessions—we cannot be free." I encourage you to purge or avoid physical triggers of negative thoughts and feelings, like that sweatshirt your ex gave you or the coffee shop where you always run into a former friend. If you don't let go physically, you won't let go emotionally.

But when a family member, a friend, or a colleague is involved, distancing ourselves is often not an option or not the first response we want to give. We need to use other strategies.

The 25/75 Principle

For every negative person in your life, have three uplifting people. I try to surround myself with people who are better than I am in some way: happier, more spiritual. In life, as in sports, being around better players pushes you to grow. I don't mean for you to take this so literally that you label each of your friends either negative or uplifting, but aim for the feeling that at least 75 percent of your time is spent with people who inspire you rather than bring you down. Do your part in making the friendship an uplifting exchange. Don't just spend time with the people you love—grow with them. Take a class, read a book, do a workshop. *Sangha* is the Sanskrit word for community, and it suggests a refuge where people serve and inspire each other.

Allocate Time

Another way to reduce negativity if you can't remove it is to regulate how much time you allow a person to occupy based on their energy. Some challenges we face only because we allow them to challenge us. There might be some people you can only tolerate for an hour a month, some for a day, some for a week. Maybe you even know a one-minute person. Consider how much time is best for you to spend with them, and don't exceed it.

Don't Be a Savior

If all someone needs is an ear, you can listen without exerting much energy. If we try to be problem-solvers, then we become frustrated when people don't take our brilliant advice. The desire to save others is ego-driven. Don't let your own needs shape your response. In *Sayings of the Fathers*, a compilation of teachings and maxims from Jewish Rabbinic tradition, it is advised, "Don't count the teeth in someone else's mouth." Similarly, don't attempt to fix a problem unless you have the necessary skills. Think of your friend as a person who is drowning. If you are an excellent swimmer, a trained lifeguard, then you have the strength and wherewithal to help a swimmer in trouble. Similarly, if you have the time and mind space to help another person, go for it. But if you're only a fair swimmer and you try to save a drowning person, they are likely to pull you down with them. Instead, you call for the lifeguard. Similarly, if you don't have the energy and experience to help a friend, you can introduce them to people or ideas that might help them. Maybe someone else is their rescuer.

REVERSE INTERNAL NEGATIVITY

Working from the outside in is the natural way of decluttering. Once we recognize and begin to neutralize the external negativities, we become better able to see our own negative tendencies and begin to reverse them.

Sometimes we deny responsibility for the negativity that we ourselves put out in the world, but negativity doesn't always come from other people and it isn't always spoken aloud. Envy, complaint, anger—it's easier to blame those around us for a culture of negativity, but purifying our own thoughts will protect us from the influence of others.

In the ashram our aspirations for purity were so high that our "competition" came in the form of renunciation ("I eat less than that monk"; "I meditated longer than everyone else"). But a monk has to laugh at himself if the last thought he has at the end of the meditation is "Look at me! I outlasted them all!" If that's where he arrived, then what was the point of the meditation? In *The Monastic Way*, a compilation of quotes edited by Hannah Ward and Jennifer Wild, Sister Christine Vladimiroff says, "[In a monastery], the only competition allowed is to outstrip each other in showing love and respect."

Competition breeds envy. In the Mahabharata, an evil warrior envies another warrior and wants him to lose all he has. The evil warrior hides a burning block of coal in his robes, planning to hurl it at the object of his envy. Instead, it catches fire and the evil warrior himself is burned. His envy makes him his own enemy.

Envy's catty cousin is Schadenfreude, which means taking pleasure in the suffering of others. When we derive joy from other people's failures, we're building our houses and pride on the rocky foundations of someone else's imperfection or bad luck. That is not steady ground. In fact, when we find ourselves judging others, we should take note. It's a signal that our minds are tricking us into thinking we're moving forward when in truth we're stuck. If I sold more apples than you did yesterday, but you sold more today, this says nothing about whether I'm improving as an apple seller. **The more we define ourselves in relation to the people around us, the more lost we are.**

We may never completely purge ourselves of envy, jealousy, greed, lust, anger, pride, and illusion, but that doesn't mean we should ever stop trying. In Sanskrit, the word *anartha* generally means "things not wanted," and to practice *anartha-nivritti* is to remove that which is unwanted. We think freedom means being able to say whatever we want. We think freedom means that we can pursue all our desires. Real freedom is letting go of things not wanted, the unchecked desires that lead us to unwanted ends.

Letting go doesn't mean wiping away negative thoughts, feelings, and ideas completely. The truth is that these thoughts will always arise—it is what we do with them that makes the difference. The neighbor's barking dog is an annoyance. It will always interrupt you. The question is how you guide that response. The key to real freedom is self-awareness.

In your evaluation of your own negativity, keep in mind that even small actions have consequences. Even when we become more aware of others' negativity and say, "She's always complaining," we ourselves are being negative. At the ashram, we slept under mosquito nets. Every night, we'd close our nets and use flashlights to confirm that they were clear of bugs. One morning, I woke up to discover that a single mosquito had been in my net and I had at least ten bites. I thought of something the Dalai Lama said, "If you think you are too small to make a difference, try sleeping with a mosquito." Petty, negative thoughts and words are like mosquitos: Even the smallest ones can rob us of our peace.

Spot, Stop, Swap

Most of us don't register our negative thoughts, much as I didn't register that sole mosquito. To purify our thoughts, monks talk about the process of awareness, addressing, and amending. I like to remember this as spot, stop, swap. First, we become aware of a feeling or issue—we *spot* it. Then we pause to address what the feeling is and where it comes from—we *stop*

to consider it. And last, we amend our behavior—we *swap* in a new way of processing the moment. **SPOT, STOP, SWAP.**

Spot

Becoming aware of negativity means learning to spot the toxic impulses around you. To help us confront our own negativity, our monk teachers told us to try not to complain, compare, or criticize for a week, and keep a tally of how many times we failed. The goal was to see the daily tally decrease. The more aware we became of these tendencies, the more we might free ourselves from them.

Listing your negative thoughts and comments will help you contemplate their origins. Are you judging a friend's appearance, and are you equally hard on your own? Are you muttering about work without considering your own contribution? Are you reporting on a friend's illness to

TRY THIS: AUDIT YOUR NEGATIVE COMMENTS.

Keep a tally of the negative remarks you make over the course of a week. See if you can make your daily number go down. The goal is zero.

call attention to your own compassion, or are you hoping to solicit more support for that friend?

Sometimes instead of reacting negatively to what is, we negatively anticipate what might be. This is suspicion. There's a parable about an evil king who went to meet a good king. When invited to stay for dinner, the evil king asked for his plate to be switched with the good king's plate. When the good king asked why, the evil king replied, "You may have poisoned this food."

The good king laughed.

That made the evil king even more nervous, and he switched the plates again, thinking maybe he was being double-bluffed. The good king just shook his head and took a bite of the food in front of him. The evil king didn't eat that night.

What we judge or envy or suspect in someone else can guide us to the darkness we have within ourselves. The evil king projects his own dishonor onto the good king. In the same way our envy or impatience or suspicion with someone else tells us something about ourselves. Negative projections and suspicions reflect our own insecurities and get in our way. If you decide your boss is against you, it can affect you emotionally—you might be so discouraged that you don't perform well at work—or practically—you won't ask for the raise you deserve. Either way, like the evil king, you're the one who will go hungry!

Stop

When you better understand the roots of your negativity, the next step is to address it. Silence your negativity to make room for thoughts and actions that add to your life instead of taking away from it. Start with your breath. When we're stressed, we hold our breath or clench our jaws. We slump in defeat or tense our shoulders. Throughout the day, observe your physical presence. Is your jaw tight? Is your brow furrowed? These are signs that we need to remember to breathe, to loosen up physically and emotionally.

The Bhagavad Gita refers to the austerity of speech, saying that we should only speak words that are truthful, beneficial to all, pleasing, and that don't agitate the minds of others. The Vaca Sutta, from early Buddhist scriptures, offers similar wisdom, defining a well-spoken statement as one that is "spoken at the right time. It is spoken in truth. It is spoken affectionately. It is spoken beneficially. It is spoken with a mind of goodwill."

Remember, saying whatever we want, whenever we want, however we want, is not freedom. Real freedom is not feeling the need to say these things.

When we limit our negative speech, we may find that we have a lot less to say. We might even feel inhibited. Nobody loves an awkward silence, but it's worth it to free ourselves from negativity. Criticizing someone else's work ethic doesn't make you work harder. Comparing your marriage to someone else's doesn't make your marriage better unless you do so thoughtfully and productively. Judgment creates an illusion: that if you see well enough to judge, then you must be better, that if someone else is failing, then you must be moving forward. In fact, it is careful, thoughtful observations that move us forward.

Stopping doesn't mean simply shunning the negative instinct. Get closer to it. Australian community worker Neil Barringham said, "The grass is greener where you water it." Notice what's arousing your negativity, over there on your frenemy's side of the fence. Do they seem to have more time, a better job, a more active social life? Because in the third step, swapping, you'll want to look for seeds of the same on your turf and cultivate them. For example, take your envy of someone else's social whirlwind and in it find the inspiration to host a party, or get back in touch with old friends, or organize an after-work get-together. It is important to find our significance not from thinking other people have it better but from being the person we want to be.

Swap

After spotting and stopping the negativity in your heart, mind, and speech, you can begin to amend it. Most of us monks were unable to completely avoid complaining, comparing, and criticizing—and you can't expect you'll be completely cured of that habit either—but researchers have found that happy people tend to complain . . . wait for it . . . mindfully. While thoughtlessly venting complaints makes your day worse, it's been shown that writing in a journal about upsetting events, giving attention to your thoughts and emotions, can foster growth and healing, not only mentally, but also physically.

We can be mindful of our negativity by being specific. When someone asks how we are, we usually answer, "good," "okay," "fine," or "bad." Sometimes this is because we know a truthful, detailed answer is not expected or wanted, but we tend to be equally vague when we complain. We might say we're angry or sad when we're offended or disappointed. Instead, we can better manage our feelings by choosing our words carefully. Instead of describing ourselves as feeling angry, sad, anxious, hurt, embarrassed, and happy, the *Harvard Business Review* lists nine more specific words that we could use for each one of these emotions. Instead of being angry, we might better describe ourselves as annoyed, defensive, or spiteful. Monks are considered quiet because they are trained to choose their words so carefully that it takes some time. We choose words carefully and use them with purpose.

So much is lost in bad communication. For example, instead of complaining to a friend, who can't do anything about it, that your partner always comes home late, communicate directly and mindfully with your partner. You might say, "I appreciate that you work hard and have a lot to balance. When you come home later than you promised, it drives me crazy. You could support me by texting me as soon as you know you're running late." When our complaints are understood—by ourselves and others—they can be more productive.

In addition to making our negativity more productive, we can also deliberately swap in positivity. One way to do this, as I mentioned, is to use our negativity—like envy—to guide us to what we want. But we can also swap in new feelings. In English, we have the words "empathy" and "compassion" to express our ability to feel the pain that others suffer, but we don't have a word for experiencing vicarious joy—joy on behalf of other people. Perhaps this is a sign that we all need to work on it. ***Mudita* is the principle of taking sympathetic or unselfish joy in the good fortune of others.**

If I only find joy in my own successes, I'm limiting my joy. But if I can take pleasure in the successes of my friends and family—ten, twenty, fifty people!—I get to experience fifty times the happiness and joy. Who doesn't want that?

The material world has convinced us that there are only a limited number of colleges worth attending, a limited number of good jobs available, a limited number of people who get lucky. In such a finite world, there's only so much success and happiness to go around, and whenever other people experience them, your chances of doing so decrease. But monks believe that when it comes to happiness and joy, there is always a seat with your name on it. In other words, you don't need to worry about someone taking your place. In the theater of happiness, there is no limit. Everyone who wants to partake in *mudita* can watch the show. With unlimited seats, there is no fear of missing out.

Radhanath Swami is my spiritual teacher and the author of several books, including *The Journey Home*. I asked him how to stay peaceful and be a positive force in a world where there is so much negativity. He said, "There is toxicity everywhere around us. In the environment, in the political atmosphere, but the origin is in people's hearts. Unless we clean the ecology of our own heart and inspire others to do the same, we will be an instrument of polluting the environment. But if we create

TRY THIS: REVERSE ENVY

Make a list of five people you care about, but also feel competitive with. Come up with at least one reason that you're envious of each one: something they've achieved, something they're better at, something that's gone well for them. Did that achievement actually take anything away from you? Now think about how it benefitted your friend. Visualize everything good that has come to them from this achievement. Would you want to take any of these things away if you could, even knowing that they would not come to you? If so, this envy is robbing you of joy. Envy is more destructive to you than whatever your friend has accomplished. Spend your energy transforming it.

purity in our own heart, then we can contribute great purity to the world around us."

KṢAMĀ: AMENDING ANGER

We've talked about strategies to manage and minimize the daily negativity in your life. But nuisances like complaining, comparing, and gossip can feel manageable next to bigger negative emotions like pain and anger. We all harbor anger in some form: anger from the past, or anger at people who continue to play a big role in our lives. Anger at misfortune. Anger at the living and the dead. Anger turned inward.

When we are deeply wounded, anger is often part of the response. Anger is a great, flaming ball of negative emotion, and when we cannot let it go, no matter how we try, the anger takes on a life of its own. The toll is enormous. I want to talk specifically about how to deal with anger we feel toward other people.

Kṣamā is Sanskrit for forgiveness. It suggests that you bring patience and forbearance to your dealings with others. Sometimes we have been wounded so deeply that we can't imagine how we might forgive the person who hurt us. But, contrary to what most of us believe, forgiveness is primarily an action we take within ourselves. Sometimes it's better (and safer and healthier) not to have direct contact with the person at all; other times, the person who hurt us is no longer around to be forgiven directly. But those factors don't impede forgiveness because it is, first and foremost, internal. It frees you from anger.

One of my clients told me, "I had to reach back to my childhood to pinpoint why I felt unloved and unworthy. My paternal grandmother set the tone for this feeling. I realized she treated me differently because she didn't like my mother. [I had to] forgive her even though she passed on already. I realized I was always worthy and always lovable. She was broken, not I."

The Bhagavad Gita describes three *gunas*, or modes of life: *tamas*, *rajas*, and *sattva*, which represent "ignorance," "impulsivity," and "goodness." I have found that these three modes can be applied to any activity—for example, when you pull back from a conflict and look for understanding, it's very useful to try to shift from *rajas*—impulsivity and passion—to *sattva*—goodness, positivity, and peace. These modes are the foundation of my approach to forgiveness.

TRANSFORMATIONAL FORGIVENESS

Before we find our way to forgiveness, we are stuck in anger. We may even want revenge, to return the pain that a person has inflicted on us. An eye for an eye. Revenge is the mode of ignorance—it's often said that you can't fix yourself by breaking someone else. Monks don't hinge their choices and feelings on others' behaviors. You believe revenge will make you feel better because of how the other person will react. But when you make your vindictive play and the person doesn't have the response you fantasized about—guess what? *You* only feel more pain. Revenge backfires.

When you rise above revenge, you can begin the process of forgiveness. People tend to think in binary terms: You either forgive someone, or you don't forgive someone, but (as I will suggest more than once in

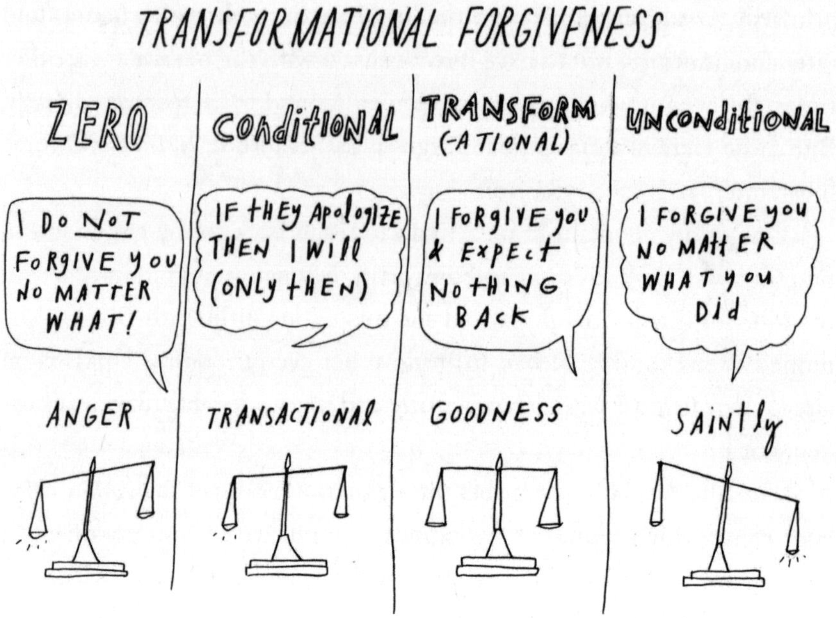

this book) there are often multiple levels. These levels give us leeway to be where we are, to progress in our own time, and to climb only as far as we can. On the scale of forgiveness, the bottom (though it is higher than revenge) is *zero forgiveness*. "I am not going to forgive that person, no matter what. I don't want to hurt them, but I'm never going to forgive them." On this step we are still stuck in anger, and there is no resolution. As you might imagine, this is an uncomfortable place to stay.

The next step is *conditional forgiveness*: If they apologize, then I'll apologize. If they promise never to do it again, I'll forgive them. This transactional forgiveness comes from the mode of impulse—driven by the need to feed your own emotions. Research at Luther College shows that forgiving appears to be easier when we get (or give) an apology, but I don't want us to focus on conditional forgiveness. I want you to rise higher.

The next step is something called *transformational forgiveness*. This is forgiveness in the mode of goodness. In transformational forgiveness, we find the strength and calmness to forgive without expecting an apology or anything else in return.

There is one level higher on the forgiveness ladder: *unconditional forgiveness*. This is the level of forgiveness that a parent often has for a child. No matter what that child does or will do, the parent has already forgiven them. The good news is, I'm not suggesting you aim for that. What I want you to achieve is transformational forgiveness.

PEACE OF MIND

Forgiveness has been shown to bring peace to our minds. Forgiveness actually conserves energy. Transformational forgiveness is linked to a slew of health improvements including: fewer medications taken, better sleep quality, and reduced somatic symptoms including back pain, headache, nausea, and fatigue. Forgiveness eases stress, because we no longer recycle the angry thoughts, both conscious and subconscious, that stressed us out in the first place.

In fact, science shows that in close relationships, there's less emotional tension between partners when they're able to forgive each other, and that promotes physical well-being. In a study published in a 2011 edition of the journal *Personal Relationships*, sixty-eight married couples agreed to have an eight-minute talk about a recent incident where one spouse "broke the rules" of the marriage. The couples then separately watched replays of the interviews and researchers measured their blood pressure. In couples where the "victim" was able to forgive their spouse, *both* partners' blood pressure decreased. It just goes to show that forgiveness is good for everyone.

Giving and receiving forgiveness both have health benefits. When we make forgiveness a regular part of our spiritual practice, we start to notice all of our relationships blossoming. We're no longer holding grudges. There's less drama to deal with.

TRY THIS: **ASK FOR AND RECEIVE FORGIVENESS**

In this exercise we try to untangle the knot of pain and/or anger created by conflict. Even if the relationship is not one you want to salvage or have the option of rebuilding, this exercise will help you let go of anger and find peace.

Before you start, visualize yourself in the other person's shoes. Acknowledge their pain and understand that it is why they are causing you pain.

Then, write a letter of forgiveness.

1. List all the ways you think the other person did you wrong. Forgiving another person honestly and specifically goes a long way toward healing the relationship. Start each item with "I forgive you for. . ." Keep going until you get everything out. We're not sending this letter, so you can repeat yourself if the same thing keeps coming to mind. Write everything you wanted to say but never had a chance. You don't have to feel forgiveness. Yet. When you write it down, what you're doing is beginning to understand the pain more specifically so that you can slowly let it go.
2. Acknowledge your own shortcomings. What was your role, if any, in the situation or conflict? List the ways you feel you did wrong, starting each with the phrase "Please forgive me for . . ." Remember you can't undo the past, but taking responsibility for your role will help you understand and let go of your anger toward yourself and the other person.
3. When you are done with this letter, record yourself reading it. (Most phones can do this.) Play it back, putting yourself in the position of the objective observer. Remember that the pain inflicted on you isn't yours. It's the other person's pain. When you squeeze an orange, you get orange juice. When you squeeze someone full of pain, pain comes out. Instead of absorbing it or giving it back, if you forgive, you help diffuse the pain.

FORGIVENESS IS A TWO-WAY STREET

Forgiveness has to flow in both directions. None of us is perfect, and though there will be situations where you are blameless, there are also times when there are missteps on both sides of a conflict. When you cause pain and others cause you pain, it's as if your hearts get twisted together into an uncomfortable knot. When we forgive, we start to separate our pain from theirs and to heal ourselves emotionally. But when we ask for forgiveness at the same time, we untwist together. This is a bit trickier, because we're much more comfortable finding fault in other people and then forgiving it. We're not used to admitting fault and taking responsibility for what we create in our lives.

FORGIVING OURSELVES

Sometimes, when we feel shame or guilt for what we've done in the past, it's because those actions no longer reflect our values. Now, when we look at our former selves, we don't relate to their decisions. This is actually good news—the reason we're hurting over our past is because we've made progress. We did the best we could then, but we can do better now. What could be better than moving forward? We're already winning. We're already crushing it.

When we wrap our heads around the fact that we can't undo the past, we begin to accept our own imperfections and mistakes, forgive

TRY THIS: **FORGIVE YOURSELF**

The exercise above can also be used to forgive yourself. Starting each line with "I forgive myself for . . . ," list the reasons you feel angry at or disappointed in yourself. Then read it out loud or record it and play it for yourself. Bring out the objective observer, and find understanding for yourself, letting go of the pain.

ourselves, and, in doing so, open ourselves up to the emotional healing we all yearn for.

ELEVATE

The pinnacle of forgiveness, true *sattva*, is to wish the person who caused you pain well.

"I became a Buddhist because I hated my husband." That's not something you hear every day, but Buddhist nun and author of *When Things Fall Apart* Pema Chödrön is only kind of kidding. After her divorce, she went into a negativity spiral where she entertained revenge fantasies because of her husband's affair. Eventually, she came across the writings of Chögyam Trungpa Rinpoche, a meditation master who founded Naropa University in Boulder, Colorado. In reading his work, she realized that the relationship had become like a malignant cell—instead of dying off, her anger and blame were causing the negativity of the breakup to spread. Once Chödrön allowed herself to "become more like a river than a rock," she was able to forgive her husband and move forward. She now refers to her ex-husband as one of her greatest teachers.

If you want the negativity between yourself and another person to dissipate, you have to hope that you both heal. You don't have to tell them directly, but send the energy of well-wishing out into the air. This is when you feel most free and at peace—because you're truly able to let go.

Negativity is a natural part of life. We tease and provoke, express vulnerability, connect over shared values and fears. It's hard to find a comedy show that isn't based on negative observations. But there is a line between negativity that helps us navigate life and negativity that puts more pain out into the world. You might talk about the problems someone's child is having with addiction because you are scared that it will happen to your family and hoping to avoid it. But you also might gossip about the same issue to judge the family and feel better about your own. Ellen DeGeneres sees the line clearly—in an interview with *Parade* magazine she said that she doesn't think it's funny to make fun of people. "The world is filled with negativity. I want people to watch me and think, 'I feel good, and I'm going to make somebody else feel good today.'" This is the spirit in which monks have fun—we are playful and laugh easily. When new monks arrived, they often took themselves too seriously (I know I did), and the senior monks would have a twinkle in their eyes when they said, "Steady now, don't waste all your energy on your first day." Whenever the priest brought out the most special sacred food—which was sweeter and tastier than the simple food we ordinarily ate—the younger monks would joke-wrestle to get to it first. And if someone fell asleep and snored during meditation, we would all glance at one another, not even trying to hide our distraction.

We needn't reduce our thoughts and words to 100 percent sunshine and positivity. But we should challenge ourselves to dig to the root of negativity, to understand its origins in ourselves and those around us, and to be mindful and deliberate in how we manage the energy it absorbs. We begin to let go through recognition and forgiveness. We spot, stop, and swap—observe, reflect, and develop new behaviors to replace the negativity in our lives, always striving toward self-discipline and bliss. When you stop feeling so curious about others' misfortunes and instead take pleasure in their successes, you're healing.

The less time you fixate on everyone else, the more time you have to focus on yourself.

Negativity, as we've discussed, often arises from fear. Next, we will explore fear itself, how it gets in our way, and how we can make it a productive part of life.

THREE

FEAR

Welcome to Hotel Earth

Fear does not prevent death. It prevents life.

—Buddha

The epic battle of Mahabharata is about to begin. The air is thick with anticipation: Thousands of warriors finger the hilts of their swords as their horses snort and paw at the ground. But our hero, Arjuna, is terrified. He has family and friends on either side of this battle, and many of them are about to die. Arjuna, among the fiercest fighters of the land, drops his bow.

The Bhagavad Gita opens on a battlefield with a warrior's terror. Arjuna is the most talented archer in the land, yet fear has caused him to totally lose connection with his abilities. The same thing happens to each of us. We have so much to offer the world, but fear and anxiety disconnect us from our abilities. This is because growing up we were taught, directly or indirectly, that fear is negative. "Don't be scared," our parents told us. "Scaredy-cat," our friends teased. Fear was an embarrassing, humiliating reaction to be ignored or hidden. But fear has a flip side, which Tom Hanks alluded to in his commencement address at Yale

University. "Fear," he told the graduates, "will get the worst of the best of us."

The truth is, we'll never live entirely without fear and anxiety. We'll never be able to fix our economic, social, and political climates to entirely eliminate conflict and uncertainty, not to mention our everyday interpersonal challenges. And that's okay, because fear isn't bad; it's simply a warning flag—your mind saying "This doesn't look good! Something might go wrong!" It's what we do with that signal that matters. We can use our fear of the effects of climate change to motivate us to develop solutions, or we can allow it to make us feel overwhelmed and hopeless and do nothing as a result. Sometimes fear is a critical warning to help us survive true danger, but most of the time what we feel is anxiety related to everyday concerns about money, jobs, and relationships. We allow anxiety—everyday fear—to hold us back by blocking us from our true feelings. The longer we hold on to fears, the more they ferment until eventually they become toxic.

I am sitting cross-legged on the floor of a cold basement room in the monastery with twenty or so other monks. I've been at the ashram for only a couple months. Gauranga Das has just discussed the scene in the Gita when Arjuna, the hero, is overcome by fear. It turns out that Arjuna's fear makes him pause instead of charging directly into battle. He's devastated that so many people he loves will die that day. The fear and anguish lead him to question his actions for the first time. Doing so provokes him into a long conversation about human morals, spirituality, and how life works according to Krishna, who is his charioteer.

When Gauranga Das concludes his lecture, he asks us to close our eyes, then directs us to relive a fear from our past: not just imagine it but feel it in our bodies—all the sights, sounds, and smells of that experience. He tells us that it's important that we not choose something minor, such as a first day at school or learning to swim (unless those experiences were truly terrifying), but something significant. He wants us to uncover, accept, and create a new relationship with our deepest fears.

We start joking around—someone makes fun of my overreaction to a snakeskin I came across on one of our walks. Gauranga Das acknowledges our antics with a knowing nod. "If you want to do this activity properly," he says, "you have to push beyond the part of your mind that's making fun of it. That's a defense mechanism keeping you from really dealing with the issue, and that's what we do with fear. We distract ourselves from it," Gauranga Das says. "You need to go past that place." The laughter fades, and I can almost feel everyone's spine straighten along with my own.

I close my eyes and my mind quiets down, but I still don't expect much. I'm not scared of anything. Not really, *I think. Then, as I drop further and further into meditation, past the noise and chatter of my brain, I ask myself,* What am I really scared of? *Flickers of truth begin to appear. I see my fear of exams as a kid. I know—that probably sounds trivial. No one likes exams, right? But exams were some of my greatest anxieties growing up. Sitting in meditation, I allow myself to explore what was behind that fear.* What am I really scared of? *I ask myself again. Gradually, I recognize that my fear focused on what my parents and my friends would think of my scores, and of me as a result. About what my extended family would say, and how I'd be compared to my cousins and pretty much everyone else around me. I don't just see this fear in my mind's eye, I feel it in my body—the tightness in my chest, the tension in my jaw, as if I am right back there.* What am I really scared of? *Then I start to delve into fear around the times when I'd gotten in trouble at school. I was so worried that I would be suspended or expelled. How would my parents react? What would my teachers think? I invite myself to go even deeper.* What am I really scared of? *I see this fear around my parents—of them not getting along and of me, at a young age, trying to mediate their marriage. Of thinking,* How can I please both of them? How can I manage them and make sure they're happy? *That's when I find the root of my fear.* What am I really scared of? *I am afraid that I can't make my parents happy. As soon as I hit that revelation, I know I've reached the true fear beneath all of the other fears. It is a full-body aha moment, like I sank deeper and deeper under water, pressure mounting against my chest, increasingly desperate to breathe, and when that realization hit me, my head popped up, and I gasped for air.*

• • •

Half an hour earlier I'd been so sure I wasn't scared of anything, and suddenly I was uncovering my deepest fears and anxieties, which I'd managed to hide completely from myself for years. By gently, but consistently, asking myself what I was scared of, I refused to let my mind dodge the question. Our brains are really good at keeping us from entering uncomfortable spaces. But by repeating a question rather than rephrasing it, we essentially corner our brain. Now, it's not about being aggressive with ourselves—this isn't an interrogation, it's an interview. You want to ask yourself the question with sincerity, not force.

Being scared of exam results was what I call a branch. As you develop your relationship with your fear, you'll have to distinguish between branches—the immediate fears that come up during your self-interview—and the root. Tracking my fear of exam results and the other "branch" fears that appeared led me to the root: fearing I couldn't make my parents happy.

THE FEAR OF FEAR

During my three years as a monk, I learned to let go of my fear of fear. Fear of punishment, humiliation, or failure—and their accompanying negative attitudes—no longer propel my misguided attempts at self-protection. I can recognize the opportunities that fear signals. Fear can help us identify and address patterns of thinking and behavior that don't serve us.

We let our fear drive us, but fear itself is not our real problem. Our real problem is that *we fear the wrong things:* What we should really fear is that we will miss the opportunities that fear offers. Gavin de Becker, one of the world's leading security experts, in *The Gift of Fear* calls it "a brilliant internal guardian that stands ready to warn you of hazards and guide you through risky situations." Often, we notice fear's warning but ignore its guidance. If we learn how to recognize what fear can teach us about ourselves and what we value, then we can use it as a tool to obtain greater meaning, purpose, and fulfillment in our lives. We can use fear to get to the best of us.

A few decades ago, scientists conducted an experiment in the Arizona desert where they built "Biosphere 2"—a huge steel-and-glass enclosure with air that had been purified, clean water, nutrient-rich soil, and lots of natural light. It was meant to provide ideal living conditions for the flora and fauna within. And while it was successful in some ways, in one it was an absolute failure. Over and over, when trees inside the Biosphere grew to a certain height, they would simply fall over. At first, the phenomenon confused scientists. Finally, they realized that the Biosphere lacked a key element necessary to the trees' health: wind. In a natural environment, trees are buffeted by wind. They respond to that pressure and agitation by growing stronger bark and deeper roots to increase their stability.

We waste a lot of time and energy trying to stay in the comfortable bubble of our self-made Biospheres. We fear the stresses and challenges of change, but those stresses and challenges are the wind that makes us stronger. In 2017, Alex Honnold stunned the world when he became the first person ever to climb Freerider—a nearly three-thousand-foot ascent up Yosemite National Park's legendary El Capitan—entirely without ropes. Honnold's unbelievable accomplishment was the subject of the award-winning documentary *Free Solo*. In the film Honnold is asked about how he deals with knowing that when he free climbs, the options are perfection or death. "People talk about trying to suppress your fear," he responded. "I try to look at it a different way—I try to expand my comfort zone by practicing the moves over and over again. I work through the fear until it's just not scary anymore." Honnold's fear prompts him to put in extensive amounts of focused work before he attempts a monumental free solo. Making his fear productive is a critical component of his training, and it's propelled Honnold to the top of his climbing game and to the top of mountains. If we can stop viewing stress and the fear that often accompanies it as negative and instead see the potential benefits, we're on our way to changing our relationship with fear.

THE STRESS RESPONSE

The first thing we need to realize about stress is that it doesn't do a good job of classifying problems. Recently I had the chance to test a virtual reality device. In the virtual world, I was climbing a mountain. As I stepped out on a ledge, I felt as scared as if I were actually eight thousand feet in the air. When your brain shouts "Fear!" your body can't differentiate between whether the threat is real or imagined—whether your survival is in jeopardy, or you're thinking about your taxes. As soon as that fear signal goes off, our bodies prepare us to fight or flee, or sometimes to freeze. If we launch into this high-alert fear state too often, all of those stress hormones start to send us downhill, affecting our immune systems, our sleep, and our ability to heal.

Yet studies show that being able to successfully deal with intermittent stressors—such as managing that big work project or moving to a new house—to approach them head-on, like those trees standing up to the wind, contributes to *better* health, along with greater feelings of accomplishment and well-being.

When you deal with fear and hardship, you realize that you're capable of dealing with fear and hardship. This gives you a new perspective: the confidence that when bad things happen, you will find ways to handle them. With that increased objectivity, you become better able to differentiate what's actually worth being afraid of and what's not.

From the fear meditation I described above, I came away with the idea that we have four different emotional reactions to fear: We panic, we freeze, we run away, or we bury it, as I had buried my anxiety about my parents. The first two are shorter-term strategies, while the second two are longer-term, but all of them distract us from the situation and prevent us from using our fear productively.

In order to change our relationship with fear, we have to change our perception of it. Once we can see the value that fear offers, we can change how we respond. An essential step in this reprogramming is learning to recognize our reaction pattern to fear.

WORK WITH FEAR

I've mentioned that monks begin the growth process with awareness. Just as we do when facing negativity, we want to externalize our fear and take a step back from it, becoming objective observers.

The process of learning to work with fear isn't just about doing a few exercises that solve everything, it's about changing your attitude toward fear, understanding that it has something to offer, then committing to doing the work of identifying and trying to shift out of your pattern of distraction every time it appears. Each of the four distractions from fear—panicking, freezing, running away, and burying—is a different version of a single action, or rather, a single *inaction*: refusing to accept our fear. So the first step in transforming our fear from a negative to a positive is doing just that.

ACCEPT YOUR FEAR

To close the gap with our fear, we must acknowledge its presence. As my teacher told us, "You've got to recognize your pain." We were still seated, and he told us to take a deep breath and silently say, "I see you," to our pain. That was our first acknowledgment of our relationship with fear, to breathe in and repeat, "I see you, my pain. I see you, my fear," and as we breathed out, we said, "I see you and I'm here with you. I see you and I am here for you." Pain makes us pay attention. Or it should. When we say "I see you," we are giving it the attention it is asking for. Just like a crying baby needs to be heard and held.

Breathing steadily while we acknowledged our fear helped us calm our mental and physical responses in its presence. Walk toward your fear. Become familiar with it. In this way we bring ourselves into full presence with fear. When you wake up to that smoke alarm going off, you would acknowledge what is happening in the moment, and then you would get out of the house. Later, in a calmer state, you would reflect on how the fire started or where it came from. You would call the insurance company. You would take control of the narrative. That is recognizing and staying in present time with fear.

TRY THIS: RATE YOUR FEAR

Draw a line with zero at one end and ten at the other. What's the worst thing you can imagine? Maybe it's a paralyzing injury or losing a loved one. Make that a ten on the line. Now rate your current fear in relation to that one. Just doing this helps give some perspective. When you feel fear crop up, rate it. Where does it fall next to something that's truly scary?

FIND FEAR PATTERNS

Along with accepting our fear, we must get personal with it. This means recognizing the situations in which it regularly appears. A powerful question to ask your fear (again, with kindness and sincerity, as many times as necessary) is "When do I feel you?" After my initial work with fear at the monastery, I continued to identify all of the spaces and situations in which my fear emerged. I consistently saw that when I was worried about my exams, when I was worried about my parents, or about my performance at school or getting in trouble, the fear always led me to the same concern: how I was perceived by others. What would they think of me? My root fear influences my decision-making. That awareness now prompts me when I reach a decisive moment to take a closer look and ask myself, "Is this decision influenced by how others will perceive me?" In this way, I can use my awareness of my fear as a tool to help me make decisions that are truly in line with my values and purpose.

Sometimes we can trace our fears through the actions we take, and sometimes it's the actions we're reluctant to take. One of my clients was a successful attorney, but she was tired of practicing law and wanted to do something new. She came to me because she was letting her fear stop her. "What if I jump and there's nothing on the other side?" she asked me. That sounded like a branch question, so I kept probing. "What are you really scared of?" I asked her, then gently kept asking until eventually she sighed and said, "I've spent so much effort and energy building this career. What if I'm just throwing it all away?" I asked again and finally we got to the root: She was afraid of failure and of being seen as less than an intelligent, capable person by others and by herself. Once she learned and acknowledged the true nature of her fear, she was on her way to recasting its role in her life, but first she needed to develop some real intimacy with it. She needed to walk into her fear.

One of the problems we identified was that she had no role models. All of the attorneys she knew were still practicing full-time. She needed to see people who had successfully done some version of what she wanted to do, so I asked her to spend time getting to know former attorneys who were now working in new careers that they loved. When she did that, she not only saw that what she dreamed of was possible, she was also delighted to learn how many of those people said they were still applying skills that they had acquired and used to practice law. She wouldn't be throwing all of her hard work away after all. I also asked her to research jobs she might consider. Through that exercise, she found that many of the "soft skills" she'd had to learn to be a successful attorney, such as communication, teamwork, and problem-solving, were highly sought after elsewhere too. By developing that intimacy with her fear—getting up close and examining what she was afraid of—she ended up with information that left her feeling more empowered and excited about the idea of switching careers.

Patterns for distracting ourselves from fear are established when we're young. They are deeply ingrained, so it takes some time and effort to uncover them. Recognizing our fear patterns helps us trace fear to the root. From there we can decipher whether there's truly any cause for urgency, or whether our fear can actually lead us to recognize opportunities to live more in alignment with our values, passion, and purpose.

THE CAUSE OF FEAR: ATTACHMENT. THE CURE FOR FEAR: DETACHMENT

Though we are developing intimacy with our fear, we want to see it as its own entity, separate from us. When we talk about our emotions, we usually say we *are* that emotion. I *am* angry. I *am* sad. I *am* afraid. Talking to our fear separates it from us and helps us understand that the fear is not us, it is just something we're experiencing. When you meet someone who gives off a negative vibe, you feel it, but you don't think that vibe *is* you. It's the same with our emotions—they are something we're feeling, but they are not us. Try shifting from I *am* angry to I *feel* angry. I *feel* sad. I *feel* afraid. A simple change, but a profound one because it puts our emotions in their rightful place. Having this perspective calms down our initial reactions and give us the space to examine our fear and the situation around it without judgment.

When we track our fears back to their source, most of us find that they're closely related to attachment—our need to own and control things. We hold on to ideas we have about ourselves, to the material possessions and standard of living that we think define us, to the relationships we want to be one thing even if they are clearly another. That is the *monkey mind* thinking. A *monk mind* practices detachment. We realize that everything—from our houses to our families—is borrowed.

Clinging to temporary things gives them power over us, and they become sources of pain and fear. But when we *accept* the temporary nature of everything in our lives, we can feel gratitude for the good fortune of getting to borrow them for a time. Even the most permanent of possessions, belonging to the most wealthy and powerful, don't actually belong to them. This is just as true for the rest of us. And for many—indeed most—of us, that impermanence causes great fear. But, as I learned in the ashram, we can shift our fear to a soaring sense of freedom.

Our teachers made a distinction between useful and hurtful fears. They told us that a useful fear alerts us to a situation we can change.

If the doctor tells you that you have poor health because of your diet, and you fear disability or disease, that's a useful fear because you can change your diet. When your health improves as a result, you eliminate your fear. But fearing that our parents will die is a hurtful fear because we can't change the truth of the matter. We transform hurtful fears into useful fears by focusing on what we can control. We can't stop our parents from dying, but we use the fear to remind us to spend more time with them. In the words of Śāntideva, "It is not possible to control all external events; but if I simply control my mind, what need is there to control other things?" This is detachment, when you observe your own reactions from a distance—with your monk mind—making decisions with a clear perspective.

There's a common misconception about detachment that I'd like to address. People often equate detachment with indifference. They think that seeing things, people, and experiences as temporary or seeing them from a distance diminishes our ability to enjoy life, but that's not the case. Imagine you're driving a luxury rental car. Do you tell yourself that you own it? Of course not. You know you only have it for the week, and in some ways, that allows you to enjoy it more—you are grateful for the chance to drive a convertible down the Pacific Coast Highway *because* it's something you won't always get to do. Imagine you're staying in the most beautiful Airbnb. It's got a hot tub, chef's kitchen, ocean views; it's so beautiful and exciting. You don't spend every moment there dreading your departure in a week. When we acknowledge that all of our blessings are like a fancy rental car or a beautiful Airbnb, we are free to enjoy them without living in constant fear of losing them. We are all the lucky vacationers enjoying our stay in Hotel Earth.

Detachment is the ultimate practice in minimizing fear. Once I identified my anxiety about disappointing my parents, I was able to detach from it. I realized I had to take responsibility for my life. My parents might be upset, they might not—I had no control over that. I could only make decisions based on my own values.

TRY THIS: AUDIT YOUR ATTACHMENTS

Ask yourself: "What am I afraid of losing?" Start with the externals: Is it your car, your house, your looks? Write down everything you think of. Now think about the internals: your reputation, your status, your sense of belonging? Write those down too. These combined lists are likely to be the greatest sources of pain in your life—your fear of having these things taken away. Now start thinking about changing your mental relationship with those things so that you are less attached to them. Remember—you can still fully love and enjoy your partner, your children, your home, your money, from a space of nonattachment. It's about understanding and accepting that all things are temporary and that we can't truly own or control anything, so that we can fully appreciate these things and they can enhance our life rather than be a source of griping and fear. What better way to accept that children eventually go off to live their own lives and call you once a week, if you're lucky?

This is a lifelong practice, but as you become more and more accepting of the fact that we don't truly own or control anything, you'll find yourself actually enjoying and valuing people, things, and experiences more, and being more thoughtful about which ones you choose to include in your life.

MANAGING SHORT-TERM FEARS

Detaching from your fears allows you to address them. Years ago, a friend lost his job. Jobs are security, and we are all naturally attached to the idea of putting food on the table. Right away, my friend went into panic mode. "Where are we going to get money? I'm never going to get hired again. I'm going to have to get two or three gigs to cover our bills!" Not only did he make grim predictions about the future, he started questioning the past. "I should have been better at my work. I should have worked harder and longer hours!"

When you panic, you start to anticipate outcomes that have not yet come to pass. Fear makes us fiction writers. We start with a premise, an idea, a fear—what will happen if . . . Then we spiral off, devising possible future scenarios. When we anticipate future outcomes, fear holds us back, imprisoning us in our imaginations. The Roman Stoic philosopher Seneca observed that "Our fears are more numerous than our dangers, and we suffer more in our imagination than reality."

We can manage acute stress if we detach on the spot. There's an old Taoist parable about a farmer whose horse ran away. "How unlucky!" his brother tells him. The farmer shrugs. "Good thing, bad thing, who knows," he says. A week later, the wayward horse finds its way home, and with it is a beautiful wild mare. "That's amazing!" his brother says, admiring the new horse with no small envy. Again, the farmer is unmoved. "Good thing, bad thing, who knows," he says. A few days later, the farmer's son climbs up on the mare, hoping to tame the wild beast, but the horse bucks and rears, and the boy, hurled to the ground, breaks a leg. "How unlucky!" his brother says, with a tinge of satisfaction. "Good thing, bad thing, who knows," the farmer replies again. The next day, the young men of the village are called into military service, but because the son's leg is broken, he is excused from the draft. His brother tells the farmer that this, surely, is the best news of all. "Good thing, bad thing, who knows," the farmer says. The farmer in this story didn't get lost in "what if" but instead focused on "what is." During my monk training, we were taught, "Don't judge the moment."

I passed along the same advice to someone I advised who'd lost his job. Instead of judging the moment, he needed to accept his situation and whatever came of it, focusing on what he could control. I worked with him on first slowing everything down, then acknowledging the facts of his situation—he had lost his job, period. From there he had a choice: He could panic or freeze, or he could take this opportunity to work with fear as a tool, using it as an indicator of what truly mattered to him and to see what new opportunities might arise.

When I asked him what he was most afraid of, he said it was that he wouldn't be able to take care of his family. I gently urged him to be more specific. He said he was worried about money. So I challenged him to think of other ways he might support his family. After all, his wife worked, so they had some money coming in; they weren't going to be out on the street. "Time," he said. "Now I have time to spend with my kids, taking them to and from school, helping them with their homework. And while they're at school, I'll actually have time to look for a new job. A better one." Because he slowed down, accepted his fear, and gained clarity around it, he was able to defuse his panic and see that fear was actually alerting him to an opportunity. Time is another form of wealth. He realized that while he had lost his job, he had gained something else very valuable. Using his newfound time, he was not only more present in his kids' lives, but he also ended up getting a new, better job. Reframing the situation stopped him from draining energy negatively and encouraged him to start applying it positively.

Still, it's hard to not judge the moment and remain open to opportunity when the unknown future spins like a whirlwind through your body and brain. Sometimes our panic or freeze responses rush ahead of us and make it difficult to suspend judgment. Let's talk about some strategies to help us amend panic and fear.

Short-Circuit Fear

Fortunately, a simple, powerful tool to short-circuit the panic response is always with us: our breath. Before I give a talk, when I'm standing offstage listening to my introduction, I'll feel my heart beat faster and my hands getting moist. I've coached people who perform in front of full arenas and people who present at everyday meetings, and, like the rest of us, they feel most of their fear physically. Whether it's performance anxiety or social fears, such as before a job interview or attending a party, our fear manifests in the body, and these bodily cues are the first signals that fear is about to take over. Panic and freezing are a disconnect between our bodies and our minds. Either our bodies go on high alert and rush ahead of our mental processes, or our minds are racing and our bodies start to shut down. As a monk, I learned a simple breathing exercise to help realign my body and mind and stop fear from stopping me. I still use it every time I'm about to give a talk to a large group, enter a stressful meeting, or go into a room full of people I don't know.

TRY THIS: DON'T PANIC! USE YOUR BREATH TO REALIGN BODY AND MIND

"Breathe to calm and relax yourself" meditation: (see page 89)

1. Inhale slowly to a count of 4.
2. Hold for a count of 4.
3. Exhale slowly to a count of 4 or more.
4. Repeat until you feel your heart rate slow down.

It's really that easy. You see, deep breathing activates a part of our nervous system called the vagus nerve, which in turn stimulates a relaxation response throughout our bodies. The simple act of controlled breathing is like flipping a switch that shifts our nervous system from the sympathetic, or fight-flight-freeze, state to the parasympathetic, or rest-and-digest, state, allowing our mind and body to get back in synch.

See the Whole Story

Breath is useful on the spot, but some fears are hard to dispel with our breath alone. When we go through a period of instability, we fear what's ahead. When we know we have a test or a job interview, we fear the outcome. In the moment, we can't see the complete picture, but when the stressful period passes, we never look back to learn from the experience. Life isn't a collection of unrelated events, it's a narrative that stretches into the past and the future. We are natural storytellers, and we can use that proclivity to our detriment—to tell horror stories about possible future events. Better to try seeing our lives as a single, long, continuing story, not just disconnected pieces. When you are hired for a job, take a moment to reflect on all the lost jobs and/or failed interviews that led to this victory. You can think of them as necessary challenges along the way. When we learn to stop segmenting experiences and periods of our life and instead see them as scenes and acts in a larger narrative, we gain perspective that helps us deal with fear.

TRY THIS: EXPAND THE MOMENT

Think of something great that happened to you. Perhaps it was the birth of a child or getting that new job you wanted. Let yourself feel that joy for a moment. Now rewind to the events that occurred just before it. What was going on in your life before the birth of your child or before you were selected for that job? Perhaps it was months and months of trying unsuccessfully to conceive or being rejected from three other jobs you'd applied for. Now try to see that narrative as a whole story—a progression from the bad to the good. Open yourself to the idea that perhaps what happened during the challenging time was actually clearing the way for what you're now celebrating, or made you feel even happier about the experience that came after it. Now take a moment to express gratitude for those challenges and weave them into the story of your life.

Admittedly, we do our best celebrating in hindsight. When we are actually experiencing challenges, it's difficult to tell ourselves, "This could end up being a good thing!" But the more we practice looking in the rear-view mirror and finding gratitude for the hard times we've experienced, the more we start to change our programming; the gap between suffering and gratitude gets smaller and smaller; and the intensity of our fear in the moments of hardship begins to diminish.

Revisit Long-Term Fears

Panic and freezing can be dealt with using breath and by reframing the circumstances, but these are short-term fear responses. It is much harder to control the two long-term strategies we use to distract us from fear: burying and running away. One of my favorite ways to understand how these strategies work involves a house on fire. Let's say you wake up in the middle of the night to your smoke detector beeping. Immediately, you're afraid, as you should be—that signal did its job, which was to get your attention. Now you smell smoke, so you gather your family and pets together and you get out of the house, right? This is fear put to its best use.

But what if, upon hearing the smoke alarm, instead of quickly assessing the situation and taking the logical next steps, you hurried over to the smoke detector, removed the battery, and went back to bed? As you can imagine, your problems are about to magnify. Yet that's what we often do with fear. Instead of assessing and responding, we deny or abandon the situation. Relationships are a space where we commonly use the "solution" of avoidance. Let's say you're having some major conflict with your girlfriend. Rather than sitting down with her and talking about what's going on (putting out the fire), or even figuring out that you aren't meant to be together (safely and calmly getting everyone out of the house), you pretend everything's fine (while the destructive fire burns on).

When we deny fear, our problems follow us. In fact, they're probably getting bigger, and bigger, and at some point something will force us to deal with them. When all else fails, pain does make us pay attention. If we don't learn from the signal that alerts us to a problem, we'll end up learning from the results of the problem itself, which is far less desirable. But if we face our fear—we stay, we deal with the fire, we have the tough conversation—we become stronger as a result.

The very first lesson the Gita teaches us is how to handle fear. In the moments before the battle starts, when Arjuna is overcome by fear, he doesn't run from it or bury it; he faces it. In the text, Arjuna is a brave and skilled warrior, yet in this moment it is fear that causes him, for the first time, to reflect. It's often said that when the fear of staying the same outweighs the fear of change, that is when we change. He asks for help in the form of insight and understanding. In that action, he has begun to shift from being controlled by his fear to understanding it. "What you run from only stays with you longer," writes the author of the novel *Fight Club*, Chuck Palahniuk, in his book *Invisible Monsters Remix*. "Find what you're afraid of most and go live there."

That day in the basement of the ashram, I opened myself to my deeply held fears about my parents. I rarely experienced panic or freeze reactions, but that didn't mean I had no fears—it meant I was pushing them down. As my teacher said, "When fear is buried, it's something we cling to, and it makes everything feel tight because we're under this burden of things we've never released." Whether you suppress them or run away from them, your fears and your problems remain with you—and they accumulate. We used to think it didn't matter if we dumped our trash in landfills without regard for the environment. If we couldn't see it or smell it, we figured it would somehow just take care of itself. Yet before regulation, landfills polluted water supplies, and even today they are one of the largest producers of human-generated methane gas in the United States. In the same way, burying our fears takes an unseen toll on our internal landscape.

TRY THIS: DIVE INTO YOUR FEARS

As we did at the ashram, take a deep dive into your fears. At first a few surface-level fears will pop up. Stay with the exercise, asking yourself *What am I really afraid of?* and larger and deeper fears will begin to reveal themselves. These answers don't usually come all at once. Typically, it takes some time to sink below the layers to the real root of your fears. Be open to the answer revealing itself over time, and maybe not even during a meditation or other focused session. You may be at the grocery store selecting avocados one day when all of a sudden it dawns on you. That's just how we operate.

Going through the processes of acknowledging fear, observing our patterns for dealing with it, addressing and amending those patterns helps us to reprogram our view of fear from something that's inherently negative to a neutral signal, or even an indicator of opportunity. When we reclassify fear, we can look past the smoke and stories to what's real, and in so doing, uncover deep and meaningful truths that can inform and empower us. When we identify our attachment-related fears and instead foster detachment, we can live with a greater sense of freedom and enjoyment. And when we channel the energy behind our fears toward service, we diminish our fear of not having enough, and feel happier, more fulfilled, and more connected to the world around us.

Fear motivates us. Sometimes it motivates us toward what we want, but sometimes, if we aren't careful, it limits us with what we think will keep us safe.

Next we will look at our primary motivators (fear is one of four) and how we can deliberately use them to build a fulfilling life.

FOUR

INTENTION

Blinded by the Gold

When there is harmony between the mind, heart,
and resolution then nothing is impossible
—Rig Veda

In our heads we have an image of an ideal life: our relationships, how we spend our time in work and leisure, what we want to achieve. Even without the noise of external influences, certain goals captivate us, and we design our lives around achieving them because we think they will make us happy. But now we will figure out what drives these ambitions, whether they are likely to make us truly happy, and whether happiness is even the right target.

I have just come out of a class where we discussed the idea of rebirth, Saṃsāra, *and now I am strolling through the quiet ashram with a senior monk and a few other students. The ashram has two locations, a temple in Mumbai and the one where I am now, a rural outpost near Palghar. This will eventually be developed into the Govardhan Ecovillage, a beautiful retreat, but for now there are just a few simple, nondescript buildings set in uncultivated land. Dry dirt footpaths divide the grasses. Here and there, monks sit on straw mats, reading or studying. The main building is open to the elements, and inside we can see monks working. As we walk, the senior monk mentions the achievements of some of the monks we pass. He points out one who can meditate for eight hours straight. A few minutes later he gestures to another: "He fasts for seven days in a row." Further along, he points. "Do you see the man sitting under that tree? He can recite every verse from the scripture."*

Impressed, I say, "I wish I could do that."

The monk pauses and turns to look at me. He asks, "Do you wish you could do that, or do you wish you could learn to do that?"

"What do you mean?" I know by now that some of my favorite lessons come not in the classroom, but in moments like this.

He says, "Think about your motivations. Do you want to memorize all of the scripture because it's an impressive achievement, or do you want the experience of having studied it? In the first, all you want is the outcome. In the second, you are curious about what you might learn from the process."

This was a new concept for me, and it blew my mind. Desiring an outcome had always seemed reasonable to me. The monk was telling me to question why I wanted to do what was necessary to reach that outcome.

THE FOUR MOTIVATIONS

No matter how disorganized we might be, we all have plans. We have an idea of what we have to accomplish in the day ahead; we probably have a sense of what the year holds, or what we hope we'll accomplish; and we all have dreams for the future. Something motivates every one of these notions—from needing to pay the rent to wanting to travel the world. Hindu philosopher Bhaktivinoda Thakura describes four fundamental motivations.

1. *Fear.* Thakura describes this as being driven by "sickness, poverty, fear of hell or fear of death."

2. *Desire.* Seeking personal gratification through success, wealth, and pleasure.
3. *Duty.* Motivated by gratitude, responsibility, and the desire to do the right thing.
4. *Love.* Compelled by care for others and the urge to help them.

These four motivations drive everything we do. We make choices, for example, because we're scared of losing our job, wanting to win the admiration of our friends, hoping to fulfill our parents' expectations, or wanting to help others live a better life.

I'm going to talk about each motivation individually, so we get a sense of how they shape our choices.

Fear Is Not Sustainable

In the last chapter we talked about fear, so I'm not going to dwell on it here. When fear motivates you, you pick what you want to achieve—a promotion, a relationship, buying a home—because you believe it will bring you safety and security.

Fear alerts and ignites us. This warning flare is useful—as we discussed, fear points out problems and sometimes motivates us. For instance, the fear of getting fired may motivate you to get organized.

The problem with fear is that it's not sustainable. When we operate in fear for a long time, we can't work to the best of our abilities. We are too worried about getting the wrong result. We become frantic or paralyzed and are unable to evaluate our situations objectively or to take risks.

The Maya of Success

The second motivation is desire. This is when we chase personal gratification. Our path to adventures, pleasures, and comforts often takes the form of material goals. *I want a million-dollar home. I want financial freedom.*

I want an amazing wedding. When I ask people to write down their goals, they often give answers describing what most people think of as success.

We think that success equals happiness, but this idea is an illusion. The Sanskrit word for illusion is *maya*, which means believing in that which is not. When we let achievements and acquisitions determine our course, we're living in the illusion that happiness comes from external measures of success, but all too often we find that when we finally get what we want, when we find success, it doesn't lead to happiness.

Jim Carrey once said, "I think everybody should get rich and famous and do everything they ever dreamed of, so they can see that it's not the answer."

The illusion of success is tied not just to income and acquisitions but to achievements like becoming a doctor or getting a promotion or . . . memorizing the scriptures. My desire in the story above—to be able to recite every verse from the scripture—is the monk's version of material desire. Like all of these "wants," my ambition was centered around an external outcome—being as impressively learned as that other monk.

American spiritual luminary Tara Brach, founder of the Insight Meditation Community of Washington, DC, writes, "As long as we keep attaching our happiness to the external events of our lives, which are ever changing, we'll always be left waiting for it."

Once, as a monk, I visited a temple in Srirangam, one of the three major holy cities in South India. I came upon a worker high up on a scaffold applying gold powder to the intricate details on the temple's ceiling. I'd never seen anything like it, and I stopped to watch. As I gazed upward, a dusting of gold floated down into my eyes. I hurried from the temple to rinse my eyes, then returned, keeping a safe distance this time. This episode felt like a lesson torn from the scriptures: Gold dust is beautiful, but come too close, and it will blur your vision.

The gilt that is used on temples isn't solid gold—it's mixed into a solution. And, as we know, it is used to cover up stone, to make it look like solid gold. It's *maya*, an illusion. In the same way, money and fame are only a facade. Because our search is never for a thing, but for the feeling we think the thing will give us. We all know this already: We see wealthy and/or famous people who seem to "have it all," but who have bad relationships or suffer from depression, and it's obvious that success didn't bring them happiness. The same is true for those of us who aren't rich and famous. We quickly tire of our smartphones and want the next model. We receive a bonus, but the initial excitement fades surprisingly fast when our lives don't really improve. We think that a new phone or a bigger house will make us feel somehow better—cooler or more satisfied—but instead find ourselves wanting more.

Material gratification is external, but happiness is internal. When monks talk about happiness, they tell the story of the musk deer, a tale derived from a poem by Kabir, a fifteenth-century Indian mystic and poet. The musk deer picks up an irresistible scent in the forest and chases it, searching for the source, not realizing that the scent comes from its own pores. It spends its whole life wandering fruitlessly. In the same way we search for happiness, finding it elusive, when it can be found within us.

Happiness and fulfillment come only from mastering the mind and connecting with the soul—not from objects or attainments. Success doesn't guarantee happiness, and happiness doesn't require success. They can feed each other, and we can have them at the same time, but they are not intertwined. After analyzing a Gallup survey on well-being, Princeton University researchers officially concluded that money does not buy happiness after basic needs and then some are fulfilled. While having more money contributes to overall life satisfaction, that impact levels off at a salary of around $75,000. In other words, when it comes to the impact of money on how you view the quality of your life, a middle-class American citizen fares about as well as Jeff Bezos.

Success is earning money, being respected in your work, executing projects smoothly, receiving accolades. Happiness is feeling good about yourself, having close relationships, making the world a better place. More than ever, popular culture celebrates the pursuit of success. TV shows aimed at adolescents focus more on image, money, and fame than in the past. Popular songs and books use language promoting individual achievement over community connection, group membership, and self-acceptance. It's no surprise that happiness rates have consistently declined among Americans adults since the 1970s. And it doesn't just boil down to income. In an interview with the *Washington Post*, Jeffrey Sachs, director of the Center for Sustainable Development and an editor of *World Happiness Report*, points out: "While the average income of people around the world definitely affects their sense of well-being, it doesn't explain all that much, because other factors, both personal and social, are very important determinants of well-being." Sachs says that while generally American incomes have risen since 2005, our happiness has fallen, in part because of social factors like declining trust in the government and our fellow Americans, and weaker social networks.

Duty and Love

If fear limits us and success doesn't satisfy us, then you've probably already guessed that duty and love have more to offer. We all have different goals, but we all want the same things: a life full of joy and meaning. Monks don't seek out the joy part—we aren't looking for happiness or pleasure. Instead, we focus on the satisfaction that comes from living a meaningful life. Happiness can be elusive—it's hard to sustain a high level of joy. But to feel *meaning* shows that our actions have purpose. They lead to a worthwhile outcome. We believe we're leaving a positive imprint. What we do matters, so we matter. Bad things happen, boring chores must get done, life isn't all sunshine and unicorns, but it is always possible to find meaning. If you lose a loved one and someone tells you to look for the positive, to be happy, to focus on the good things in your life—well, you might want to punch that person. But we can survive the worst tragedies by looking for *meaning* in the loss. We might honor a loved one by giving to the community. Or discover a new gratitude for life that we pass on to those who have supported us. Eventually, the value that we see in our actions will lead to a sense of meaning. In the Atharva Veda it says,

"Money and mansions are not the only wealth. Hoard the wealth of the spirit. Character is wealth: good conduct is wealth; and spiritual wisdom is wealth."

Purpose and meaning, not success, lead to true contentment. When we understand this, we see the value of being motivated by duty and/or love. When you act out of duty and love, you know that you are providing value.

The more we upgrade from trying to fulfill our selfish needs to doing things out of service and love, the more we can achieve. In her book *The Upside of Stress*, author Kelly McGonigal says that we can better handle discomfort when we can associate it with a goal, purpose, or person we care about. For example, when it comes to planning a child's birthday party, a parent might be more than willing to endure the unpleasantness of staying up late. The pain of lost sleep is offset by the satisfaction of being a loving mother. But when it comes to working late at a job that same woman hates? She is miserable. We can take on more when we're doing it for someone we love or to serve a purpose we believe in rather than from the misguided idea that we will find happiness through success. When we perform work with the conviction that what we do matters, we can live intensely. Without a reason for moving forward, we have no drive. When we live intentionally—with a clear sense of why what we do matters—life has meaning and brings fulfillment. Intention fills the car with gas.

THE WHY LADDER

Fear, desire, duty, and love are the roots of all intentions. In Sanskrit the word for intention is *sankalpa*, and I think of it as the reason, formed by one's own heart and mind, that one strives for a goal. To put it another way, from your root motivation you develop intentions to drive you forward. Your intention is who you plan to be in order to act with purpose and feel that what you do is meaningful. So if I'm motivated by fear, my intention might be to protect my family. If I'm motivated by desire, my

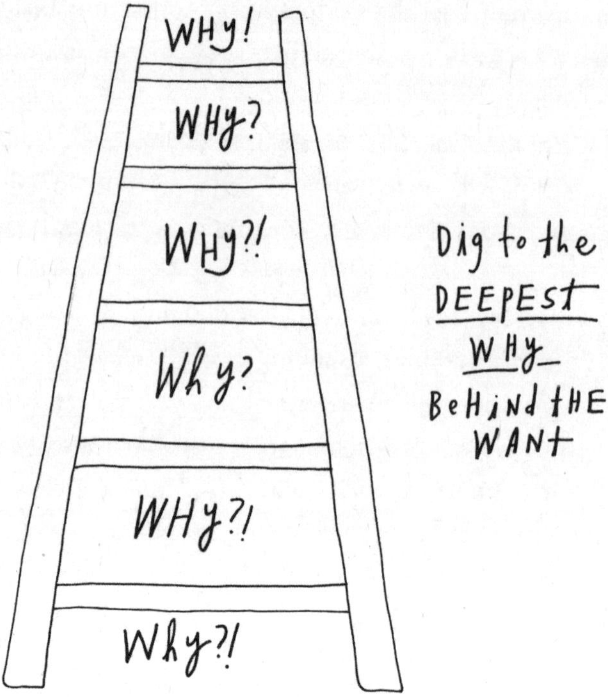

intention might be to gain worldwide recognition. If I'm motivated by duty, my intention might be to help my friends no matter how busy I am. If I'm motivated by love, my intention might be to serve where I am most needed.

There are no rules attaching certain intentions to certain motivations. You can also perform service to make a good impression (desire, not love). You can support your family out of love, not fear. You can want to get rich in order to serve. And none of us has just one motivation and one intention. I want us to learn how to make big and small choices intentionally. Instead of forever climbing the mountain of success, we need to descend into the valley of our true selves to weed out false beliefs.

To live intentionally, we must dig to *the deepest why behind the want*. This requires pausing to think not only about *why* we want something, but also who we are or need to be to get it, and whether being that person appeals to us.

Most people are accustomed to looking for answers. Monks focus on questions. When I was trying to get close to my fear, I asked myself "What am I afraid of?" over and over again. When I'm trying to get to the root of a desire, I start with the question "Why?"

This monkish approach to intention can be applied to even the worldliest goals. Here's a sample goal I've chosen because it's something we never would have contemplated in the ashram and because the intention behind it isn't obvious: *I want to sail solo around the world.*

Why do you want to sail around the world?

It will be fun. I'll get to see lots of places and prove to myself that I'm a great sailor.

It sounds like your intention is to gratify yourself, and that you are motivated by *desire.*

But, what if your answer to the question is:

It was always my father's dream to sail around the world. I'm doing it for him.

In this case, your intention is to honor your father, and you are motivated by *duty and love.*

I'm sailing around the world so I can be free. I won't be accountable to anyone. I can leave all my responsibilities behind.

This sailor intends to escape—he is driven by *fear.*

Now let's look at a more common want:

My biggest want is money, and here's Jay, probably about to tell me to become kind and compassionate. That's not going to help.

Wanting to be rich for the sake of being rich is fine. It's firmly in the category of material gratification, so you can't expect it to give an internal sense of fulfillment. Nonetheless, material comforts are undeniably part of what we want from life, so let's get to the root of this goal rather than just dismissing it.

Wealth is your desired outcome. Why?

I don't ever want to have to worry about money again.

Why do you worry about money?

I can't afford to take the vacations I dream about.

Why do you want those vacations?

I see everyone else on exotic trips on social media. Why should they get to do that when I can't?

Why do you want what they want?

They're having much more fun than I have on my weekends.

Aha! So now we are at the root of the want. Your weekends are unfulfilling. What's missing?

I want my life to be more exciting, more adventurous, more exhilarating.

Okay, your intention is to make your life more exciting. Notice how different that is from "I want money." Your intention is still driven by the desire for personal gratification, but now you know two things: First, you can add more adventure to your life right now without spending more money. And second, you now have the clarity to decide if that's something you want to work hard for.

If a person went up to my teacher and said, "I just want to be rich," my teacher would ask, "Are you doing it out of service?" His reason for asking would be to get to the root of the desire.

If the man said, "No, I want to live in a nice house, travel, and buy whatever I want." His intention would be to have the financial freedom to indulge himself.

My teacher would say, "Okay, it's good that you're honest with yourself. Go ahead, make your fortune. You'll come to service anyway. It may take you five or ten years, but you'll get to the same answer." Monks believe that the man won't be fulfilled when he finds his fortune, and that if he continues his search for meaning, the answer will always, eventually, be found in service.

Be honest about what your intention is. The worst thing you can do is pretend to yourself that you're acting out of service when all you want is material success.

When you follow the whys, keep digging. Every answer provokes deeper questions. Sometimes it helps to sit with a question in the back of your mind for a day, even a week. Very often you'll find that what you are ultimately searching for is an internal feeling (happiness, security, confidence, etc.). Or maybe you'll find that you're acting out of envy, not the most positive emotion, but a good alert to the need you are trying to fill. Be curious about that discovery. Why are you envious? Is there something—like adventure—that you can start working on right away? Once you're doing that, the external wants will be more available to you—if they still matter at all.

TRY THIS: A QUESTION MEDITATION

Take a desire you have and ask yourself why you want it. Keep asking until you get to the root intention.

Common answers are:

To look and feel good
Security
Service
Growth

Don't negate intentions that aren't "good," just be aware of them and recognize that if your reason isn't love, growth, or knowledge, the opportunity may fulfill important practical needs, but it won't feel emotionally meaningful. We're most satisfied when we are in a state of progress, learning, or achievement.

SEEDS AND WEEDS

As monks, we learned to clarify our intentions through the analogy of seeds and weeds. When you plant a seed, it can grow into an expansive tree that provides fruit and shelter for everyone. That's what a broad intention, like love, compassion, or service, can do. The purity of your intention has nothing to do with what career you choose. A traffic officer can give a speeding ticket making a show of his power, or he can instruct you not to speed with the same compassion a parent would have when telling a child not to play with fire. You can be a bank teller and execute a simple transaction with warmth. But if our intentions are vengeful or self-motivated, we grow weeds. Weeds usually grow from ego, greed, envy, anger, pride, competition, or stress. These might look like normal plants to begin with, but they will never grow into something wonderful.

If you start going to the gym to build a revenge body so your ex regrets breaking up with you, you're planting a weed. You haven't properly addressed what you want (most likely to feel understood and loved, which would clearly require a different approach). You'll get strong, and reap the health benefits of working out, but the stakes of your success are tied to external factors—provoking your ex. If your ex doesn't notice or care, you'll still feel the same frustration and loneliness. However, if you start going to the gym because you want to feel physically strong after your breakup, or if, in the course of working out, your intention shifts to this, you'll get in shape *and* feel emotionally satisfied.

Another example of a weed is when a good intention gets attached to the wrong goal. Say my intention is to build my confidence, and I decide that getting a promotion is the best way to do it. I work hard, impress my boss, and move up a level, but when I get there, I realize there's another level, and I still feel insecure. External goals cannot fill internal voids. No external labels or accomplishments can give me true confidence. I have to find it in myself. We will talk about how to make internal changes like this in Part Two.

THE GOOD SAMARITANS

Monks know that one can't plant a garden of beautiful flowers and leave it to thrive on its own. We have to be gardeners of our own lives, planting only the seeds of good intentions, watching to see what they become, and removing the weeds that spring up and get in the way.

In a 1973 experiment called "From Jerusalem to Jericho," researchers asked seminary students to prepare short talks about what it meant to be a minister. Some of them were given the parable of the Good Samaritan to help them prep. In this parable, Jesus told of a traveler who stopped to help a man in need when nobody else would. Then some excuse was made for them to switch to a different room. On their way to the new room, an actor, looking like he needed help, leaned in a doorway. Whether a student had been given materials about the Good Samaritan made no difference in whether the student stopped to help. The researchers did find that if students were in a hurry they were much less likely to help, and "on several occasions, a seminary student going to give his talk on the parable of the Good Samaritan literally stepped over the victim as he hurried on his way!"

The students were so focused on the task at hand that they forgot their deeper intentions. They were presumably studying at seminary with the intention to be compassionate and helpful, but in that moment anxiety or the desire to deliver an impressive speech interfered. As Benedictine monk Laurence Freeman said in his book *Aspects of Love*, "Everything you do in the day from washing to eating breakfast, having meetings, driving to work . . . watching television or deciding instead to read . . . *everything* you do is your spiritual life. It is only a matter of how consciously you do these ordinary things . . ."

LIVE YOUR INTENTIONS

Of course, simply having intentions isn't enough. We have to take action to help those seeds grow. I don't believe in wishful "manifesting," the idea that if you simply believe something will happen, it will. We can't sit around with true intentions expecting that what we want will fall into our laps. Nor can we expect someone to find us, discover how amazing we are, and hand us our place in the world. Nobody is going to create our lives for us. Martin Luther King Jr., said, "Those who love peace must learn to organize as effectively as those who love war." When people come to me seeking guidance, I constantly hear, "I wish . . . I wish . . . I wish . . ." *I wish my partner would be more attentive. I wish I could have the same job but make more money. I wish my relationship were more serious.*

We never say, "I wish I could be more organized and focused and could do the hard work to get that." We don't vocalize what it would actually take to get what we want. **"I wish" is code for "I don't want to do anything differently."**

There's an apocryphal story about Picasso that perfectly illustrates how we fail to recognize the work and perseverance behind achievement. As the tale goes, a woman sees Picasso in a market. She goes up to him and says, "Would you mind drawing something for me?"

"Sure," he says, and thirty seconds later hands her a remarkably beautiful little sketch. "That will be thirty thousand dollars," he says.

"But Mr. Picasso," the woman says, "how can you charge me so much? This drawing only took you thirty seconds!"

"Madame," says Picasso, "it took me thirty years."

The same is true of any artistic work—or, indeed, any job that's done well. The effort behind it is invisible. The monk in my ashram who could easily recite all the scriptures put years into memorizing them. I needed to consider that investment, the life it required, before making it my goal.

When asked who we are, we resort to stating what we do: "I'm an accountant." "I'm a lawyer." "I'm a housewife/househusband." "I'm an athlete." "I'm a teacher." Sometimes this is just a useful way to jump-start a conversation with someone you've just met. But life is more meaningful when we define ourselves by our intentions rather than our achievements. If you truly define yourself by your job, then what happens when you lose your job? If you define yourself as an athlete, then an injury ends your career, you don't know who you are. Losing a job shouldn't destroy our identities, but often it does. Instead, if we live intentionally, we sustain a sense of purpose and meaning that isn't tied to what we accomplish but who we are.

If your intention is to help people, you have to embody that intention by being kind, openhearted, and innovative, by recognizing people's strengths, supporting their weaknesses, listening, helping them grow, reading what they need from you, and noticing when it changes. If your intention is to support your family, you might decide that you have to be generous, present, hardworking, and organized. If your intention is to live your passion, maybe you have to be committed, energetic, and truthful. (Note that in Chapter One we cleared out external noise so that we could see our values more clearly. When you identify your intentions, they reveal your values. The *intentions* to help people and to serve mean you *value* service. The *intention* to support your family means you *value* family. It's not rocket science, but these terms get thrown around and used interchangeably, so it helps to know how they connect and overlap.)

Living your intention means having it permeate your behavior. For instance, if your goal is to improve your relationship, you might plan dates, give your partner gifts, and get a haircut to look better for them. Your wallet will be thinner, your hair might look better, and your relationship may or may not improve. But watch what happens if you make internal changes to live your intention. In order to improve your relationship, you try to become calmer, more understanding, and more inquisitive. (You can still go to the gym and get a haircut.) If the changes you make are internal, you'll feel better about yourself and you'll be a better person. If your relationship doesn't improve, you'll still be the better for it.

DO THE WORK

Once you know the *why* behind the want, consider the *work* behind the want. What will it take to get the nice house and the fancy car? Are you interested in that work? Are you willing to do it? Will the work itself bring you a sense of fulfillment even if you don't succeed quickly—or ever? The monk who asked me why I wanted to learn all of the scripture by heart didn't want me to be mesmerized by the superpowers of other monks and to seek those powers out of vanity. He wanted to know if I was interested in the work—in the life I would live, the person I would be, the meaning I would find in the process of learning the scriptures. The focus is on the process, not the outcome.

The Desert Fathers were the earliest Christian monks, living in

TRY THIS: ADD TO-BE'S TO YOUR TO-DO'S

Alongside your to-do list, try making a to-be list. The good news is you're not making your list longer—these are not items you can check off or complete—but the exercise is a reminder that achieving your goals with intention means living up to the values that drive those goals.

EXAMPLE 1

Let's say my goal is to be financially free. Here's my to-do list:

- Research lucrative job opportunities requiring my skill set
- Rework CV, set up informational meetings to identify job openings
- Apply for all open positions that meet my salary requirements

But what do I need to *be*? I need to be:

- Disciplined
- Focused
- Passionate

EXAMPLE 2

Let's say I want to have a fulfilling relationship. What do I need to do?

- Plan dates
- Do nice things for my partner
- Improve my appearance

But what do I need to *be*?

- More calm
- More understanding
- More inquisitive about my partner's day and feelings

hermitage in the deserts of the Middle East. According to these monks, "We do not make progress because we do not realize how much we can do. We lose interest in the work we have begun, and we want to be good without even trying." If you don't care deeply, you can't go all in on the process. You're not doing it for the right reasons. You can reach your goals, get everything you ever wanted, be successful by anyone's terms, only to discover you still feel lost and disconnected. But if you're in love with the day-to-day process, then you do it with depth, authenticity, and a desire to make an impact. You might be equally successful either way, but if you're driven by intention, you will feel joy.

And if you have a clear and confident sense of why you took each step, then you are more resilient. Failure doesn't mean you're worthless—it means you must look for another route to achieving worthwhile goals. Satisfaction comes from believing in the value of what you do.

ROLE MODELS

The best way to research the work required to fulfill your intention is to look for role models. If you want to be rich, study (without stalking!) what the rich people you admire are being and doing, read books about how they got where they are. Focus especially on what they did at your stage, in order to get where they are now.

You can tour an entrepreneur's office or visit an expat's avocado ranch and decide it's what you want, but that doesn't tell you anything about the journey to get there. Being an actor isn't about appearing on screen and in magazines. It's about having the patience and creativity to perform a scene sixty times until the director has what she wants. Being a monk isn't admiring someone who sits in meditation. It's waking up at the same time as the monk, living his lifestyle, emulating the qualities he displays. Shadow someone at work for a week and you'll gain some sense of the challenges they face, and whether those are challenges you want to take on.

In your observations of people doing the work, it's worth remembering that there can be multiple paths to achieve the same intention. For example, two people might have helping the earth as an intention. One could do it through the law, working with the nonprofit Earthjustice; the other could do it through fashion, like Stella McCartney, who has helped popularize vegan leather. In the next chapter we'll talk about tapping into the method and pursuit that fits you best, but this example shows that if you lead with intention, then you open up the options for how to reach your goal.

And, as we saw with the example of sailing around the globe, two identical acts can have very different intentions behind them. Let's say two people give generous donations to the same charity. One does it because she cares deeply about the charity, a broad intention, and the other does it because he wants to network, a narrow intention. Both donors are commended for their gifts. The one who truly wanted to make a difference feels happy and proud and a sense of meaning. The one who wanted to network only cares whether he met anyone useful to his career or social status. Their different intentions make no difference to the charity—the gifts do good in the world either way—but the internal reward is completely different.

It should be said that no intentions are completely pure. My charitable acts might be 88 percent intended to help people and 8 percent to feel good about myself and 4 percent to have fun with my other charitable friends. There's nothing intrinsically wrong with cloudy or multifaceted intentions. We just need to remember that the less pure they are, the less likely they are to make us happy, even if they make us successful. When people gain what they want but aren't happy at all, it's because they did it with the wrong intention.

LETTING GO TO GROW

The broadest intentions often drive efforts to help and support other people. Parents working overtime to put food on the table for their families. Volunteers devoting themselves to a cause. Workers who are motivated to serve their customers. We sense these intentions from the people we encounter, whether it's the hairdresser who really wants to find a style that suits you or the doctor who takes the time to ask about your life. Generous intentions radiate from people, and it's a beautiful thing. Time and again we see that if we're doing it for the external result, we won't be happy. With the right intention, to serve, we can feel meaning and purpose every day.

Living intentionally means stepping back from external goals, letting go of outward definitions of success, and looking within. Developing a meditation practice with breathwork is a natural way to support this intention. As you cleanse yourself of opinions and ideas that don't make sense with who you are and what you want, I recommend using breathwork as a reminder to live at your own pace, in your own time. Breathwork helps you understand that your way is unique—and that's as it should be.

MEDITATION

BREATHE

The physical nature of breathwork helps drive distractions from your head. Breathwork is calming, but it isn't always easy. In fact, the challenges it brings are part of the process.

I'm sitting on a floor of dried cow dung, which is surprisingly cool. It's not uncomfortable, but it's not comfortable. My ankles hurt. I can't keep my back straight. God, I hate this, it's so difficult. It's been twenty minutes and I still haven't cleared my mind. I'm supposed to be bringing awareness to my breath, but I'm thinking about friends back in London. I sneak a peek at the monk closest to me. He's sitting up so straight. He's nailing this meditation thing. "Find your breath," the leader is saying. I take a breath. It's slow, beautiful, calm.

Oh, wait. Oh okay. I'm becoming aware of my breath.
Breathing in . . . breathing out . . .
Oh I'm there . . .
Okay, this is cool . . .
This is interesting . . .
Okay.

This . . .

Works . . .

Wait, I've an itch on my back—

Breathing in . . . breathing out.

Calm.

My first trip to the ashram was two weeks long, and I spent it meditating with Gauranga Das every morning for two hours. Sitting for that long, often much longer, is uncomfortable and tiring and sometimes boring. What's worse, unwanted thoughts and feelings started drifting into my head. I worried that I wasn't sitting properly and that the monks would judge me. In my frustration, my ego spoke up: I wanted to be the best meditator, the smartest person at the ashram, the one who made an impact. These weren't monk-like thoughts. Meditation definitely wasn't working the way I had thought it would. It was turning me into a bad person!

I was shocked and, to be frank, disappointed to see all the unresolved negativity inside myself. Meditation was only showing me ego, anger, lust, pain—things I didn't like about myself. Was this a problem . . . or was it the point?

I asked my teachers if I was doing something wrong. One of them told me that every year the monks meticulously cleaned the Gundicha Temple in Puri, checking every corner, and that when they did it, they visualized cleaning their hearts. He said that by the time they finished, the temple was already getting dirty again. That, he explained, is the feeling of meditation. It was work, and it was never done.

Meditation wasn't making me a bad person. I had to face an equally unappealing reality. In all that stillness and quiet, it was amplifying what was already inside me. In the dark room of my mind, meditation had turned on the lights.

In getting you where you want to be, meditation may show you what you don't want to see.

Many people run from meditation because they find it difficult and unpleasant. In the Dhammapada the Buddha says, "As a fish hooked and left on the sand thrashes about in agony, the mind being trained in meditation trembles all over." But the point of meditation is to examine what makes it challenging. There is more to it than closing your eyes for fifteen minutes a day. It is the practice of giving yourself space to reflect and evaluate.

By now I've had many beautiful meditations. I've laughed, I've cried, and my heart has felt more alive than I knew possible. The calming, floating, quiet bliss comes eventually. Ultimately, the process is as joyous as the results.

BREATHWORK FOR THE BODY AND MIND

As you've probably noticed, your breathing changes with your emotions. We hold our breath when we're concentrating, and we take shallow breaths when we're nervous or anxious. But these responses are instinctive rather than helpful, meaning that to hold your breath doesn't really help your concentration, and shallow breathing actually makes the symptoms of anxiety worse. Controlled breathing, on the other hand, is an immediate way to steady yourself, a portable tool you can use to shift your energy on the fly.

For millennia, yogis have practiced breathing techniques (called *prāṇāyāma*) to do things like stimulate healing, raise energy, and focus on the present moment. The Rig Veda describes breath as the path beyond the self to consciousness. It states that breath is "the life, like one's own son," or as Abbot George Burke (also known as Swami Nirmalananda Giri) describes it, "the extension of our inmost life." In the Mahāsatipaṭṭhāna Sutta, the Buddha described *ānāpānasati* (which roughly translated means "mindfulness of breathing") as a way to gain enlightenment. Modern science backs up the effectiveness of *prāṇāyāma* for myriad effects including improving cardiovascular health, lowering overall stress, and even improving academic test performance. The meditations I present here and elsewhere in the book are universally used in therapy, coaching, and other meditation practices throughout the world.

When you align with your breath, you learn to align with yourself through every emotion—calming, centering, and de-stressing yourself.

Once or twice a day, I suggest setting aside time for breathwork. Additionally, breathwork is such an effective way to calm yourself down that I use it, and suggest others use it, at points throughout the day when you feel short of breath or that you're holding your breath. You don't need to be in a relaxing space in order to meditate (though it is obviously helpful and appropriate when you are new to meditation). You can do it anywhere—in the bathroom at a party, when getting on a plane, or right before you make a presentation or meet with strangers.

TRY THIS: BREATHWORK

Here are powerful breathing patterns that I use every day. They can be used as needed to either induce focus or increase calm.

BREATHWORK PREPARATION

For the calming and energizing breathing exercises I describe below, begin your practice with the following steps.

1. Find a comfortable position—sitting in a chair, sitting upright with a cushion, or lying down
2. Close your eyes
3. Lower your gaze (yes, you can do this with your eyes closed)
4. Make yourself comfortable in this position
5. Roll back your shoulders
6. Bring your awareness to

   Calm
   Balance
   Ease

(continued on next page)

Stillness
Peace

Whenever your mind wanders just gently and softly bring it back to

Calm
Balance
Ease
Stillness
Peace

7. Now become aware of your natural breathing pattern. Don't force or pressure your breath, just become aware of your natural breathing pattern.

   At the ashram we were taught to use diaphragmatic breathing. To do so, place one hand on your stomach and the other on your chest, and:

   Breathe in through your nose, and out through your mouth
   When you inhale, feel your stomach expand (as opposed to your chest)
   When you exhale, feel your stomach contract
   Continue this in your own pace, at your own time
   When you inhale, feel that you are taking in positive, uplifting energy
   When you exhale, feel that you are releasing any negative, toxic energy

8. Lower your left ear to your left shoulder as you breathe in . . . and bring it back to the middle as you breathe out.
9. Lower your right ear to your right shoulder as you breathe in . . . and bring it back to the middle as you breathe out.

10. Really feel the breath, with no rush or force, in your own pace, at your own time

Breathe to calm and relax yourself

Do this after you've done the breathwork preparation above:

Breathe in for a count of 4 through your nose in your own time at your own pace

Hold for a count of 4

Exhale for a count of 4 through your mouth

Do this for a total of ten breaths.

Breathe for energy and focus (*kapalabhati*)

Do this after you've done the breathwork preparation above:

Breathe in through your nose for a count of 4

Then exhale powerfully through your nose for less than a second (You will feel a sort of engine pumping in your lungs.)

Breathe in again through your nose for a count of 4

Do this for a total of ten breaths.

Breathe for sleep

Breathe in for 4 seconds

Exhale for longer than 4 seconds

Do this until you are asleep or close to it.

PART TWO

GROW

FIVE

PURPOSE

The Nature of the Scorpion

When you protect your dharma,
your dharma protects you.
—Manusmriti 8:15

From the outside, being a monk looks like it's fundamentally about letting go: the baldness, the robes, stripping away distractions. In fact, the asceticism was less a goal than it was a means to an end. Letting go opened our minds.

We spent our days in service; which was also designed to expand our minds. In the course of this service, we weren't supposed to gravitate to our favorite ways to serve, but rather to help out wherever and however it was needed. To experience and emphasize our willingness and flexibility, we rotated through various chores and activities instead of choosing roles and becoming specialists: cooking, cleaning, gardening, caring for the cows, meditating, studying, praying, teaching, and so on. It took some work for me to truly see all activities as equal—I much preferred to study than to clean up after the cows—but we were told to see society as the organs of a body. No one organ was more important than another; all of them worked in concert, and the body needed them all.

In spite of this equitable coexistence, it became clear that each of us had natural affinities. One might be drawn to tending the animals (not me!), another might take pleasure in cooking (again, not me, I'm an eat-to-live kind of guy), another might get great satisfaction from gardening. We undertook such a breadth of activities that, although we didn't indulge our particular passions, we could observe and reflect on where they lay. We could experiment with new skills, study them, see how improving them made us feel. What did we like? What felt natural and fulfilling? Why?

If something, like cleaning up after the cows, made me uncomfortable, instead of turning away, I pushed myself to understand the feelings that lay at the root of my discomfort. I quickly identified my hatred for some of the most mundane chores as an ego issue. I thought them a waste of time when I could be learning. Once I admitted this to myself, I could explore whether cleaning had anything to offer me. Could I learn from a mop? Practice Sanskrit verse while planting potatoes? In the course of my chores, I observed that mop heads need to be completely flexible in order to get into every space and corner. Not every task is best served by something sturdy like a broom. To my monk mind, there was a worthwhile lesson in that: We need flexibility in order to access every corner of study and growth. When it came to planting potatoes, I found that the rhythm of it helped me remember verse, while the verse brought excitement to the potatoes.

Exploring our strengths and weaknesses in the self-contained universe of the ashram helped lead each of us to our *dharma*. Dharma, like many Sanskrit terms, can't be defined by a single English word, though to say something is "your calling" comes close. My definition of dharma is an effort to make it practical to our lives today. I see dharma as the combination of *varna* and *seva*. Think of *varna* (also a word with complex meanings) as passion and skills. *Seva* is understanding the world's needs and selflessly serving others. When your natural talents and passions (your *varna*) connect with what the universe needs (*seva*) and become your purpose, you are living in your dharma.

When you spend your time and energy living in your dharma, you have the satisfaction of using your best abilities and doing something that matters to the world. **Living in your dharma is a certain route to fulfillment.**

In the first part of this book we talked about becoming aware of and letting go of the influences and distractions that divert us from a fulfilling life. Now we'll rebuild our lives around our guiding values and deepest intentions. This growth begins with dharma.

Two monks were washing their feet in a river when one of them realized that a scorpion was drowning in the water. He immediately picked it up and set it upon the bank. Though he was quick, the scorpion stung his hand. He resumed washing his feet. The other monk said, "Hey, look. That foolish scorpion fell right back in." The first monk leaned over, saved the scorpion again, and was again stung. The other monk asked him, "Brother, why do you rescue the scorpion when you know its nature is to sting?"

"Because," the monk answered, "to save it is my nature."

The monk is modeling humility—he does not value his own pain above the scorpion's life. But the more relevant lesson here is that "to save" is so essential to this monk's nature that he is compelled and content to do it even knowing the scorpion will sting him. The monk has so much faith in his dharma that he is willing to suffer in order to fulfill it.

DISCOVERING DHARMA

It is my first summer at the ashram. I've cleaned bathrooms, cooked potato curry, harvested cabbages. I've washed my own clothes by hand, which is not an easy chore—our robes have as much material as bedsheets, and to scrub out food or grass stains would have qualified as a CrossFit workout of the day.

One day I'm scrubbing pots with the gusto of an overeager apprentice when a senior monk comes up to me.

"We'd like you to lead a class this week," he says. "The topic is this verse from

the Gita: 'Whatever action is performed by a great man, common men follow in his footsteps, and whatever standards he sets by exemplary acts, all the world pursues.'"

I agree to do it, and as I return to scrubbing I think about what I'll say. I understand the basic gist of the scripture—we teach by example. It taps into my understanding that who you are is not what you say, but how you behave—and it reminds me of a quote often attributed to Saint Francis of Assisi: "Preach the Gospel at all times. When necessary, use words."

Many of the other monks, like me, didn't enter the ashram at age five. They've been to mainstream schools, had girlfriends and boyfriends, watched TV and movies. They won't have trouble grasping the meaning of the verse, but I'm excited to figure out how I can make it feel fresh and relevant to their experiences outside the ashram.

The aging computers in our library have an excruciatingly slow internet connection. I'm in India, in the middle of nowhere, and it seems like every image takes an hour to download. After having done research on the speedy computers of a college library, I find the wait painful. But I know that, over in the kitchen, my fellow monks are patiently waiting for water to boil. As they're doing, I try to respect the process.

During my research, I become fascinated by the psychology of communication. I find studies by Albert Mehrabian showing that 55 percent of our communication is conveyed by body language, 38 percent is tone of voice, and a mere 7 percent is the actual words we speak. (That's a general guideline, but even in situations where those percentages shift, the fact remains that most of our communication is nonverbal.) I lose myself in exploring how we convey our messages and values, analyzing the communication styles of various leaders, and figuring out how it all adds up to be relevant in our lives. Among others, I read about Jane Goodall, who never intended to become a leader. She first entered the wilds of Tanzania to study chimpanzees in 1960, but her research and ongoing work have significantly redefined conservation, attracted women to her field, and inspired hundreds of thousands of young people to get involved in conservation.

Our class gathers in a medium-sized room. I take my place on an elevated, cushioned seat, and the students sit on cushions in front of me. I don't see myself as above them in any way, except for my elevated seat. We monks have already learned that everyone is always simultaneously a student and a teacher.

When I finish giving my talk, I'm pleased with how it's gone. I enjoyed sharing the ideas as much as I enjoyed researching them. People thank me, telling me that they appreciated the examples and how I made the ancient verse feel relevant. One or two ask me how I prepared—they've noticed how much work I put into it. As I bask in the glow of my satisfaction and their appreciation, I am beginning to realize my dharma—studying, experimenting with knowledge, and speaking.

Everyone has a psychophysical nature which determines where they flourish and thrive. Dharma is using this natural inclination, the things you're good at, your thrive mode, to serve others. You should feel passion when the process is pleasing and your execution is skillful. And the response from others should be positive, showing that your passion has a purpose. This is the magic formula for dharma.

Passion + Expertise + Usefulness = Dharma.

If we're only excited when people say nice things about our work, it's a sign that we're not passionate about the work itself. And if we indulge our interests and skills, but nobody responds to them, then our passion is without purpose. If either piece is missing, we're not living our dharma.

When people fantasize about what they want to do and who they want to be, they don't often investigate fully enough to know if it suits their dharma. People think they want to be in finance because they know it's lucrative. Or they want to be a doctor because it's respected *and* honorable. But they move forward with no idea whether those professions suit them—if they will like the process, the environment, and the energy of the work, or whether they're any good at it.

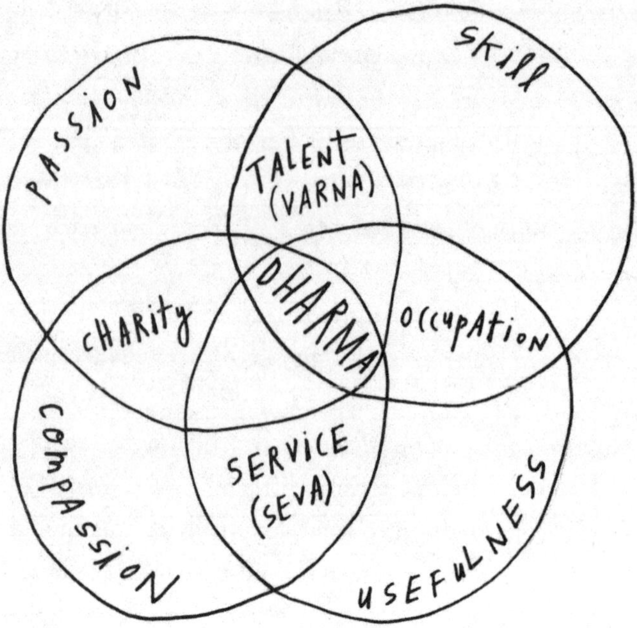

EVERYTHING YOU ARE

There are two lies some of us hear when we're growing up. The first is "You'll never amount to anything." The second is "You can be anything you want to be." The truth is—

You can't be anything you want.

But you can be everything you are.

A monk is a traveler, but the journey is inward, bringing us ever closer to our most authentic, confident, powerful self. There is no need to embark on an actual Year-in-Provence-type quest to find your passion and purpose, as if it's a treasure buried in some distant land, waiting to be discovered. Your dharma is already with you. It's always been with you. It's woven into your being. If we keep our minds open and curious, our dharmas announce themselves.

Even so, it can take years of exploration to uncover our dharma. One of our biggest challenges in today's world is the pressure to perform big, right now. Thanks to the early successes of folks like Facebook founder

Mark Zuckerberg and Snapchat cofounder Evan Spiegel (who became the youngest billionaire in the world at age twenty-four), along with celebs such as Chance the Rapper and Bella Hadid, many of us feel that if we haven't found our calling and risen to the top in our fields in our twenties, we've failed.

Putting all of this pressure on people to achieve early is not only stressful, it can actually hinder success. According to *Forbes* magazine publisher Rich Karlgaard, in his book *Late Bloomers*, the majority of us don't hit our stride quite so early, but society's focus on academic testing, getting into the "right" colleges, and developing and selling an app for millions before you even get your degree (if you don't drop out to run your multimillion-dollar company) is causing high levels of anxiety and depression not only among those who haven't conquered the world by age twenty-four, but even among those who've already made a significant mark. Many early achievers feel tremendous pressure to maintain that level of performance.

But, as Karlgaard points out, there are plenty of fantastically successful people who hit their strides later in life: *The Bluest Eye*, Toni Morrison's first novel, wasn't published until she was thirty-nine. And after a ten-year stint in college and time spent working as a ski instructor, Dietrich Mateschitz was forty before he created blockbuster energy drink company Red Bull. Pay attention, cultivate self-awareness, feed your strengths, and you *will* find your way. And once you discover your dharma, pursue it.

OTHER PEOPLE'S DHARMA

The Bhagavad Gita says that it's better to do one's own dharma imperfectly than to do another's perfectly. Or, as Steve Jobs put it in his 2005 Stanford commencement address, "Your time is limited, so don't waste it living someone else's life."

In his autobiography, Andre Agassi dropped a bombshell on the world: The former world's number one tennis player, eight-time grand slam champion, and gold medal winner *didn't like tennis*. Agassi was pushed into playing by his father, and though he was incredible at the game, he hated playing. The fact that he was tremendously successful and made loads of money didn't matter; it wasn't his dharma. However, Agassi has transitioned his on-court success into his true passion—instead of serving aces, he's now serving others. Along with providing other basic services for children in his native Nevada, the Andre Agassi Foundation runs a K-12 college preparatory school for at-risk youth.

Our society is set up around strengthening our weaknesses rather than building our strengths. In school, if you get three As and a D, all the adults around you are focused on that D. Our grades in school, scores on standardized tests, performance reviews, even our self-improvement efforts—all highlight our insufficiencies and urge us to improve them. But what happens if we think of those weaknesses not as our failures but as *someone else's dharma*? Sister Joan Chittister, a Benedictine nun, wrote, "It is trust in the limits of the self that makes us open and it is trust in the gifts of others that makes us secure. We come to realize that we don't have to do everything, that we can't do everything, that what I can't do is someone else's gift and responsibility. . . . My limitations make space for the gifts of other people." Instead of focusing on our weaknesses, we lean into our strengths and look for ways to make them central in our lives.

Here are two important caveats: First, following your dharma doesn't mean you get a free pass. When it comes to skills, you should lean into your strengths. But if your weaknesses are emotional qualities like empathy, compassion, kindness, and generosity, you should never stop developing them. There's no point in being a tech wizard if you're not compassionate. You don't get to be a jerk just because you're skilled.

Second, a bad grade in school doesn't mean you get to ditch the subject altogether. We have to be careful not to confuse inexperience with weakness. Some of us live outside our dharma because we haven't figured out what it is. It is important to experiment broadly before we reject options, and much of this experimentation is done in school and elsewhere when we're young.

My own dharma emerged from some experiences I found extremely unpleasant. Before I taught that class at the ashram, I had a distaste for public speaking. When I was seven or eight years old, I took part in a school assembly where kids shared their cultural traditions. My mother dressed me as an Indian king, wrapping me in an ill-fitting sari-like getup that did nothing for my awkward body. The minute I walked on stage, kids started to laugh. I can't carry a tune for the life of me, and when I started to sing a prayer in transliterated Sanskrit, they lost it. I wasn't even two minutes in, and five hundred kids and all the teachers were laughing at me. I forgot the lyrics and looked down at the sheet in front of me, but I couldn't read the words through my tears. My teacher had to walk out onto the stage, put her arm around me, and lead me away as everyone continued to laugh. It was mortifying. From that moment, I hated the stage. Then, when I was fourteen, my parents forced me to attend a public speaking/drama afterschool program. Three hours, three times a week, for four years gave me the skills to stand up on stage, but I had nothing to talk about and took no pleasure in it. I was and still am shy, but that public speaking course changed my life because once that skill connected to my dharma, I ran with it.

After my first summer at the ashram ended, I was not yet a full-time monk. I returned to college and decided to try my hand at teaching again. I set up an extracurricular club called "Think Out Loud," where every week people would come to hear me speak on a philosophical, spiritual, and/or scientific topic, and then we'd discuss it. The topic for the first meeting was "Material Problems, Spiritual Solutions." I planned to explore how as humans we experience the same challenges, setbacks, and issues in life, and how spirituality can help us find the answer. Nobody showed up. It was a small room, and when it stayed empty, I thought, *What can I learn from this?* Then I carried on—I gave my talk to the empty room with my full energy, because I felt the topic deserved it. Ever since then I have been doing the same thing in one medium or another—starting a conversation about who we are and how we can find solutions to our daily challenges.

For the next meeting of "Think Out Loud," I did a better job of distributing flyers and posters, and about ten people showed up. The topic for my second attempt was the same, "Material Problems, Spiritual Solutions," and I opened the discussion by playing a clip of the comedian Chris Rock doing a bit about how the pharmaceutical industry doesn't really want to cure diseases—it actually wants us to have a *prolonged* need for the medications that it produces. I tied this to a discussion of how we are looking for instant fixes instead of doing the real work of growth. I've always loved drawing from funny and contemporary examples to relate monk philosophy to our daily lives. "Think Out Loud" did just that every week for the next three years of college. By the time I graduated, the club had grown to one hundred people and become a weekly three-hour workshop.

We've all got a special genius inside of us, but it may not be on the path that opens directly before us. There may be no visible path at all. My dharma was not in one of the job tracks that were common at my school but rather in the club that I founded there after a chance assignment at the ashram hinted at my dharma. Our dharmas don't hide, but sometimes we need to work patiently to recognize them. As researchers Anders Ericsson and Robert Pool underscore in their book *Peak*, mastery requires deliberate practice, and lots of it. But if you love it, you do it. Picasso experimented with other forms of art but kept painting as his focus. Michael Jordan did a stint at baseball, but basketball was where he really thrived. Play hardest in your area of strength and you'll achieve depth, meaning, and satisfaction in your life.

ALIGN WITH YOUR PASSION

In order to unveil our dharma, we have to identify our passions—the activities we both love and are naturally inclined to do well. It's clear to anyone who looks at the Quadrants of Potential that we should be spending as much time as possible at the upper right, in Quadrant Two: doing things that we're both good at and love. But life doesn't always work out that way. In fact, many of us find ourselves spending our careers in Quadrant One: working on things that we're good at, but don't love. When we

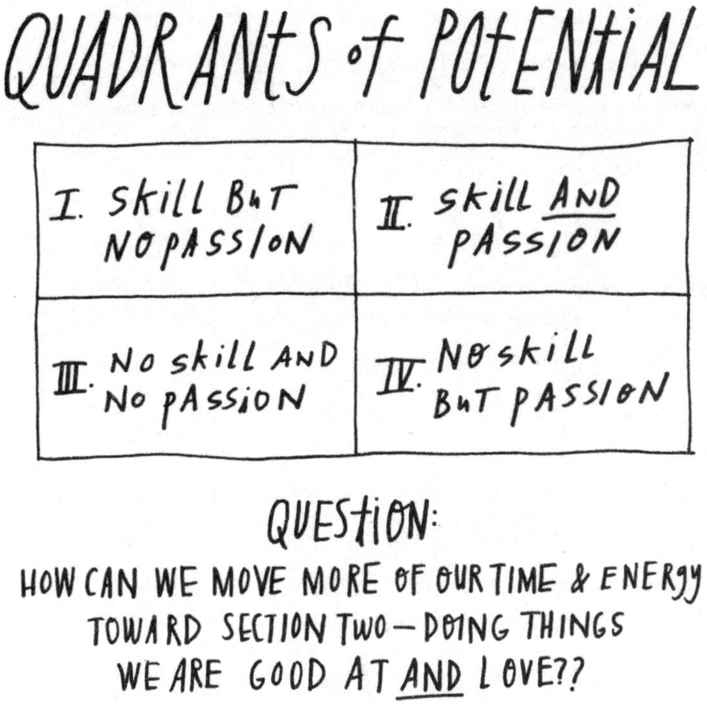

have time to spare, we hop over to Quadrant Four to indulge the hobbies and extracurriculars that we love, even though we never have enough time to become as good at them as we would like. Everyone can agree that we want to spend as little time as possible in Quadrant Three. It's super-depressing to hang out there, doing things we don't love and aren't good at. So the question is: How can we move more of our time toward Quadrant Two: doing things we are good at and love? (You'll notice that I don't discuss the quadrants in numerical order. This is because Quadrants One and Four both offer half of what we want, so it makes sense to discuss them first.)

Quadrant One: Good at, but Don't Love

Getting from here to Quadrant Two is easier said than done. Say you don't love your job. Most of us can't just leap into a job we love that miraculously comes with a generous salary. A more practical approach is to find innovative ways to move toward Quadrant Two within the jobs that we already have. What can you do to bring your dharma where you are?

When I first left the ashram, I took a consulting job at Accenture, a global management consulting firm. We were constantly dealing with numbers, data, and financial statements, and it quickly became clear that a talent for Excel was essential in order to excel in my position. But Excel was not my thing. In spite of my efforts, I couldn't force myself to get better at it. I just wasn't interested. As far as I was concerned, it was worse than mucking out the cow stalls. So, while I continued to do my best, I thought about how I could demonstrate what I was good at. My passion was wisdom and tools for life like meditation and mindfulness, so I offered to teach a mindfulness class to my working group. The lead managing director loved the idea, and the class I gave was popular enough that she asked me to speak about mindfulness and meditation at a company-wide summer event for analysts and consultants. I would speak in front of a thousand people at Twickenham Stadium, the home stadium of England's national rugby team.

When I got to the stadium, I found out that my turn at the podium was sandwiched between words from the CEO and Will Greenwood, a rugby legend. I sat in the audience listening to the lineup, thinking *Crap, everyone's going to laugh at me. Why did I agree to this?* All the other speakers were at the top of their fields and so articulate. I started to have second thoughts about what I had planned to say and how to deliver it. Then I went through my breathing exercises, calmed myself down, and two seconds before I went on stage, I thought, *Just be yourself.* I would do my own dharma perfectly instead of trying to do anyone else's. I went up, did my thing, and afterward the response couldn't have been better. The director who had organized it said, "I've never heard an audience of consultants and analysts stay so quiet you could hear a pin drop." Later, she invited me to teach mindfulness all across the company in the UK.

This was a tipping point for me. I saw that I hadn't just spent three years of my life learning some weird monk-only philosophy that was irrelevant outside the ashram. I could take all my skills and put them into practice. I could actually fulfill my dharma in the modern world. P.S. I still don't know how to use Excel.

Instead of making a huge career change, you can try my approach: look for opportunities to do what you love in the life you already have. You never know where it might lead. Leonardo DiCaprio hasn't given up acting or producing, yet he also directs significant energy toward environmental advocacy because it's part of his dharma. A corporate assistant might volunteer to do design work; a bartender can run a trivia contest. I worked with a lawyer whose true passion was to be a baker on *The Great British Bake Off*. That goal felt unrealistic to her, so she got a group of her colleagues obsessed with the show, and they started "Baking Mondays," where every Monday someone on her team brought in something they'd made. She still worked just as hard and performed well at a job that she found slightly tedious, but bringing her passion to the water cooler made her team stronger and made her feel more energized throughout the day. If you have two kids and a mortgage and can't quit your job, do as the lawyer did and find a way to bring the energy of your dharma into the workplace, or look for ways to bring it into other aspects of your life like your hobbies, home, and friendships.

Also, consider why you don't love your strengths. Can you find a reason to love them? I often encounter people working corporate jobs who have all the skills required to do good work, but they find the work meaningless. The best way to add meaning to an experience is to look for how it might serve you in the future. If you tell yourself: "I'm learning how to work in a global team," or "I'm getting all the budgeting skills I'll need if I open a skate shop one day," then you can nurture a passion for something that may not be your first choice. Link the feeling of passion to the experience of learning and growth.

Psychologist Amy Wrzesniewski from the Yale School of Management and colleagues studied hospital cleaning crews to understand how they experienced their work. One crew described the work as not particularly satisfying and not requiring much skill. And when they explained the tasks they performed, it basically sounded like the job description from the personnel manual. But when the researchers talked to another cleaning crew, they were surprised by what they heard. The second group enjoyed their work, found it deeply meaningful, and described it as being highly skilled. When they described their tasks, the reason for the distinction between the crews started to become clear. The second crew talked not just about typical custodial chores, but also about noticing which patients seemed especially sad or had fewer visitors and making a point to start a conversation or check in on them more often. They related incidents where they escorted elderly visitors through the parking structure so they wouldn't get lost (even though the custodians technically could have gotten fired for that). One woman said she periodically switched the pictures on the walls among different rooms. When asked if this was part of her job, she replied, "That's not part of my job. But that's part of me."

From this study and subsequent research, Wrzesniewski and her colleagues created the phrase "job crafting" to describe "what employees do to redesign their own jobs in ways that foster engagement at work, job satisfaction, resilience, and thriving." According to the researchers, we can reengineer our tasks, relationships, or even just how we perceive what we do (such as custodians thinking of themselves as "healers" and "ambassadors"). The intention with which we approach our work has a tremendous impact on the meaning we gain from it and our personal sense of purpose. Learn to find meaning now, and it will serve you all your life.

Quadrant Four: Not Good at, but Love

When our passions aren't lucrative, we de-prioritize them. Then we feel frustrated that we love an activity but can't do it well or frequently enough to fully enjoy it. The surest route to improving skills is always time. Can you use coaching, take courses, or get training to improve at what you love?

"Impossible," you say. "If I had time to do that, believe me, I would." We will talk about how to find nonexistent time in the next chapter, but for now I will say this: Everyone has time. We commute or we cook or we watch TV. We may not have three hours, but we have ten minutes to listen to a podcast or learn a new technique from a YouTube video. You can do a lot in ten minutes.

Sometimes when we tap into our dharma, it carves out the time for us. When I first started making videos, I worked on them after I got home from my corporate job. Five hours a day, five days a week, I focused on editing five-minute videos. For a long time, the return-on-investment was pitiful, but I wasn't willing to write myself off before trying to make the most of my skill.

In the years since, I've seen people monetize the weirdest things. Spend any amount of time on Etsy, and you'll be amazed at how many people have found ways to make money off their passions. However, if the world is sending you a very strong message that it won't pay for or does not otherwise need or want your passion, then fine. Accept that. There's a *critical* need for soccer in the world, but there's no need for *me* to play soccer. Still, the soccer matches I organized at Accenture were the highlight of my week. If it's not your dharma, it can still give you joy.

Quadrant Three: Not Good at, Don't Love

Do whatever you can to crawl out of this soul-sucking quadrant. You will always have unpleasant chores, but they shouldn't be the biggest part of your life. If at all possible, you should work toward outsourcing the chores in this category. Hurt the pocket, save the mind. And remember, just because you don't like it doesn't mean nobody likes it. Can you work out a trade with a friend or colleague, where you take on each other's least favorite tasks?

If you can't offload the chore, remember the lesson I learned at the ashram—every task is an essential organ. None is less important than the others, and none of us is too important to do any chore. If you think you're too good for something, you succumb to the worst egotistical impulses, and you devalue anyone who does that chore. When you're satisfied in your dharma, you can, without envy or ego, appreciate others who are good at another skill. I have great respect for people who can do Excel, I just don't want to do it myself. When I encounter doctors or soldiers or people in any number of other careers, I think, *That's extraordinary. It's amazing. But it's not me.*

TRY THIS: IDENTIFY YOUR QUADRANT OF POTENTIAL

You may have been doing this exercise in your head as you read about the Quadrants of Potential. Nonetheless, I want you to go through the exercise of acknowledging how close you are to living your dharma today.

Do you like your job?
Do you love your job?
Are you good at your job?
Do other people need and appreciate your work?
Is your greatest skill or passion outside your work?
What is it?
Do you dream of making it your work?
Do you think this is an attainable dream?
Do you think there might be ways you could bring your passion to your work?
Write down any ideas you have for bringing your passion to the universe.

Quadrant Two: Vedic Personality

We want to live in Quadrant Two, where we spend our time using our talents to do what we love. If we aren't there, we examine the problem the monk way—instead of looking at specific skills you've developed and specific activities that you love, we look beyond them, to their roots. The Bhagavad Gita contemplates dharma by dividing us into four personality types—what it calls *varnas*. There are four *varnas*, and knowing your *varna* tells you your nature and competence. In relatively recent history (during the nineteenth century), when British leaders imposed their own rigid class system on Indian society, the *varnas* emerged as the basis for the caste system. Though castes—a hierarchy of job categories—were based on the *varnas*, this is a misinterpretation of the text. I'm not talking about the caste system here—I believe that all of us are equal; we just have different talents and skills. My discussion of the *varnas* is about how to harness these skills and talents to live to your fullest potential. The different personality types are meant to work together in a community, like the organs in a body—all essential and none superior to the others.

Varnas aren't determined by birth. They're meant to help us understand our true nature and inclinations. You're not creative just because your parents are.

No one *varna* is better than another. We all seek different types of work, fun, love, and service. There is no hierarchy or segregation. If two people are both acting in their best dharma, living for the service of others, then neither is better than the other. Is a cancer researcher better than a fireman?

TRY THIS: THE VEDIC PERSONALITY TEST

This simple test is not an absolute determination of your personality type, but it will help as you seek out your dharma.

See the appendix for The Vedic Personality Test.

THE VARNAS

The four *varnas* are the Guide, the Leader, the Creator, and the Maker. These labels aren't directly tied to specific jobs or activities. Sure, certain activities bring us pleasure because they fulfill our dharma, but there are many different ways to live in our dharma. A Guide, as you will see on page 112, is compelled to learn and share knowledge—you could be a teacher

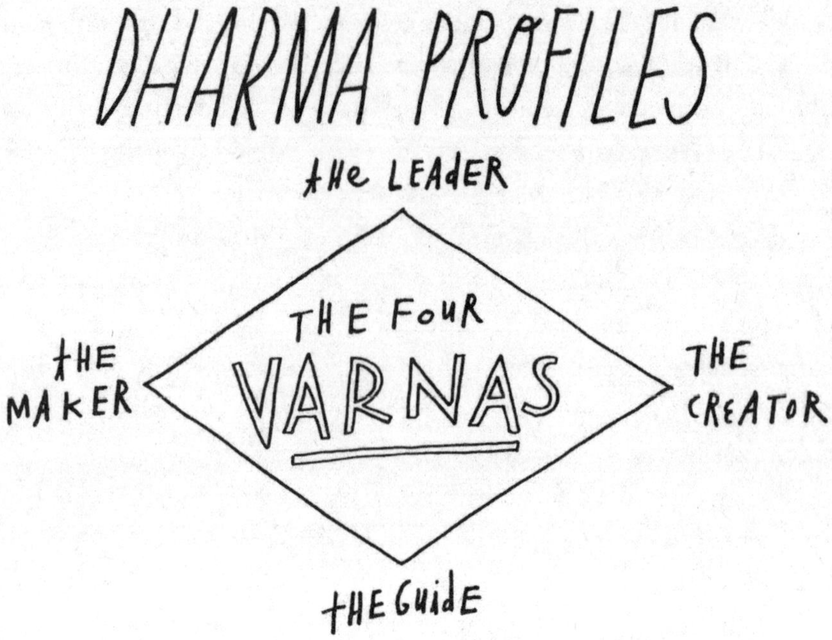

or a writer. A Leader likes to influence and provide, but that doesn't mean you have to be a CEO or a lieutenant—you could be a school principal or shop manager. A Creator likes to make things happen—this could be at a start-up or in a neighborhood association. A Maker likes to see things tangibly being built—they could be a coder or a nurse.

Remember the *gunas*: *tamas*, *rajas*, and *sattva*—ignorance, impulsivity, and goodness. For each of the *varnas* I describe what their behavior looks like in each *guna* mode. We strive toward *sattva* through letting go of ignorance, working in our passion, and serving in goodness. The more time we spend in *sattva*, the more effective and fulfilled we become.

Creators

Originally: merchants, businesspeople
Today: marketers, salespeople, entertainers, producers, entrepreneurs, CEOs
Skills: brainstorming, networking, innovating

- Make things happen
- Can convince themselves and others of anything
- Great at sales, negotiation, persuasion
- Highly driven by money, pleasure, and success
- Very hardworking and determined
- Excel in trade, commerce, and banking
- Always on the move
- Work hard, play hard

Mode of Ignorance

- Become corrupt and sell things with no value / Lie, cheat, steal to sell something
- Beaten down by failure
- Burned out, depressed, moody, due to overwork

Mode of Impulse

- Status-driven
- Dynamic, charismatic, and captivating
- Hustler, goal-oriented, tireless

Mode of Goodness

- Use money for greater good
- Create products and ideas that make money but also serve others
- Provide jobs and opportunities for others

Makers

Originally: artists, musicians, creatives, writers

Today: social workers, therapists, doctors, nurses, COOs, heads of human resources, artists, musicians, engineers, coders, carpenters, cooks

Skills: inventing, supporting, implementing

Mode of Ignorance

- Depressed by failure
- Feel stuck and unworthy
- Anxious

Mode of Impulse

- Explore and experiment with new ideas
- Juggle too many things at the same time
- Lose focus on expertise and care; focus more on money and results

Mode of Goodness

- Driven by stability and security
- Generally content and satisfied with the status quo
- Choose meaningful goals to pursue
- Work hard but always maintain balance with family commitments
- Best right-hand man or woman
- Lead team gatherings
- Support those in need
- Highly skilled at manual professions

Connections

Makers and Creators complement each other

Makers make Creators focus on detail, quality, gratitude, and contentment

Creators help Makers think bigger, become more goal-oriented

Guides

Originally and today: teachers, guides, gurus, coaches, mentors

Skills: learning, studying, sharing knowledge, and wisdom

- A coach and a mentor no matter what role they play
- Want to bring out the best in the people in their life

- Value knowledge and wisdom more than fame, power, money, security
- Like having space and time to reflect and learn
- Want to help people find meaning, fulfillment, and purpose
- Like to work alone
- Enjoy intellectual pursuits in their spare time—reading, debate, discussion

Mode of Ignorance

- Don't practice what they preach
- Don't lead by example
- Struggle with implementation

Mode of Impulse

- Love to debate and destroy others' arguments
- Use knowledge for strength and power
- Intellectually curious

Mode of Goodness

- Use knowledge to help people find their purpose
- Aspire to better themselves in order to give more
- Realize knowledge is not theirs to use alone, but that they are here to serve

Leaders

Originally: kings, warriors
Today: military, justice, law enforcement, politics
Skills: governing, inspiring, engaging others

- Natural leaders of people, movements, groups, and families
- Directed by courage, strength, and determination
- Protect those who are less privileged

- Led by higher morals and values and seek to enforce them across the world
- Provide structures and frameworks for the growth of people
- Like to work in teams
- Great at organization, focus, and dedication to a mission

Mode of Ignorance

- Give up on change due to corruption and hypocrisy
- Develop a negative, pessimistic viewpoint
- Lose moral compass in drive for power

Mode of Impulse

- Build structures and frameworks for fame and money, not meaning
- Use their talents to serve themselves not humanity
- Focus on short term goals for themselves

Mode of Goodness

- Fight for higher morals, ethics, and values
- Inspire people to work together
- Build long-term goals to support society

Connections

Guides and Leaders complement each other
Guides give wisdom to Leaders
Leaders give structure to Guides

The point of the *varnas* is to help you understand yourself so you can focus on your strongest skills and inclinations. Self-awareness gives you more focus. When I look at my Guide tendencies, it makes sense to me that I succeed when I focus on strategy. Creators and Makers are better at implementation, so I've surrounded myself with people who can help me with that. A musician might be a Maker, driven by security. In order to succeed, they might need to be surrounded by strategists. Invest in your strengths and surround yourself with people who can fill in the gaps.

When you know your *varna*—your passion and skills—and you serve with that, it becomes your dharma.

TRY THIS: REFLECTED BEST-SELF EXERCISE

1. Choose a group of people who know you well—a diverse mix of people you've worked with, family, and friends. As few as three will work, but ten to twenty is even better.
2. Ask them to write down a moment when you were at your best. Ask them to be specific.
3. Look for patterns and common themes.
4. Write out a profile of yourself, aggregating the feedback as if it weren't about you.
5. Think about how you can turn your best skills into action. How can you use those skills this weekend? In different circumstances or with different people?

TEST-DRIVE YOUR DHARMA

The Vedic Personality Test helps you begin to see your *varna*, but just like a horoscope, it can't tell you what's going to happen tomorrow. It's up to you to test these *varnas* in the real world through exploration and experimentation. If your *varna* is Leader, try to take on that role at work, or by organizing your kid's birthday party. Do you genuinely take joy in the process?

Think about the level of awareness we have when we eat something. We immediately do a sense check and decide if we like it, and we wouldn't have trouble rating it on a scale of one to ten if asked to do so. Furthermore, we might have different feelings about it the next day. (When I have my favorite chocolate brownie sundae on a Sunday night, I feel pretty happy about it, but by Monday morning I no longer think it was the best thing in the world to put in my body.) With both immediate and long-term reflection, we form nuanced opinions about whether we want to make that food part of our regular diet. All of us do this with food, we do it when we leave a movie theater ("Did you like it?"), and some of us do it on Yelp. But we don't think to measure our compatibility with and taste for how we spend our time. When we get in the habit of identifying what empowers us, we have a better understanding of ourselves and what we want in life. This is exactly what we're going to do to refine our understanding of our *varna*.

The first and most critical question to ask when you're exploring your *varna* is:

Did I enjoy the process?

Test the description of your *varna* against your experience to pinpoint what you enjoyed about it. Instead of saying, "I love taking pictures," find the root of it. Do you like helping families put together a Christmas card that makes them proud? (Guide) Do you like to document human struggles or other meaningful situations in order to promote change? (Leader) Or do you love the technical aspects of lighting, focus, and developing film? (Maker) As monks, every time we completed an activity or thought exercise like the ones in this book, we asked ourselves questions: *What did I like about that? Am I good at it? Do I want to read about it, learn about it, and spend a lot of my time doing it? Am I driven to improve? What made me feel comfortable or uncomfortable? If I was uncomfortable, was it in a positive way—a challenge that made me grow—or a negative way?* This awareness

TRY THIS: **KEEP AN ACTIVITY JOURNAL**

Take note of every activity you take part in through the course of a few days. Meetings, walking the dog, lunch with a friend, writing emails, preparing food, exercising, spending time on social media. For every activity, answer the two questions fundamental to dharma: Did I enjoy the process? Did other people enjoy the result? There are no right or wrong answers. This is an observation exercise to amplify your awareness.

gives us a much more nuanced view of where we thrive. Instead of sending us on one and only one path, that awareness opens us to new ways we can put our passions to use.

EMBRACE YOUR DHARMA

Our heads might try to convince us that we've only ever made the best choices, but our true nature—our passion and purpose—isn't in our heads, it's in our hearts. In fact, our heads often get in the way of our passions. Here are some of the excuses that we use to close our minds:

> "I'm too old to start my own business."
> "It would be irresponsible of me to make this change."
> "I can't afford to do this."
> "I already know that."
> "I've always done it this way."
> "That way won't work for me."
> "I don't have time."

Past beliefs, false or self-deceiving, sneak in to block our progress. Fears prevent us from trying new things. Our egos get in the way of learning new information and opening ourselves to growth. (More on this in Chapter Eight.) And nobody ever has time for change. But miracles happen when you embrace your dharma.

Growing up, Joseph Campbell had no model of a career that fit his diverse interests. As a child in the early 1900s, he became fascinated by Native American culture and studied everything he could about it. During college, he became entranced with the rituals and symbols of Catholicism. While studying abroad, his interests expanded to include the theories of Jung and Freud, and he developed an interest in modern art. Back at Columbia, Campbell told his dissertation advisors that he wanted to blend ancient stories about the Holy Grail with ideas in art and psychology. They rejected that idea. He abandoned work on his thesis and in 1949 found a job teaching literature at Sarah Lawrence College, which he held for thirty-eight years. Meanwhile, he published hundreds of books and articles, and did a deep dive into ancient Indian mythology and philosophy. But it was in *The Hero with a Thousand Faces* that he first discussed his groundbreaking ideas about what he called "the hero's journey"—a concept that established Campbell as one of the foremost authorities on mythology and the human psyche. As someone who followed his dharma, it's no surprise that Joseph Campbell is the original source of the advice "Follow your bliss." He wrote, "Now, I came to this idea of bliss because in Sanskrit, which is the great spiritual language of the world, there are three terms that represent the brink, the jumping-off place to the ocean of transcendence: Sat, Chit, Ananda. The word 'Sat' means being. 'Chit' means consciousness. 'Ananda' means bliss or rapture. I thought, 'I don't know whether my consciousness is proper consciousness or not; I don't know whether what I know of my being is my proper being or not; but I do know where my rapture is. So let me hang on to rapture, and that will bring me both my consciousness and my being.' I think it worked." If you follow your bliss, he said, "doors will open for you that wouldn't have opened for anyone else."

Protective instincts hold us back or steer us toward practical decisions (Campbell did teach literature for thirty-eight years), but we can see past them and follow our dharma if we know what to look for.

DHARMA IS OF THE BODY

Instead of listening to our minds, we must pay attention to how an idea or activity feels in our bodies. First, when you visualize yourself in a process, do you feel joy? Does the idea of it appeal to you? Then, when you actually do the activity, how does your body respond? When you're in your element, you can feel it.

1. *Alive.* For some people, being in their dharma means they feel a calm, confident satisfaction. For others, there is a thrill of joy and

excitement. In either case, you feel alive, connected, with a smile on your face. A light comes on.

2. *Flow.* In dharma, there is a natural momentum. You feel like you're in your lane, swimming with the current, instead of struggling through a resistant surf. When you are truly aligned, there is a sense of flow—you come out of your own head and lose track of time.
3. *Comfort.* In your dharma, you don't feel alone or out of place, no matter who comes or goes or where you are physically; where you are feels right, even if the place where you feel right is traveling the world. I don't like the feeling of danger, but I have a friend who loves fast cars and Jet Skis. The danger—the worst-case scenario—is the same for both of us, but for him it is worth it, or the danger itself is a joy. On stage, I'm in my element, but someone else would shut down.
4. *Consistency.* If you have a great time snorkeling on vacation, that doesn't mean snorkeling, or being on vacation for that matter, is your dharma. Being in your dharma bears repeating. In fact, it gets better the more you do it. But a single event is a clue to what energy you like, when and how you feel alive.
5. *Positivity and growth.* When we're aware of our own strengths, we're more confident, we value others' abilities more, and we feel less competitive. The inclination to compare yourself to others may not go away completely, but it shrinks because you only compare yourself to people within your area of expertise. Rejection and criticism don't feel like assaults. They feel like information that we can accept or reject, depending on whether they help us move forward.

DHARMA IS YOUR RESPONSIBILITY

Once you have a sense of your dharma, it's up to you to set up your life so that you can live it. We're not always going to be in a place or a situation where others recognize our dharma and bend over backward to help us fulfill it. As we all have experienced at one time or another, bosses don't always tap into their employees' potential. If you're reading this chapter thinking *My manager needs to understand dharma—then she'll give me the promotion*, you've missed the point. We will never live in an idyllic world where everyone constantly lives their dharma, with occasional pauses for their bosses to call and ask if they're truly fulfilled.

It is our responsibility to demonstrate and defend our dharma. The Manusmriti says that dharma protects those who protect it. Dharma brings you stability and peace. When we have the confidence to know where we thrive, we find opportunities to demonstrate that. This creates a feedback loop. When you safeguard your dharma, you constantly strive to be in a place where you thrive. When you thrive, people notice, and you reap rewards that help you stay in your dharma. Your dharma protects your joy and your sense of purpose and helps you grow.

STRETCH YOUR DHARMA

A person who isn't living their dharma is like a fish out of water. You can give the fish all the riches in the world, but it will die unless it's returned to the water. Once you discover your dharma, strive to play that role in every aspect of your life. Follow your passion in the workplace. Take up community issues using the same skill set. Be in your dharma with your family, in sports, in relationships, during days out with friends. If my dharma is to be a leader, I'm probably the one who should be planning the family holidays. I will feel meaning in that role. But if I'm a leader and I'm not playing that role, I'll feel insignificant and frustrated.

Perhaps you are thinking, *Jay, it makes no sense to stick to your dharma. Everyone knows that you should push yourself. Try new things. Venture out of your comfort zone.* Though your dharma is your natural state, its range is further than your comfort zone. For instance, if your dharma is to be a speaker, you can go from an audience of ten to an audience of a hundred, scaling the size of your impact. If you speak to students, you can start speaking to CEOs.

It's also important to stretch your dharma. I'm not the most outgoing person in the world, but I go to events and meetings because I know connecting with people serves my purpose. Going against your dharma is a bit like roller skating. You feel off-balance, slightly out of control, and exhausted afterward. But the more you understand yourself, the more solid your footing. You can consciously skate off in a new direction for a higher purpose. Understanding your dharma is key to knowing when and how to leave it behind.

Our dharmas evolve with us. A British expat, Emma Slade, lived in Hong Kong, where she worked as an investor for a global bank managing accounts worth more than a billion dollars. "I loved it," says Slade. "It was fast, it was exciting. . . . I ate balance sheets for breakfast." Then in September 1997, Slade was on a business trip in Jakarta, Indonesia, when an armed man pushed a gun into her chest, robbed her, and held her hostage in her hotel room. She says that as she lay cowering on the floor, she learned the value of a human life. Fortunately, police arrived before Slade was physically harmed. Later, when police officers showed her a photograph of the man slumped against the hotel wall surrounded by spatters of blood, Slade was shocked to feel sadness and compassion for him. That feeling stuck with her and led her to pursue the question of her real purpose.

Slade quit her job and began exploring yoga and the nature of mind. In 2011, she traveled to Bhutan, where she met a monk who left an indelible impression on her (been there!). In 2012, she became a Buddhist nun, and Slade (now also known as Pema Deki) felt she'd finally found peace. Yet that feeling of compassion she'd felt for the man who attacked her returned, and Slade realized she needed to do something to put her compassion into action. So in 2015 she founded a UK-based charity called Opening Your Heart to Bhutan, which seeks to meet the basic needs of people in rural areas of East Bhutan. Though she found fulfillment in becoming a nun, it was never her dharma to sit in a cave and meditate for the rest of her life. She now deploys her financial acumen in a way that serves herself and others more richly. Says Slade, "The skills of old have been very useful in bringing me now a very meaningful and happy life." Slade compares her experience to the lotus flower, which begins in the mud then grows upward through the water as it seeks light. In Buddhism, the lotus represents the idea that the mud and muck of life's challenges can provide fertile ground for our development. As the lotus grows, it rises through the water to eventually blossom. The Buddha says, "Just like a red, blue, or white lotus—born in the water, grown in the water, rising up above the water—stands unsmeared by the water, in the same way I—born in the world, grown in the world, having overcome the world—live unsmeared by the world."

"Jakarta was my mud," Slade says in her TEDx Talk, "but it was also the seed of my future development."

Remember the whole equation of dharma. Dharma isn't just passion and skills. Dharma is *passion in the service of others.* Your passion is for you. Your purpose is for others. Your passion becomes a purpose when you use it to serve others. Your dharma has to fill a need in the world. As I've said, monks believe that you should be willing to do whatever is needed when there's a higher purpose (and monks live this fully), but if you're not a monk the way to see it is that the pleasure you feel in doing your passion should equal how much others appreciate it. If others don't think you're effective, then your passion is a hobby, which can add richness to your life.

This doesn't mean every activity outside your dharma is a waste of time. For all of us there are activities in life that are competence-building and activities that are character-building. When I was first asked to give talks, I built competence in my dharma. But when I was asked to take out the trash, it built my character. To build your competence without regard for character is narcissistic, and to build character without working on skills is devoid of impact. We need to work on both in order to serve our souls and a higher purpose.

Knowing your purpose and fulfilling it is easier and more fruitful when you use your time and energy wisely every day. In the next chapter we will talk about how to get the best start to your day and how to follow through from there.

SIX

ROUTINE

Location Has Energy; Time Has Memory

Every day, think as you wake up, today I am fortunate to be alive, I have a precious human life, I am not going to waste it.

—the Dalai Lama

There are twelve of us, maybe more, sleeping on the floor, each on a thin yoga-type pad, covered by a simple sheet. The walls of the room are made of packed cow dung that feels like rough plaster and gives the place a not-unpleasant earthy smell. The unfinished stone floors are worn smooth, but a far cry from memory foam. There are no finished windows in this building—we're in an interior room that keeps us dry in the rainy season and has plenty of doors for ventilation.

Although I sleep here every night, there is no particular space that I consider "mine." We steer clear of ownership here—no possessions, no material attachments. Right now the room is dark as a cave, but from the tenor of the birds outside, our bodies know that it's 4 a.m.—time to wake up. We're due at collective prayers in half an hour. Without speaking a word, we move to the locker room, some of us showering, some of us pulling on our robes. We wait in line to brush our teeth at one of the four communal sinks. No one from the outside world is witness to our activity, but if they were, they would see a group of seemingly well-rested men, all of whom appear perfectly content to be getting up at this early hour.

It wasn't always that easy. Every morning my brain, desperate to remain shut down just a little bit longer, thought of a different excuse for why I should sleep in. But I pushed myself to adopt this new routine because I was committed to the process. The fact that it was hard was an important part of the journey.

Eventually, I learned the one infallible trick to successfully getting up earlier: *I had to go to sleep earlier.* That was it. I'd spent my entire life pushing the limits of each day, sacrificing tomorrow because I didn't want to miss out on today. But once I finally let that go and started going to sleep earlier, waking up at four became easier and easier. And as it became easier, I found that I could do it without the help of anyone or anything besides my own body and the natural world around it.

This was a revelatory experience for me. I realized I had never in my life begun my day without being startled in one way or another. When I was a teenager, my morning summons came in the form of my mother screaming "Jay, wake up!" from downstairs. In later years, an alarm clock performed the same thankless task. Every day of my life had begun with a sudden, jarring intrusion. Now, however, I was waking up to the sounds of birds, trees rustling in the wind, a stream of water. I woke to the sounds of nature.

At last I came to understand the value in it. The point of waking up early wasn't to torture us—it was to start the day off with peace and tranquility. Birds. A gong. The sound of flowing water. And our morning routine never varied. The simplicity and structure of ashram mornings spared us from the stressful complexity of decisions and variation. Starting our days so simply was like a mental shower. It cleansed us of the challenges of the previous day, giving us the space and energy to transform greed into generosity, anger into compassion, loss into love. Finally, it gave us resolve, a sense of purpose to carry out into the day.

In the ashram, every detail of our life was designed to facilitate the habit or ritual we were trying to practice. For example, our robes: When we rose, we never had to think about what to wear. Like Steve Jobs, Barack Obama, and Arianna Huffington, all of whom have been known to have their own basic uniforms, monks simplify their clothing so as not to waste energy and time on dressing for the day. We each had two sets of robes—one to wear and one to wash. In similar fashion, the early morning wake-up was designed to launch the day in the right spirit. It was an ungodly hour, yet it was spiritually enlightening.

I would never wake up that early, you may be thinking. *I can't think of a worse way to start the day*. I understand that perspective since I used to feel the same way! But let's take a look at how most people currently start their day: sleep researchers say 85 percent of us need an alarm clock to wake up for work. When we wake up before our bodies are ready, the hormone melatonin, which helps to regulate sleep, is usually still at work, which is one of the reasons we grope for the snooze button.

Unfortunately, our productivity-driven society encourages us to live like this. Maria Popova, a writer who's best known as the curator of *Brain Pickings*, writes, "We tend to wear our ability to get by on little sleep as some sort of badge of honor that validates our work ethic. But what it *is* is a profound failure of self-respect and of priorities."

Then, once we've woken up after too little sleep, nearly a quarter of us do something else that starts us out on the second wrong foot of the day—*we reach for our cell phones within one minute of waking up*. Over half of us are checking messages within ten minutes. A majority of people go from out cold to processing mountains of information within minutes every morning.

There are only six cars that can go from zero to sixty miles per hour in under two seconds. Like most cars, humans are not built for that kind of sudden transition, mentally or physically. And the last thing you need to do when you've just woken up is to stumble straight into tragedy and pain courtesy of news headlines or friends venting about gridlock on their commute. Looking at your phone first thing in the morning is like inviting one hundred chatty strangers into your bedroom before you've showered, brushed your teeth, fixed your hair. Between the alarm clock and the world inside your phone, you're immediately overwhelmed with stress, pressure, anxiety. Do you really expect yourself to emerge from that state and have a pleasant, productive day?

In the ashram, we started each morning in the spirit of the day we planned to have, and we trained ourselves to sustain that deliberateness and focus all day long. Sure, that's all fine and good if your daily schedule involves prayer, meditation, study, service, and chores, but the outside world is more complex.

EARLY TO RISE

Here is my first recommendation: Wake up one hour earlier than you do now. "No way!" you say. "Why would I want to wake up any earlier than I do right now? I don't get enough sleep as it is. Besides, yuck!" But hear me out. None of us wants to go to work tired and then get to the end of the day feeling like we could have done more. The energy and mood of the morning carries through the day, so making life more meaningful begins there.

We're used to waking up just before we have to get to work, or to a class, or to a workout, or to shuttle children off to school. We leave ourselves just enough time to shower, eat breakfast, pack up, etc. But having "just enough time" means *not* having enough time. You run late. You skip breakfast. You leave the bed unmade. You can't take the time to enjoy your shower, brush your teeth properly, finish your breakfast, or put everything away so you'll return to a tidy home. You can't do things with purpose and care if you have to speed through them. When you start the morning with high pressure and high stress, you're programming your body to operate in that mode for the rest of the day, through conversations, meetings, appointments.

Waking up early leads to a more productive day. Successful businesspeople are already onto this. Apple CEO Tim Cook starts his day at 3:45 a.m. Richard Branson is up at 5:45. Michelle Obama rises at 4:30. But it's important to note that while lots of high-impact people rise early, there's also a movement among top executives to reclaim sleep. Amazon CEO Jeff Bezos makes it a priority to get eight hours of sleep every night, saying that less sleep might give you more time to produce, but the quality will suffer. So if you're going to rise early, you need to turn in at an hour that allows you to get a full night's rest.

Life gets more complicated if you have kids or a night job, so if these or other circumstances make the idea of waking up an hour earlier unfathomable, don't despair. Start with manageable increments (see the Try This below). And notice I didn't name a specific time for you to get up. I'm not asking for 4 a.m. The hour doesn't even have to be early—the goal is to give you enough time to move with intention and do things completely. That spirit will carry through the day.

Create a time cushion at the beginning of the day or you'll spend the rest of the day searching for it. I guarantee you will never find that extra time in the middle of the day. Steal it from your morning sleep and give that sleep back to yourself at night. See what changes.

TRY THIS: EASE INTO AN EARLIER WAKE-UP

This week, wake up just fifteen minutes earlier. You'll probably have to use an alarm, but make it a gentle one. Use low lighting when you first wake up; put on quiet music. Don't pick up your phone for at least those bonus fifteen minutes. Give your brain this time to set a tone for the day ahead. After one week of this, roll your wake time back another fifteen minutes. Now you have half an hour that is all yours. How will you choose to spend it? You might take a longer shower. Sip your tea. Go for a walk. Meditate. Spend a moment cleaning up after yourself before you step out the door. At night, turn off the TV and phone and get in bed whenever you feel the first twinge of fatigue.

FOUND TIME

Once you've created space in the morning, it is yours alone; nobody else controls how you use it. Given how much of our time is controlled by our obligations—job, family, etc.—this free time is one of the greatest gifts we can give ourselves. You might go about your ordinary routine, but feel the space and leisure created by more time. Maybe you have time to make your own coffee instead of grabbing it en route. You can have a conversation over breakfast, read the paper, or use your newfound time to exercise. If you have a meditation, you can start the day with a gratitude visualization practice. Maybe, as health experts are fond of recommending, you'll park further from work to add a bit of a walk to your morning. When you create the space, you'll realize it fills with what you lack most of all: time for yourself.

TRY THIS: A NEW MORNING ROUTINE

Every morning make some time for:

Thankfulness. Express gratitude to someone, some place, or something every day. This includes thinking it, writing it, and sharing it. (See Chapter Nine.)

Insight. Gain insight through reading the paper or a book, or listening to a podcast.

Meditation. Spend fifteen minutes alone, breathing, visualizing or with sound. (More about sound meditation at the end of Part 3.)

Exercise. We monks did yoga, but you can do some basic stretches or a workout.

Thankfulness. Insight. Meditation. Exercise. T.I.M.E. A new way to put time into your morning.

THE EVENING ROUTINE

At the ashram, I learned that the morning is defined by the evening. It's natural for us to treat each morning like a new beginning, but the truth is that our days circle on themselves. You don't set your alarm in the morning—you set it the night before. It follows that if you want to wake up in the morning with intention, you need to start that momentum by establishing a healthy, restful evening routine—and so the attention we've given the mornings begins to expand and define the entire day.

There is "no way" you have time to wake up one hour earlier, but how often do you switch on the TV, settle on one show or another, and end up watching until past midnight? You watch TV because you're "unwinding." You're too tired to do anything else. But earlier sleep time can put you in a better mood. Human growth hormone (HGH) is kind of a big deal. It plays a key role in growth, cell repair, and metabolism, and without it we might even die sooner. As much as 75 percent of the HGH in our bodies is released when we sleep, and research shows that our highest bursts of HGH typically come between 10 p.m. and midnight, so if you're awake during those hours, you're cheating yourself of HGH. If you have a job that goes past midnight, or little kids who keep you up, feel free to ignore me, but waking up before the demands of your day begin should not be at the expense of good sleep. If you spent that ten to midnight getting real rest, it wouldn't be so hard to find those hours in the morning.

In the ashram, we spent the evenings studying and reading and went to sleep between eight and ten. We slept in pitch darkness, with no devices in the room. We slept in T-shirts and shorts, never in our robes, which carried the energy of the waking day.

Morning sets the tone of the day, but a well-planned evening prepares you for morning. In an interview on CNBC's Make It, Instagram *Shark Tank* star Kevin O'Leary said that before he goes to sleep he writes down three things he wants to do the next morning before he talks to anyone besides his family. Take his cue and before you go to sleep, figure out the first things you want to achieve tomorrow. Knowing what you're tackling first will simplify your morning. You won't have to push or force your mind when it's just warming up. (And, bonus, those tasks won't keep you up at night if you know you're going to handle them.)

Next, find your version of a monk's robe, a uniform that you'll put on in the morning. I have a bigger selection of clothes now, and to my wife's relief none of them are orange robes, but I favor similar sets of clothes in different colors. The point is to remove challenges from the morning. Insignificant as they may seem, if you're spending your morning deciding what to eat, what to wear, and what tasks to tackle first, the accumulating choices complicate things unnecessarily.

Christopher Sommer, a former US National Team gymnastics coach, with forty years' experience, tells his athletes to limit the number of decisions they have to make because each decision is an opportunity to stray from their path. If you spend your morning making trivial decisions, you'll have squandered that energy. Settle into patterns and make decisions the night before, and you'll have a head start on the morning and will be better able to make focused decisions throughout the day.

Finally, consider what your last thoughts are before going to sleep. Are they *This screen is going blurry, I'd better turn off my phone* or *I forgot to wish my mother "Happy Birthday"*? Don't program yourself to wake up with bad energy. Every night when I'm falling asleep, I say to myself, "I am relaxed, energized, and focused. I am calm, enthusiastic, and productive." It has a yoga-robot vibe when I put it on paper, but it works for me. I am programming my mind to wake up with energy and conviction. **The emotion you fall asleep with at night is most likely the emotion you'll wake up with in the morning.**

A STONE ON THE PATH

The goal of all this preparation is to bring intentionality to the entire day. The moment you leave your home, there will be more curveballs, whatever your job may be. You're going to need the energy and focus you cultivated all morning. Monks don't just have morning routines and

TRY THIS: **VISUALIZATION FOR TOMORROW**

Just as an inventor has to visualize an idea before building it, we can visualize the life we want, beginning by visualizing how we want our mornings to be.

After you do breathwork to calm your mind, I want you to visualize yourself as your best self. Visualize yourself waking up in the morning healthy, well rested, and energized. Imagine the sunlight coming through the windows. You get up, and as your feet touch the ground, you feel a sense of gratitude for another day. Really feel that gratitude, and then say in your mind, "I am grateful for today. I am excited for today. I am joyful for today."

See yourself brushing your teeth, taking your time, being mindful to brush every tooth. Then, as you go into the shower, visualize yourself feeling calm, balance, ease, stillness. When you come out of the shower, because you chose what you were going to wear the night before, it's not a bother to dress. Now see yourself setting your intentions, writing down, "My intention today is to be focused. My intention today is to be disciplined. My intention today is to be of service."

Visualize the whole morning again as realistically as you can. You may add some exercise, some meditation. Believe it. Feel it. Welcome it into your life. Feeling fresh, feeling fueled.

Now visualize yourself continuing the day as your best self. See yourself inspiring others, leading others, guiding others, sharing with others, listening to others, learning from others, being open to others, their feedback and their thoughts. See yourself in this dynamic environment, giving your best and receiving your best.

Visualize yourself coming home at the end of the day. You're tired, but you're happy. You want to sit down and rest, but you're grateful for whatever you have: a job, a life, family, friends, a home. You have more than so many people. See yourself in the evening; instead of being on your phone or watching a show, you come up with new ideas to spend that time meaningfully.

When you visualize yourself getting into bed at a good time, see yourself

(continued on next page)

looking up and saying, "I'm grateful for today. I will wake up tomorrow feeling healthy, energized, and rested. Thank you." Then visualize yourself scanning throughout your body and thanking each part of your body for helping you throughout the day.

When you're ready, in your own time, at your own pace, slowly and gently open your eyes.

Note: Life messes up your plans. Tomorrow is not going to go as you visualize it. Visualization doesn't change your life, but it changes how you see it. You can build your life by returning to the ideal that you imagined. Whenever you feel that your life is out of alignment, you realign it with the visualization.

nighttime routines; we use routines of time and location every moment of the day. Sister Joan Chittister, the Benedictine nun I've already mentioned, says, "People living in the cities and suburbs . . . can make choices about the way they live, though most of them don't see that, because they are conditioned to be on the go all the time. . . . Imagine for a moment what America would look like, imagine the degree of serenity we'd have, if laypeople had something comparable to the daily schedule of the cloistered life. It provides scheduled time for prayer, work, and recreation." **Routines root us.** The two hours I spend meditating support the other twenty-two hours of my day, just as the twenty-two hours influence my meditation. The relationship between the two is symbiotic.

In the ashram we took the same thirty-minute walk on the same path at least once a day. Every day the monk asked us to keep our eyes open for something different, something we'd never before seen on this walk that we had taken yesterday, and the day before, and the day before that.

Spotting something new every day on our familiar walk was a reminder to keep our focus on that walk, to see the freshness in each "routine," to be aware. Seeing something is not the same as noticing it. Researchers at UCLA asked faculty, staff, and students in the Department of Psychology whether they knew the location of the nearest fire extinguisher. Only 24 percent could remember where the closest one was, even though, for 92 percent of the participants, a fire extinguisher was just a few feet from where they filled out the survey (which was usually their own office or a classroom they frequently visited). One professor didn't realize that there was a fire extinguisher just inches from the office he'd occupied for twenty-five years.

Truly noticing what's around us keeps our brains from shifting to autopilot. At the ashram we were trained to do this on our daily walk.

I have taken this walk for hundreds of days now. It is hot, but not unpleasant in my robes. The forest is leafy and cool, the dirt path feels soothing underfoot. Today a senior monk has asked us to look for a new stone, one that we have never noticed before. I am slightly disappointed. For the past week or so we've been asked to look for a new flower every day, and yesterday I lined up an extra one for today, a tiny blue flower cupping a drop of dew that seemed to wink at me as if it were in on my plan. But no, our leader is somehow onto me and has switched things up. And so the hunt is on.

Monks understand that routine frees your mind, but the biggest threat to that freedom is monotony. People complain about their poor memories, but I've heard it said that we don't have a *re*tention problem, we have an *at*tention problem. By searching for the new, you are reminding your brain to pay attention and rewiring it to recognize that there's something to learn in everything. Life isn't as certain as we assume.

How can I advocate both for establishing routines and seeking out novelty? Aren't these contradictory? But it is precisely doing the familiar that creates room for discovery. The late Kobe Bryant was onto this. The basketball legend had started showing his creative side, developing books and a video series. As Bryant told me on my podcast, *On Purpose*, having a routine is critical to his work. "A lot of the time, creativity comes from structure. When you have those parameters and structure, then within that you can be creative. If you don't have structure, you're just aimlessly doing stuff." Rules and routines ease our cognitive burden so we have bandwidth for creativity. Structure enhances spontaneity. And discovery reinvigorates the routine.

This approach leads to delight in small things. We tend to anticipate the big events of life: holidays, promotions, birthday parties. We put pressure on these events to live up to our expectations. But if we look for small joys, we don't have to wait for them to come up on the calendar. Instead they await us every day if we take the time to look for them.

And I've found it! Here, a curious orange-y stone that has seemingly appeared out of nowhere since yesterday. I turn it over in my palm. Finding the stone isn't the end of our discovery process. We observe it deeply, describe the color, the shape, immerse ourselves in it in order to understand and appreciate it. Then we might describe it again to be sure we've experienced it fully. This isn't an exercise, it's real. A deep experience. I smile before returning it to the edge of the path, half-hidden, but there for someone else to find.

To walk down the same old path and find a new stone is to open your mind.

CHEW YOUR DRINKS AND DRINK YOUR FOOD

Monk training wasn't just about spotting the new. It was about doing familiar things with awareness.

One afternoon a senior monk told us, "Today we will have a silent lunch. Remember to chew your drinks and drink your food."

"What does that mean?" I asked.

"We don't take the time to consume our food properly," the monk said. "When you drink your food, grind the solids into liquid. When you chew your drink, instead of gulping it down take each sip as if it is a morsel to be savored."

TRY THIS: SAME OLD, SAME NEW

Look for something new in a routine that you already have. What can you spy on your commute that you have never seen before? Try starting a conversation with someone you see regularly but haven't ever engaged. Do this with one new person every day and see how your life changes.

If a monk can be mindful of a single sip of water, imagine how this carries through to the rest of daily life. How can you rediscover the everyday? When you exercise, can you see the route that you run or feel the rhythms of the gym differently? Do you see the same woman walking her dog every day? Could you greet her with a nod? When you shop for food, can you take the time to choose the perfect apple—or the most unusual one? Can you have a personal exchange with the cashier?

In your physical space, how can you look at things freshly? There are articles all around our homes and our workspaces that we have put out because they please us: photos, knickknacks, art objects. Look at yours closely. Are these a true reflection of what brings you joy? Are there other favorites that deserve a turn in the spotlight and inject some novelty into your familiar surroundings? Add flowers to a vase or rearrange your furniture to find new brightness and purpose in familiar possessions. Simply choosing a new place for incoming mail can change it from clutter to part of an organized life.

We can awaken the familiarity of home by changing things up. Have music playing when your partner comes home if that's something you don't usually do. Or vice versa, if you usually put on music or a podcast when you get home, try silence instead. Bring a strange piece of fruit home from the store and put it in the middle of the dinner table. Introduce a topic of conversation to your dinner companions or take turns reporting three surprising moments in the day. Switch the lightbulb to a softer or clearer light. Flip the mattress. Sleep on the "wrong" side of the bed.

Appreciating the everyday doesn't even have to involve change so much as finding value in everyday activities. In his book *At Home in the World*, the monk Thich Nhat Hanh writes, "To my mind, the idea that doing dishes is unpleasant can occur only when you aren't doing them. . . . If I am incapable of washing dishes joyfully, if I want to finish them quickly so I can go and have dessert or a cup of tea, I will be equally incapable of enjoying my dessert or my tea when I finally have them. . . . Each thought, each action in the sunlight of awareness becomes sacred. In this light, no boundary exists between the sacred and the profane."

TRY THIS: TRANSFORM THE MUNDANE

Even a task as quotidian as doing the dishes can transform if you let it. Allow yourself to be in front of the sink, committed to a single task. Instead of putting on music, focus all your senses on the dishes—watch their surfaces go from grimy to clean, smell the dish soap, feel the steam of the hot water. Observe how satisfying it is to see the sink go from full to empty. There is a Zen koan that says, "Before enlightenment, chop wood, carry water. After enlightenment, chop wood, carry water." No matter how much we grow, we are never free of daily chores and routines, but to be enlightened is to embrace them. The outside may look the same, but inside you are transformed.

EVERY MOMENT OF THE DAY

We've talked about taking an ordinary, familiar moment and finding new ways to appreciate it. To take that presence to another level, we try to string these moments together, so that we're not picking and choosing certain walks or dishwashing episodes to make special—we're elevating our awareness of every moment, at every moment.

We're all familiar with the idea of being in the moment. It's not hard to see that if you're running a race, you won't be able to go back and change how fast you ran at Mile 2. Your only opportunity to succeed is in that moment. Whether you are at a work meeting or having dinner with friends, the conversations you have, the words you choose—you won't ever have another opportunity just like that one. In that moment you can't change the past, and you're deciding the future, so you might as well be where you are. Kālidāsa, the great Sanskrit writer of the fifth century, wrote, "Yesterday is but a dream. Tomorrow is only a vision. But today well lived makes every yesterday a dream of happiness, and every tomorrow a vision of hope."

We may all agree that living in the present makes sense, but the truth is that we're only willing to have *selective presence*. We're willing to be present at certain times—during a favorite show or a yoga class, or even during the mundane task we've chosen to elevate—but we still want to be distracted when we choose to be distracted. We spend time at work dreaming about going on a beach vacation, but then, on the beach, long-awaited drink in hand, we're annoyed to find that we can't stop thinking about work. Monks learn that these two scenarios are connected. A desired distraction at work bleeds into unwanted distraction on vacation. Distraction at lunch bleeds into the afternoon. We are training our minds to be where we physically aren't. If you allow yourself to daydream, you will always be distracted.

Being present is the only way to live a truly rich and full life.

LOCATION HAS ENERGY

It is easier to see the value of being present throughout an ordinary day, and easier to be truly present if you understand and appreciate the benefits that routine has to offer. Routines aren't just about actions; they're also about the locations in which those actions take place. There's a reason people study better in libraries and work better in offices. New York City imparts its hustle and bustle, while LA makes you feel laid back. Each environment—from the biggest city to the smallest corner of a room—has its own particular energy. Every location gives off a different feeling, and your dharma thrives—or falters—in specific environments.

We are constantly experiencing a range of activities and environments, but we don't pause to contemplate which ones most appeal to us. Do you thrive in busy environments or in solitude? Do you like the safety of cozy nooks or spacious libraries? Do you prefer to be surrounded by stimulating artwork and music, or does uncluttered simplicity help you concentrate? Do you like to bounce ideas off others or to get feedback after completing a job? Do you prefer familiarity or a change of scenery? Having this self-awareness serves your dharma. It means that when you step into a job interview, you have a better sense of how you will perform at this job and whether it's a good match. It means that when you plan a date, you can choose a space where you will be most comfortable. When you imagine different careers within your skill set, you know which ones are best suited to your sensibilities.

TRY THIS: ENVIRONMENTAL AWARENESS

For every environment where you spend time this week, ask yourself the following questions. If possible, ask them right after the experience, then again at the end of the week.

What were the key features of the space?
Quiet or loud?
Big or small?
Vibrant or plain?
In the center of an active space or removed?
Close to other people or isolated?
How did I feel in this space: productive? relaxed? distracted?
Did the activity I was doing fit well with the place where I was doing it?
Was I in the best mindset for what I set out to do?
If not, is there another place where I am more comfortable accomplishing what I planned?

The more your personal spaces are devoted to single, clear purposes, the better they will serve you, not just in the fulfillment of your dharma but in your mood and productivity. Just as the room where we monks slept was designed for nothing but sleep, so every place in the ashram was devoted to a single activity. We didn't read or meditate where we slept. We didn't work in the refectory.

In the world outside an ashram, to watch Netflix and/or eat in your bedroom is to confuse the energy of that space. If you bring those energies to your bedroom, it becomes harder to sleep there. Even in the tiniest apartment, you can dedicate spaces to different activities. Every home should have a place to eat. A place to sleep. A sacred space that helps you feel calm and a space that feels comforting when you are angry. Create spaces that bring you the energy that matches your intention. A bedroom should have few distractions, calm colors, soft lighting. Ideally, it should not contain your workspace. Meanwhile, a workspace should be well lit, uncluttered, and functional, with art that inspires you.

When you identify where you thrive, focus on expanding those opportunities. If you're drawn to the energy of a nightclub in your leisure time, would you do better in a career that is equally vibrant? If you're a rock musician but you thrive in quiet, then maybe you should be composing music instead of performing. If you have the "perfect job" working from home, but you prefer the activity of an office, look to move your work to a café or shared workspace. The point is to be aware about where you thrive, where you're at your best, and to figure out how to spend the most time in that place.

Of course, we are all obligated to do activities we don't like in environments that aren't ideal—especially work—and we've all experienced the negative energies that these activities generate. With elevated awareness, we understand what has made us impatient, stressed, or drained, and develop guidelines for what living in our dharma, in the right environment, with the right energy, would look like. This should be the long-term goal.

Sound Design Your Life

Your location and your senses speak to each other. This is most obvious when we think about the sounds that we encounter every day. In monk life the sounds we hear relate directly to what we are doing. We wake up to birds and winds. We hear chanting as we walk into a meditation. There is no painful noise.

But the modern world is getting louder. Planes howl overhead, dogs bark, drills whine. We're subjected to uncontrollable noise all day. We think we're ignoring the honk and clatter of daily life, but all of it adds to our cognitive load. The brain processes sound even when we don't consciously hear it. At home, many of us retreat to silence, so we live in the extremes of silence and noise.

Instead of tuning out the noise in your life—sound design it. Start by picking the best alarm tone in the world. Begin the day with a song that makes you happy. On your way to work, listen to a beloved audiobook, a favorite podcast, or your go-to playlist. Choose sounds that make you feel happier and healthier, the better to replicate the highly curated life in an ashram.

TIME HAS MEMORY

When we tailor our locations for specific purposes, we're better able to summon the right kind of energy and attention. The same is true for time. Doing something at the same time every day helps us remember to do it, commit to it, and do it with increasing skill and facility. If you're accustomed to going to the gym every morning at the same time, try going in the evening for a change and you'll see what a challenge it is. When we do something at the same time every day, that time keeps that memory for us. It holds the practice. It saves the space. When you want to incorporate a new habit into your routine, like meditating or reading, don't make it more difficult by trying to do it whenever you have a free moment. Slot it into the same time every day. Even better, link the new practice to something that's already a habit. A friend of mine wanted to incorporate daily yoga into her schedule so she laid a mat right next to her bed. She literally rolled out of bed and into her yoga practice. Marrying habits is a way of circumventing excuses.

Location has energy; time has memory.

If you do something at the same time every day, it becomes easier and natural.

If you do something in the same space every day, it becomes easier and natural.

SINGLE-TASKING

Time and location help us maximize the moment, but there is one essential component to being wholly present in that moment: single-tasking. Studies have found that only 2 percent of us can multitask effectively; most of us are terrible at it, especially when one of those tasks requires a lot of focus. When we think we're multitasking, what's usually happening is that we're shifting rapidly among several different things, or "serial tasking." This fragmented attention actually erodes our ability to focus, so doing just one thing at a time without distraction becomes harder. Researchers from Stanford University took a group of students and divided them into two groups—those who frequently switch among multiple streams of media (checking email, social media, and headline news, for instance) and those who don't. They put the groups through a series of attention and memory tasks, such as remembering sequences of letters and focusing on certain colored shapes while ignoring others, and the media multitaskers consistently performed poorly. They even did worse on a test of task-switching ability.

To make single-tasking easier for myself, I have "no tech" zones and times. My wife and I don't use tech in the bedroom or at the dining table, and try not to between 8 p.m. and 9 a.m. I try to practice single-tasking with mundane tasks in order to strengthen the habit. I used to brush my teeth without thought. They were white enough; they looked great. But then the dentist told me that I'd damaged my gums. Now I spend four seconds on each tooth. I count in my head, *one, two, three, four*, which gives me something to do. I'm still spending the same amount of time brushing my teeth, but I'm doing it in a more effective way. If I think about business when I'm brushing my teeth or in the shower, it doesn't feel nourishing and energizing, and I don't take care with my gums. When you're brushing, just brush. When you're showering, just shower.

We don't have to be focused like a laser beam on every task every time. It's okay to listen to music while cleaning the bathroom or talk with your partner while eating together. Just as some instruments sound great together, certain habits complement each other. But single-tasking as much as possible keeps your brain in the habit of focusing on one thing at a time, and you should pick certain routines where you always single-task, like walking the dog, using your phone (one app at a time!), showering, or folding the laundry, in order to build the skill.

GOING ALL THE WAY

Routines become easier if you've done something immersively. If you want to bring a new skill into your life, I recommend that you kick it off with single-pointed focus for a short period of time. If I play Ping-Pong every day for an hour, I'm definitely going to be better at it. If you want to start a daily meditation, a weeklong meditation retreat will give you a strong base on which to build. Throughout this book I suggest many changes you can make to your life. But if you try to change everything at the same time, they will all become small, equal priorities. Change happens with small steps and big priorities. Pick one thing to change, make it your number one priority, and see it through before you move on to the next.

Monks try to do everything immersively. Our lunches were silent. Our meditations were long. We didn't do anything in just five minutes. (Except for showering. We weren't showering immersively.) We had the luxury of time, and we used it to single-task for hours on end. That same level of immersion isn't possible in the modern world, but the greater your investment, the greater your return. If something is important, it deserves to be experienced deeply. And everything is important.

We all procrastinate and get distracted, even monks, but if you give yourself more time, then you can afford to get distracted and then refocus. In your morning routine, having limited time means that you're one phone call or spilled coffee away from being late to work. If you're frustrated with learning a new skill, understanding a concept, or assembling a piece of Ikea furniture, your instinct will be to pull away, but go all in and you'll accomplish more than you thought possible. (Even the Hemnes dresser—allegedly Ikea's most difficult build.)

As it turns out, periods of deep focus are also good for your brain. When we switch tasks compulsively (like the multitaskers who showed poor memory and focus in the Stanford study), it erodes our ability to focus. We overstimulate the dopamine (reward) channel. That's also the addiction pathway, so we are compelled to stimulate it more and more to get the same feel-good hit, and that leads to more and more distraction. But ultimately, ironically, the feel-good of dopamine bums us out—too much dopamine can keep our bodies from making and processing serotonin, the contentment chemical. If you've ever spent the day jumping on and off calls, in and out of meetings, ordering this book from Amazon and checking that thread on Snapchat, you know that feeling of exhaustion you have at the end of it all? It's a dopamine hangover.

When we allow ourselves to have immersive experiences—through meditation, focused periods of work, painting, doing a crossword puzzle, weeding a garden, and many other forms of *contemplative single-tasking*—we're not only more productive, we actually feel better.

There are plenty of magazine articles and phone apps that encourage you to meditate for five minutes a day. I'm not against that, but I'm also not surprised if it does nothing for you. In our culture, it is commonplace to devote five to ten minutes to one daily practice or another, but the truth is you achieve very little in five minutes. I've had more than one friend complain to me: "Jay, I've been meditating for five minutes a day for seven months and it's not working."

Imagine you were told you could spend five minutes a day for a whole month with someone you were attracted to. At the end of the month you'd still barely know them. You definitely wouldn't be in love. There's a reason we want to talk to someone all night when we're falling in love. Maybe sometimes it's even the other way around: We fall in love *because* we talked to someone all night. The ocean is full of treasures, but if you swim on the surface, you won't see them all. If you start a meditation practice with the idea that you can instantly clear your mind, you'll soon learn that immersion takes time and practice.

When I began to meditate, it took me a good fifteen minutes to settle physically and another fifteen to settle down the mental chatter. I've been meditating for one to two hours a day for thirteen years, and it *still* takes me ten minutes to switch off my mind. I'm not saying you have to meditate two hours a day for thirteen years to get the benefit. That's not the point. I have confidence that any process can work if you do it immersively. After you break the barrier and commit yourself wholly, you start experiencing the benefits. You lose track of time. The feeling of being fully engaged is often so rewarding that when it's time to stop, you want to return to the experience.

I recommend using immersive experience as a kickoff or reinvigoration for a regular practice. To my friend who was frustrated with his five minutes-a-day meditation practice, I said, "I get it. Time is tough to find, but if you feel like you're not getting enough from it, try taking an hour-long class. Then return to your ten-minute practice. You might find it has become more powerful. If you want, you could try a daylong retreat." I talked to him about falling in love, how eventually you aren't compelled to stay up all night anymore because you've gotten to know the person. Five minutes goes a lot further when you're married. I told him, "Maybe you and meditation could use a romantic getaway."

Routines are counterintuitive—instead of being boring and repetitive, doing the same tasks at the same time in the same place makes room for creativity. The consistent energy of location and memory of time help us be present in the moment, engaging deeply in tasks instead of getting distracted or frustrated. Build routines and train yourself as monks do, to find focus and achieve deep immersion.

Once we quell our external distractions, we can address the most subtle and powerful distractions of all, the voices inside our heads.

SEVEN

THE MIND

The Charioteer's Dilemma

When the five senses and the mind are stilled, when the reasoning intellect rests in silence, then begins the highest path.
—the Katha Upanishad

It is raining. Though it's September and monsoon season is over, it's coming down hard. I really need a shower before morning meditation. About a hundred of my fellow monks and I arrived here in South India last night after a two-day train ride from Mumbai. We had the cheapest tickets available, of course, sleeping in close quarters with strangers, and the bathrooms were so foul that I decided to fast for the entire trip in order to avoid them. We are on a pilgrimage, staying in a warehouse-type building near the seashore. After morning meditation we will go straight to classes, so now is my best chance to shower.

I ask for directions to the shower, and someone points to a wet, muddy dirt pathway through the low shrubs. "It's about a twenty-minute walk," he says.

I look down at my flip-flops. Great. My feet will get even dirtier on the way to the shower than they are right now. What's the point?

Then another voice comes into my head: "Don't be lazy. You have to get ready for morning meditation. Just go take the shower."

I duck my head and start down the path. Squelching through the mud, I try not to slip. Every step is unpleasant, not just because of the conditions but because the first voice in my head keeps discouraging me, saying "See? You're getting muddy on your way to the showers, and you'll get dirty again on the way back."

The other voice urges me onward: "You are doing the right thing. Honor your commitment."

Finally, I reach the showers, a row of white stalls. I open the door to one and look up. Rain pours down from the still-dark sky. There is no roof. Seriously? I step into the stall and don't even bother to turn on the faucet. We bathe in cold water anyway, and that's exactly what the rain is delivering.

Standing in the shower, I wonder what the hell I am doing here. In this miserable excuse for a shower, on that filthy train yesterday, on this trip, living this life. I could be dry and warm in a nice apartment in London right now, making fifty thousand pounds a year. Life could be so much easier.

But as I walk back, the other voice returns with some interesting ideas about the value of what I've just accomplished. Going to the shower in the rain wasn't a notable achievement. It didn't require physical strength or bravery. But it tested my ability to tolerate external difficulties. It gave me an idea of how much frustration I could handle in one morning. It may not have cleansed or refreshed me, but it did something more valuable: It strengthened my resolve.

THE MONKEY MIND

In the Hitopadeśa, an ancient Indian text by Nārāyana, the mind is compared to a drunken monkey that's been bitten by a scorpion and haunted by a ghost.

We humans have roughly seventy thousand separate thoughts each day. Ernst Pöppel, a German psychologist and neuroscientist, has shown through his research that our minds are only in present time for about three seconds at a time. Other than that, our brains are thinking forward and backward, filling in ideas about present time based on what we've experienced in the past and anticipating what is to come. As Lisa Feldman Barrett, author of *How Emotions Are Made*, describes it on a podcast, most of the time "your brain is not reacting to events in the world, it's predicting . . . constantly guessing what's going to happen next." The Samyutta Nikaya describes each thought as a branch, and our minds as monkeys, swinging from one branch to the next, often aimlessly. This almost sounds like fun, but, as we all know, it is anything but. Usually those thoughts are fears, concerns, negativity, and stress. What will happen this week at work? What should I eat for dinner? Have I saved enough for a holiday this year? Why is my date five minutes late? Why am I here? These are all genuine questions that deserve answers, but none of them will be resolved while we swing from branch to branch, thought to thought. This is the jungle of the untrained mind.

The Dhammapada is a collection of verses probably collected by Buddha's disciples. In it, the Buddha says, "As irrigators lead water where they want, as archers make their arrows straight, as carpenters carve wood, the wise shape their minds." True growth requires understanding the mind. It is the filter, judge, and director of all our experiences, but, as evidenced by the conflict I felt on my shower adventure, we are not always of one mind. The more we can evaluate, understand, train, and strengthen our relationship with the mind, the more successfully we navigate our lives and overcome challenges.

This battle in our mind is waged over the smallest daily choices (Do I have to get up right now?) and the biggest (Should I end this relationship?). All of us face such battles every single day.

A senior monk once told me an old Cherokee story about these dilemmas which all of us agonize over: "An elder tells his grandson, 'Every choice in life is a battle between two wolves inside us. One represents anger, envy, greed, fear, lies, insecurity, and ego. The other represents peace, love, compassion, kindness, humility, and positivity. They are competing for supremacy.'

"'Which wolf wins?' the grandson asks. 'The one you feed,' the elder replies."

"But how do we feed them?" I asked my teacher.

The monk said, "By what we read and hear. By who we spend time with. By what we do with our time. By where we focus our energy and attention."

The Bhagavad Gita states, "For him who has conquered the mind, the mind is the best of friends; but for one who has failed to do so, his very mind will be the greatest enemy." The word *enemy* may seem too strong to describe the voice of dissent in your head, but the definition rings true: An enemy, according to the Oxford English Dictionary, is "a person who is actively opposed or hostile to someone or something," and "a thing that harms or weakens something." Sometimes our own minds work against us. They convince us to do something, then make us feel guilty or bad about it, often because it's gone against our values or morals.

A pair of researchers from Princeton University and the University of Waterloo have shown that the weight of a bad decision isn't just metaphorical. They asked study participants to remember a time they'd done something unethical, then asked them to rate their perception of their body weight. People who'd been asked to recall an unethical action said they felt physically heavier than those who'd been asked to recall a neutral memory. Other times we want to focus on something—a project at work, an artistic endeavor, a home repair, a new hobby—and our minds just won't let us get around to it. When we procrastinate, there's a conflict between what researchers call our "should-self," or what we feel we should do because it's good for us, and our "want-self," what we actually want to do in the moment. "I know I *should* get started on that business proposal, but I *want* to watch the US Open quarterfinals."

Before I became a monk, my own mind stopped me from doing what I loved because it was too risky. It allowed me to consume a chocolate bar and a liter of soda daily even though I wanted to be healthy. It made me compare myself to other people instead of concentrating on my own growth. I blocked myself from reaching out to people I had hurt because I did not want to appear weaker. I allowed myself to be angry at people I loved because I cared more about being right than being kind.

In the introduction to his translation of the Dhammapada, Eknath Easwaran writes that in our everyday swirl of thoughts "we have no more idea of what life is really like than a chicken has before it hatches. Excitement and depression, fortune and misfortune, pleasure and pain, are storms in a tiny, private, shell-bound realm which we take to be the whole of existence." It makes sense, then, that when the Buddha finally reached "the realm utterly beyond the reach of thought," he described feeling like a chick breaking out of its shell.

At the ashram, I learned something that has been crucial in curbing these dangerous, self-destructive thoughts. Our thoughts are like clouds passing by. The self, like the sun, is always there. We are not our minds.

THE PARENT AND THE CHILD

As my teachers explained, visualizing the mind as a separate entity helps us work on our relationship with it—we can think of the interaction as making a friend or negotiating peace with an enemy.

As in any interaction, the quality of our communication with the mind is based on the history of our relationship with it. Are we hotheaded combatants or stubborn and unwilling to engage? Do we have the same arguments over and over again, or do we listen and compromise? Most of us don't know the history of this internal relationship because we've never taken the time to reflect on it.

The monkey mind is a child and the monk mind is an adult. A child cries when it doesn't get what it wants, ignoring what it already has. A child struggles to appreciate real value—it would happily trade a stock certificate for some candy. When something challenges us in some way, the childlike mind reacts immediately. Maybe you feel insulted and make a sour face, or you start defending yourself. A conditioned, automatic reaction like this is ideal if someone pulls out a knife. You feel scared, and you bolt. But it's not ideal if we're being emotionally defensive because someone has said something we don't want to hear. We don't want to be controlled by automatic reactions in every case, nor do we want to eliminate the child mind altogether. The child mind enables us to be spontaneous, creative, and dynamic—all invaluable qualities—but when it rules us, it can be our downfall.

The impulsive, desire-driven child mind is tempered by the judicious, pragmatic adult mind, which says, "That's not good for you," or "Wait until later." The adult mind reminds us to pause and assess the bigger picture, taking time to weigh the default reaction, decide if it's appropriate, and propose other options. The intelligent parent knows what the child needs versus what it wants and can decide what is better for it in the long term.

Framing inner conflict this way—parent and child—suggests that when the childlike mind is fully in control it's because our monk mind has not been developed, strengthened, or heard. The child gets frustrated, throws tantrums, and we quickly give in to it. Then we get mad at ourselves. *Why am I doing this? What is wrong with me?*

The parent is the smarter voice. If well trained, it has self-control, reasoning power, and is a debating champ. But it can only use the strength that we give it. It's weaker when tired, hungry, or ignored.

When the parent isn't supervising, the child climbs on the counter near the hot stove to get to the cookie jar, and trouble follows. On the other hand, if the parent is too controlling, the child gets bitter, resentful, and risk-averse. As with all parent-child relationships, striking the right balance is an ongoing challenge.

This, then, is the first step to understanding our minds—simply becoming aware of the different voices inside us. Starting to differentiate what you're hearing will immediately help you make better decisions.

DRIVE THE CHARIOT OF THE MIND

When you begin to sort out the multiple voices in your head, the level of conflict may surprise you. It doesn't make sense. Our minds *should* work in our own best interest. Why would we stand in our own way? The complication is that we are weighing input from different sources: our five

senses, telling us what appeals in the moment; our memories, recalling what we have experienced in the past; and our intellects, synthesizing and evaluating the best choice for the long term.

Beyond the parent-child model, the monk teachings have another analogy for the competing voices in our heads. In the Upanishads the working of the mind is compared to a chariot being driven by five horses. In this analogy, the chariot is the body, the horses are the five senses, the reins are the mind, and the charioteer is the intellect. Sure, this description of the mind is more complicated, but bear with me.

In the untrained state, the charioteer (the intellect) is asleep on the job, so the horses (the senses) have control of the reins (mind) and lead the body wherever they please. Horses, left to their own devices, react to what's around them. They see a tasty-looking shrub, they bend to eat it. Something startles them, they spook. In the same way, our senses are activated in the moment by food, money, sex, power, influence, etc. If the horses are in control, the chariot veers off the road in the direction of temporary pleasure and instant gratification.

In the trained state, the charioteer (the intellect) is awake, aware, and attentive, not allowing the horses to lead the way. The charioteer uses the reins of the mind to carefully steer the chariot along the correct route.

MASTER THE SENSES

Think about those five unruly horses, harnessed to the chariot of a lazy driver, snorting and tossing their heads impatiently. Remember that they represent the five senses, always our first point of contact with the external. The senses are responsible for our desires and attachments, and they pull us in the direction of impulsivity, passion, and pleasure, destabilizing the mind. Monks calm the senses in order to calm the mind. As Pema Chödrön says, "You are the sky. Everything else—it's just the weather."

Shaolin monks are a wonderful example of how we can train our minds to subdue the senses. (Note: I never lived or trained as a Shaolin monk, although I might want to try!)

The Shaolin Temple in China dates back more than fifteen hundred years, and Shaolin monks regularly demonstrate the impossible. They balance on the blade of a sword, break bricks with their heads, and lie on beds of nails and blades without apparent effort or injury. It seems like magic, but the Shaolin monks actually push their limits through rigorous physical and mental regimes.

Children may begin study at the Shaolin monastery as early as age three. They spend long days in training and meditation. Through breathing techniques and Qi Gong, an ancient healing technique, the monks develop the ability to accomplish superhuman feats of strength and to endure uncomfortable situations—from attack to injury. By cultivating their inner calm, they can ward off mental, physical, and emotional stress.

It's not only the Shaolin monks who've demonstrated incredible sensory control. Researchers took a different group of monks, along with people who'd never meditated, and secured a thermal stimulator to their wrists—a device designed to induce pain through intense heat. The plate warms slowly, then stays at maximum heat for ten seconds before cooling. During the experiment, as soon as the plate began to heat, the pain matrix in the non-monks' brains started firing like crazy, as if the plate were already at maximum heat. Researchers call this "anticipatory anxiety," and the monks showed none of it. Instead, as the plate heated, their brain activity remained pretty much the same. When the plate reached full heat, activity in the monks' brains spiked, but only in areas that registered the physical sensations of pain. You see for most of us, pain is a twofold sensation—we feel some of it physically and some of it emotionally. For the monks the heat was painful, but they didn't assign negative feelings to the experience. They felt no *emotional pain.* Their brains also recovered from the physical pain faster than the non-meditators.

This is a remarkable level of sensory control—more than most of us are committed to developing—but do think about your senses as paths to the mind. Most of our lives are governed by what we see, hear, smell, touch, and taste. If you smell your favorite dessert, you want to eat it. If you see photo of a beach, you start daydreaming about vacation. You hear a certain phrase and flash to the person who used to say it all the time.

The monkey mind is reactive, but the monk mind is proactive. Let's say that whenever you go on YouTube to watch one video, you end up going down a rabbit hole. You drift from a cute animal video to a shark attack compilation, and before you know it you're watching Sean Evans eating hot sauce with a celebrity guest. Senses recklessly transport our minds away from where we want them to be. Don't tease your own senses. Don't set yourself up to fail. A monk doesn't spend time in a strip club. We want to minimize the mind's reactive tendencies, and the easiest way to do that is for the intellect to proactively steer the senses away from stimuli that could make the mind react in ways that are hard to control. It's up to the intellect to know when you're vulnerable and to tighten the reins, just as a charioteer does when going through a field of tasty grass.

Any sensory input can trigger emotions—a tempting or upsetting or sad reminder that lures those wild horses off the charioteer's chosen path. Social media might suck away time you wanted to spend otherwise; a photo might remind you of a lost friend in a moment when you don't have time for grief; an ex's sweatshirt might re-break your heart. Within reason, I recommend removing unwanted sensory triggers from your home (or deleting the apps). As you do, visualize yourself removing them from your mind. You can do the same thing when you hit an unwanted mental trigger—a word that you used to hear from a parent, a song from your past. Visualize yourself removing that from your life as you would a physical object. When you remove those mental and physical triggers, you can stop giving in to them. Needless to say, we can never remove all senses and all triggers. Nor would we want to. Our goal is not to silence the mind or even to still it. We want to figure out the meaning of a thought. That's what helps us let go. But temporarily, while we're strengthening our relationship with our minds, we can take steps to avoid triggering places and people by adjusting what we see, listen to, read, absorb.

From a monk's perceptive, the greatest power is self-control, to train the mind and energy, to focus on your dharma. Ideally, you can navigate anything that seems tough, challenging, or fun with the same balance and equanimity, without being too excited in pleasure or too depressed by pain.

Ordinarily our brains turn down the volume on repeated input, but when we train our minds, we build the ability to focus on what we want regardless of distractions.

Meditation is an important tool that allows us to regulate sensory input, but we can also train the mind by building the relationship between the child and the adult mind. When a parent says, "Clean your room," and the child doesn't, that's like your monk mind saying, "Change your course," and the monkey mind saying, "No thanks, I'd rather listen to loud music on my headphones." If the parent gets angry at the child and says, "I told you to clean your room! Why haven't you done it yet?" the child retreats further. Eventually, the child may follow orders, but the exchange hasn't built a connection or a dialogue.

The more a frustrated parent and petulant child do battle, the more alienated from each other they feel. When you are fighting an internal battle, your monkey mind is an adversary. View it as a collaborator, and you can move from battle to bond, from rejected enemy to trusted friend. A bond has its own challenges—there can still be disagreement—but at least all parties want the same outcome.

In order to reach such a collaboration, our intellect must pay closer attention to the automatic, reactive patterns of the mind, otherwise known as the subconscious.

THE STUBBORN SUBCONSCIOUS

The mind already has certain instinctive patterns that we never consciously chose. Imagine you have an alarm on your phone set to ring at the same time every morning. It's an excellent system until a national holiday comes along, and the alarm goes off anyway. That alarm is like our subconscious. It's already been programmed and defaults to the same thoughts and actions day after day. We live much of our lives following the same path we've always taken, for better or worse, and these thoughts and behaviors will never change unless we actively reprogram ourselves.

Joshua Bell, a world-famous violinist, decided to busk outside a DC subway station during the morning rush hour. Playing on a rare and precious instrument, he opened up his case for donations and performed some of the most difficult pieces ever written for the violin. In about forty-five minutes, barely anyone stopped to listen or donate. He made about $30. Three days before the subway performance he had played the same violin at Boston's Symphony Hall, where the decent seats went for $100.

There are many reasons people might not stop to hear a brilliant musician playing, but one of them is certainly that they were on autopilot, powering through the rush hour crowds. How much do we miss when we're in default mode?

"Insanity is doing the same thing again and again, expecting different results." (This quote is often attributed to Einstein, although there's no proof that he ever said it.) How many of us do the same thing, year after year, hoping our lives will transform?

Thoughts repeat in our minds, reinforcing what we believe about ourselves. Our conscious isn't awake to make edits. The narration playing in your mind is stuck in its beliefs about relationships, money, how you feel about yourself, how you should behave. We all have had the experience of someone saying, "You look amazing today," and our subconscious responding, "I don't look amazing. They're saying that to be nice." When someone says, "You really deserved that," perhaps you say to yourself, "Oh no, I'm not sure I can do it again." These habitual reactions pepper our days. Change begins with the words inside your head. We are going to work on hearing, curating, choosing, and switching our thoughts.

TRY THIS: WAKE UP THE SUBCONSCIOUS

Write down all the noise you hear in your mind on a daily basis. Noise that you know you don't want to have. This should not be a list of your problems. Instead, write the negative, self-defeating messages your mind is sending you, such as:

- You're not good enough.
- You can't do this.
- You don't have the intelligence to do this.

These are the times when the charioteer is asleep at the wheel.

INVEST IN THE CONSCIOUS MIND

Just as you are not your mind, you are not your thoughts. Saying to yourself "I don't deserve love" or "My life sucks" doesn't make it a fact, but these self-defeating thoughts are hard to rewire. All of us have a history of pain, heartbreak, and challenges, whatever they may be. Just because we've been through something and it's safely in the past doesn't mean it's over. On the contrary, it will persist in some form—often in self-defeating thoughts—until it teaches us what we need to change. If you haven't healed your relationship with your parents, you'll keep picking partners who mirror the unresolved issues. If you don't deliberately rewire your mindset, you are destined to repeat and re-create the pain you've already endured.

It may sound silly, but the best way to overwrite the voices in your head is to start talking to them. Literally.

Start talking to yourself every day. Feel free to address yourself with your name and to do it out loud wherever you're comfortable doing so (so maybe not on a first date or a job interview). Sound is powerful, and hearing your own name grabs your attention.

If your mind says, "You can't do this," respond by saying to yourself, "You can do it. You have the ability. You have the time."

Talking yourself through a project or task enhances focus and concentration. Those who do it function more efficiently. In a series of studies, researchers showed volunteers groups of pictures, then asked them to locate specific items from among those pictured. Half of the subjects were told to repeat the names of the items to themselves out loud as they searched, and the other half were told to stay silent. Those who repeated the items were significantly faster than the silent searchers. The researchers concluded that talking to yourself not only boosts your memory, it also helps you focus. Psychologist Linda Sapadin adds that talking to yourself "helps you clarify your thoughts, tend to what's important and firm up any decisions you're contemplating."

Let's consider some ways you can find a new perspective to shift your mind in a productive way.

REFRAME

If you're like most other humans, your intellect excels at telling your mind where it goes wrong, but rarely bothers to tell your mind where it goes right. What kind of parenting is that?

> Nothing's going to get better
> Nobody understands me
> I'm not good enough
> I'm not attractive enough
> I'm not smart enough

We look for the worst in ourselves and tell ourselves that it will never change. This is the least encouraging approach we could pick. There are three routes to happiness, all of them centered on knowledge: learning, progressing, and achieving. Whenever we are growing, we feel happy and free of material yearnings. If you're unsatisfied, or criticizing yourself, or feeling hopeless, don't let that stall you out. Identify the ways you're making progress, and you will begin to see, feel, and appreciate the value of what you are doing.

Reframe your self-criticism in terms of knowledge. When you hear yourself say, "I'm bored, I'm slow, I can't do this," respond to yourself: "You are working on it. You are improving." This is a reminder to yourself that you are making progress. Build a relationship with that pessimistic child's voice. Your adult voice will get stronger as you read, research, apply, and test. Turn up the volume on recognizing what your mind gets right. Rather than amplifying your failures, amplify your progress. If you managed to wake up early two days out of seven, encourage yourself as you would a child who was just beginning to make a change. If you accomplished half of what you planned, call it a glass half-full.

In addition to amplifying our growth, we can use "positive direction" to reframe unwanted thoughts. Our monkey mind often creates chatter like "I can't do this." This can be reworded to "I can do this by . . ."

"I can't do this" becomes "I can do this by . . ."
"I'm bad at this" becomes "I'm investing the time I need to get better"
"I'm unlovable" becomes "I'm reaching out to new people to make new connections"
"I'm ugly" becomes "I'm taking steps to be my healthiest"
"I can't handle everything" becomes "I'm prioritizing and checking items off my list"

Putting a solution-oriented spin on your statement reminds you to be proactive and take responsibility rather than languishing in wishful thinking.

We can take action instead of using words alone to reframe our state of mind. A simple way of overcoming this is to learn one new thing every day. It doesn't have to be big. You don't need to teach yourself how to code or learn quantum mechanics. You could read an article about a person, a city, or a culture, and you'll feel a burst of self-esteem. You have something to contribute to the next conversation you have. Even if you just learn one new word . . . here's one: the Inuit word *iktsuarpok* refers to the feeling of anticipation you have when you're waiting for a guest and you keep going to the window to check and see if they've arrived. Just sharing a new word in conversation can bring richness to the dinner table.

Many of the frustrations we endure can be seen as blessings because they urge us to grow and develop. Try putting negative thoughts and circumstances on the perspective continuum. The same way doctors evaluate pain, I ask people to rate an individual concern on a scale of one to ten. Zero is no worries. Ten is the worst thing in the world, something as awful as: "I worry that my whole family will die." Actually, that's probably an eleven.

Problems of all sorts can feel like they deserve a ten rating, especially in the middle of the night. Not getting promoted feels like a ten. Losing a treasured watch—another ten. But if you've ever experienced the pain of losing someone you love (and we all have or will), the scale shifts; your whole perspective shifts. Suddenly, losing your job is not great, but tolerable. The watch is gone, but it was just an object. Your body may be imperfect, but it's given you some great experiences. Use the awareness of what deep pain really is to keep smaller disruptions in perspective. And when you must face a truly devastating ten, own it, take the time to heal it. This is not about reducing the impact of all negative experiences; it's about gaining a clearer view of them. And sometimes a ten is a ten.

SLOW IT DOWN

Sometimes reframing works best on paper. Imagine a monkey swinging from branch to branch at full throttle. It takes effort to grab its attention and force it to focus. When your mind is anxious and racing, when your thoughts are repetitive and unproductive, when you feel like you need to press pause, take fifteen minutes to write down every thought that enters your mind.

For a study, a group of college students spent fifteen minutes a day for four days writing their "deepest thoughts and feelings" about the most traumatic experience of their lives. Not only did the students say they found the experience to be valuable, 98 percent said they'd like to do it again. But they didn't just enjoy the writing, it also improved their health. Students who'd written about traumatic experiences had fewer visits to the university health center after the study. The researchers concluded that one of the benefits of the writing may have been helping students render their worst experiences as a coherent narrative. Distancing themselves from the moment in this way allowed them to see the experiences objectively and, one hopes, to conjure a happy ending.

Writer Krysta MacGray was terrified of flying. She tried white knuckling it. She tried logic. She even tried having a few drinks. But every time she knew she'd have to fly, she spent weeks in advance imagining what her kids' lives would be like after she went down in a fiery crash. MacGray started blogging about this fear as a means of trying to gain perspective, and it was then she realized she was on track to become her grandmother, who refused to fly and missed out on a lot because of it. So MacGray started listing everything she wanted to do in her life that would be worth flying for. Though she hasn't totally conquered her fear, she did manage to take a bucket-list vacation to Italy with her husband. Writing by itself doesn't solve all of our problems, but it can help us gain critical perspective we can use to find solutions.

If you don't like writing, you can speak into your phone, then play back the audio file or read the transcript (many phones can transcribe spoken words into text). Recording yourself puts you in an observer mindset, making you deal more objectively with yourself.

Another option is to simply repeat an ancient samurai saying that the monks use: "Make my mind my friend," over and over in your head. When you repeat a phrase, it quiets the default mode network—the area of the brain associated with mind wandering and thinking about yourself. The monkey will be forced to stop and listen.

FIND SELF-COMPASSION

When the anxious monkey mind stops to listen, you can tweak the internal monologue with self-compassion. When anxious thoughts arise, instead of indulging them, we respond with compassion. "I know you're worried and upset, and you feel like you can't handle this, but you are strong. You can do it." Remember, it's about observing your feelings without judging them.

With my friends at the branding company Shareability, I did an exercise with a small group of teenage girls and their sisters. I asked the girls to write down negative thoughts they had that affected their self-esteem. They wrote down things like "You are scared," "You are worthless," "You are unimportant." Then I asked them to read what they'd written to their sisters, as if it were about them.

They all refused. "It's not very nice." One pointed out that it was normal in her head, but completely different when she spoke it.

We say things to ourselves that we would never say to people we love. We all know the Golden Rule: Do unto others as you would have them do unto you. To that I would add: **Treat yourself with the same love and respect you want to show to others.**

TRY THIS: NEW SCRIPTS FOR THE CHARIOTEER

1. Write a list of the negative things you say to yourself. Next to each one write down how you would present that idea to someone you care about. For example, these are the negative thoughts the sisters wrote down about themselves along with how they might have presented them to their sisters:

"You are scared"	"It's okay to feel scared. How can I help you through this?"
"You are worthless"	"You feel worthless—let's talk about what you love about yourself."
"You are unimportant"	"These things make you feel unimportant. Before we talk about how to change that, let's list what makes you feel important."

2. Imagine you found out that your child or best friend or cousin or someone who is dear to you was getting a divorce. What is your first reaction? What would you say to the person? What advice would you give them? You might say, "I'm sorry, I know this is a hard time." Or "Congratulations. I know you're going through a lot, but people rarely ever regret getting divorced." We would never tell a loved one, "You're an idiot. You must be a loser if you married that loser." We give love and support, maybe offering ideas and solutions. This is how we should talk to ourselves.

We are defined by the narrative that we write for ourselves every day. Is it a story of joy, perseverance, love, and kindness, or is it a story of guilt, blame, bitterness, and failure? Find a new vocabulary to match the emotions and feelings that you want to live by. Talk to yourself with love.

STAY PRESENT

It can be hard to know what to tell your monkey mind when it's dwelling on the past or spinning into the future. Father Richard Rohr writes, "All spiritual teaching—this is not an oversimplification—is about how to be present to the moment. . . . But the problem is, we're almost always somewhere else: reliving the past or worrying about the future."

We all have happy memories that we enjoy revisiting and painful memories that we can't let go. But both nostalgia and remorse can be traps, closing us off from new experiences and keeping us locked in the unresolved past and/or the good old days. Just as the past is unchangeable, the future is unknowable. A certain amount of planning is useful and good preparation for the various scenarios ahead, but when these thoughts tip into repetitive anxiety and worry or unrealistic aspirations, they are no longer productive.

Whether it feels like the world's falling down around you or you're just having a bad day at work, the challenges to presence abound. Realistically, you'll never reach a point in your life when you're present 100 percent of the time—that's not the goal. After all, thinking about good times we've had or valuable lessons we've learned in the past and planning for our future are excellent uses of our mental bandwidth. What we don't want to do is waste time on regret or worry. Practicing presence helps us do as spiritual teacher Ram Dass advised and "*be here now.*"

When your mind continually returns to thoughts of the past or the future, look for clues in the present. Is your mind seeking to shield or distract you? Instead of thinking about what mattered in the past or what the future might hold, gently guide your mind back to the moment. Ask yourself questions about right now.

What is missing from this moment?

What is unpleasant about today?

What would I like to change?

Ideally, when we talk to ourselves about the present, we look back on the negative and positive elements of the past as the imperfect road that brought us to where we are—a life that we accept, and from which we can still grow. And, ideally, we also think of the future in context of the present—an opportunity to realize the promise of today.

NOTHING OWNS YOU

When we talk to ourselves as we would to a loved one, just as when we observe the argument between the child mind and the adult mind, we're creating a distance between ourselves and our own minds in order to see more clearly. We've discussed this approach before; instead of reacting emotionally, monks gain perspective by stepping out of a situation to become objective observers. In Chapter Three, we talked about stepping away from fear, and we gave this action a name—detachment.

The crane stands still in water, ignoring the small fish as they pass by. Her stillness allows her to catch the bigger fish.

Detachment is a form of self-control that has infinite benefits across every form of self-awareness that I talk about in this book, but its origin is always in the mind. The Gita defines detachment as doing the right thing for its own sake, because it needs to be done, without worrying about success or failure. That sounds simple enough, but think about what it takes to do the right thing for its own sake. It means detaching from your selfish interest, from being right, from being seen in a certain way, from what you want right now. Detaching means escaping the hold of the senses, of earthly desires, of the material world. You have the perspective of an objective observer.

Only by detaching can we truly gain control of the mind.

I've remixed some Zen stories, introducing new characters so that they're more relatable. One of them is about a monk who arrives at the entrance to a palace. She's a known holy woman, so she is brought to the king, who asks the monk what she wants. "I would like to sleep in this hotel for the night," says the monk.

The king is rather taken aback at this unexpected lack of respect. "This is not a hotel, it is my palace!" he says haughtily.

The monk asks, "Who owned this place before you?"

The king folds his arms across his chest. "My father. I am heir to the throne," he declares.

"Is he here now?"

"He is not. He is dead. What is the meaning of this?"

"And before your father, who was the owner?"

"*His* father," the king shouts.

The monk nods. "Ah," she says, "so people who come to this place, stay here for a while, and then continue their journey. Sounds like a hotel to me."

This story gives a window into the illusion of permanence with which we all live. A more recent window is *Tidying Up with Marie Kondo*, the show where Kondo helps people "declutter" their lives, and at the end, over and over again, you'll see people weeping with relief and joy at having purged so much. That's because they've just dramatically decreased the number of things they're *attached* to. Attachment brings pain. If you think something is yours or you think you are something, then it hurts to have it taken away from you.

A quote from Alī, cousin and son-in-law of the Prophet Muhammed, best explains the monk idea of detachment: "Detachment is not that you own nothing, but that nothing should own you." I love how this summarizes detachment in a way that it's not usually explained. Usually people see detachment as being removed from everything, not caring. Marie Kondo isn't telling people to stop caring—she is telling them to look for joy. Actually, the greatest detachment is being close to everything and not letting it consume and own you. That's real strength.

Like most monk endeavors, detachment is not a destination one arrives at, but a process one must constantly, consciously undertake. It's hard enough to detach in an ashram, where monks own almost nothing but our ideas and identities. In the modern world we can strive for detachment—particularly when we face a challenge like an argument or a decision—and hope to achieve it fleetingly.

DON'T TRY THIS AT HOME

Monks go to extremes to achieve detachment. I don't expect you to do this, but after we look at how it works, we'll talk about more practical, even fun, ways to experiment with detachment and the benefits it yields.

Experiments in discomfort—like fasting, silence, meditating in heat or cold, and others we've discussed—detach you from the body because they make you realize how much of the discomfort is in the mind. Another way we monks tested our detachment was to travel with nothing. No food, no shelter, no money. We had to fend for ourselves and recognize that we needed very little to get by. It also made us more grateful for all that we had. All of these exercises helped us push ourselves to the limit—mentally and physically—to build resolve, resilience, grit, to strengthen our ability to control our minds.

The first time I did a full-day fast, consuming no food or water, I spent the first few hours feeling desperately hungry. We weren't supposed to take naps while we were fasting—the point was to have the experience, not to avoid it with sleep. I had to use my intellect to soothe myself. I had to become absorbed in something higher to let go of these hungry thoughts.

As the day went on, I realized that because my body didn't need to think about what to eat, to prepare for a meal, to consume, or to digest, I actually had more of a different sort of energy.

When we fast, we detach from the body and all the time we spend attending to its demands. When we remove eating, we can let go of hunger and satiety, pain and pleasure, failure and success. We redirect our energy and attention to focus on the mind. In future fasts, I got in the habit of using that energy to study, research, make notes, or prepare a talk. Fasting became a creative time, free of distractions.

At the end of the fast, I felt physically tired, but mentally stronger. In functioning without something my body relied on, I had broken a limit that existed in my mind. I gained flexibility and adaptability and resourcefulness. That experience with fasting bled into the rest of my life.

Fasting is a physical challenge driven by the intellect. Being silent for long periods of time brought up completely different issues—who was I when I detached from other people?

I am on Day Nine of thirty days of silence and I think I'm losing my mind. Before this I've definitely never kept my mouth shut for an entire day, much less a whole month. Now, along with the group of monks who joined the ashram at the same time as I did, I've gone for more than a week without speaking, watching, hearing, or communicating in any other way. I'm a talker. I love sharing and hearing others' experiences. In the silence, my mind is going wild. In quick succession I think of:

- *rap lyrics to songs I haven't heard in a while*
- *everything I have to read and learn for monk school*
- *how everyone else is possibly enduring this*
- *a random conversation I once had with an ex-girlfriend*
- *what I would be doing at this very moment if I had taken a job instead of becoming a monk counting down the days 'til I can speak again.*

This is all in ten minutes.

In my month-long silent retreat there is no outlet. I have no option but to go inward. I must face my monkey mind and start conversations. I ask myself questions: Why do I need to talk? Why can't I just be in my thoughts? What can I find in silence that I can't get anywhere else? When my mind wanders, I return to my questioning.

I find, initially, that the silence and stillness help me discover new details in familiar routines. More revelations follow, not as words but as experiences: I find myself attuned to every part of my body. I feel the air against my skin, my breath traveling through my body. My mind empties.

Over time, other questions emerge: I want to be part of a conversation. Why? I want to connect with other people. Why? I need friendship to feel whole. Why do I feel that friendship as an immediate need rather than a long-term comfort? My ego uses friendship to feel secure in my choices. And then I see the work I need to do on my ego.

Often, in the emptiness, I repeat to myself "make your mind your friend," and I imagine that my mind and I are at a networking event. It's loud, it's hectic, there's a lot going on, but the only way to build a friendship is to start a conversation. And that's what I do.

Fasting and the other austerities that monks practice remind us that we can bear greater hardship than we thought possible, that we can overcome the demands of the senses with self-control and resolve. Regardless of their faith, most monks are celibate, eat a highly restricted diet, and live apart from mainstream society. Then there are the extremes. Jain monk Shri Hansratna Vijayji Maharaj Saheb fasted for 423 days (with a few breaks). *Sokushinbutsu* is the name for a Japanese style of self-mummification practice where monks would eat a diet of pine needles, tree bark, and resins, then give up food and water while they continued to chant mantras until eventually their bodies petrified.

You don't have to take vows or eat pine needles to explore your limits. Often all that holds us back from achieving the impossible is the belief that it is impossible. From 1850 (when the first accurately measured circular running tracks were made) until 1954, the record for running a mile never dropped below four minutes. Nobody had done it in less, and it was thought that nobody could. Then, in 1954, British Olympian Roger Bannister set out to do it. He ran a mile in 3:59.4 minutes, breaking the four-minute barrier for the first time. Ever since, runners have been breaking subsequent records at a much quicker pace. Once people realized there was no limit, they pushed further and further.

There are everyday people, as well, who use austerities to up their game. People consistently report that experimenting with extremes helps them be more thoughtful and positive in their everyday lives. Let's explore how you can use austerities to detach.

HOW TO DETACH

All of the ways we've already talked about training the mind involve detaching: becoming an objective observer of the competing voices in your head, having new conversations with the conscious mind to reframe thoughts, finding compassion for yourself, staying in the moment. Instead of reactively doing what we want, we proactively evaluate the situation and do what is right.

Think of austerities as a detachment boot camp. Disconnect from the ideas that limit you, open your mind to new possibilities, and, like a soldier training for battle, you will find that your intellect gets stronger. You'll find that you're capable of more than you ever imagined.

There are infinite austerities or challenges you can try: giving up TV or your phone, sweets or alcohol; taking on a physical challenge; abstaining from gossip, complaining, and comparing. The austerity that was most powerful for me was meditating in cold or heat. The only way to escape the cold was to go inward. I had to learn to redirect my attention from the physical discomfort by talking to my mind. I still use this technique at the gym. If I'm doing crunches, I bring awareness to a part of my body that doesn't hurt. I don't recommend this for psychological pain—I'm not a stoic! But the skill of removing yourself from physical pain allows you to tolerate it in a positive sense. When you know the pain has value—you're getting stronger at the gym; you're serving food to children on a very hot day—you are able to push yourself mentally and physically. You can focus on what is important instead of being distracted by your discomfort.

We start with awareness. Spot the attachment. When do you experience it? When are you most vulnerable to it? Let's say you want to detach from technology. Do you use it out of boredom, laziness, fear of missing out, loneliness? If you want to stop drinking, look at the frequency and time of day. Are you using it to unwind, to connect, to reward yourself, or to check out?

Once you have diagnosed the attachment, the next step is to stop and rethink it. What do you want to add and what do you want to subtract? How much time do you want to dedicate to technology, and in what form? Are there certain apps you want to eliminate entirely, or do you want to limit the time that you spend using your phone? For drinking, you might look at whether you think you need to quit entirely, whether you want to experiment with a dry month to see what you learn about yourself, or whether you want to limit yourself.

The third step is to swap in new behavior. There are two general approaches that I recommend—choose the one that best suits your personality. The monk way is to go all in. If immersion and extremes work best for you, you might commit to eliminating social media entirely for a week or a month. Or you might, as I mention above, go on the wagon for a month. If you work better in slow, gradual iterations, make a small change and build on it. In the case of technology, you could limit the amount of time you allow yourself to be online, or perhaps limit, but don't fully eliminate, certain apps.

Decide how you want to spend your newfound time. If you want to minimize your YouTube time, look for another way to find that relaxation or decompression. Meditation is my first go-to. If you're cutting back on social media, do you want to spend the time interacting with friends in real life rather than online? Perhaps, as a project, you could select which of those Instagram photos deserve to go in an album or on your walls. Use your found time to fulfill the same need or to accomplish the projects and to-dos that always linger on the back burner.

At first, when we make a change, the mind may rebel. Look for ways to ease the transition. If I want to eat less sugar, reading studies linking sugar to cancer strengthens my intellect and motivates me to persist. At the same time, my wife sets up what I call "The worst snack drawer of all time." There is nothing "bad" in it, no junk food. My senses don't have access to snacks. I also look for natural habits that curb my desire. I notice that after I go to the gym, I eat less sugar. For me, going to the gym wakes up the charioteer. Realizing that I turn to sugar to increase my energy and improve my mood, I look for other, healthier activities that have a similar effect.

Once the initial pangs of desire abate, you'll begin to feel the benefits of detachment. You'll find new clarity and perspective. You'll feel more control over the monkey mind, but you will also stop trying to control that which you can't control. The mind will quiet and you will make decisions without fear, ego, envy, or greed. You will feel confident and free from illusion. Though life remains imperfect, you accept it as it is and see a clear path ahead.

MIND MAINTENANCE

Detachment doesn't mean we completely ignore our bodies and our minds. The body is a vessel. It contains us, so it's important. We have to take care of it, feed it, keep it healthy, but the vessel is just a carrier. What it carries is the real value. And the mind, as we've talked about, is an important counterbalance to the intellect's control and restraint. Without his chariot, horse, and reins, the charioteer's options are limited. She is slow. Or he can't travel far on his own. Or she can't pick up a weary traveler and help them on their journey. We do not want to eliminate the voices in our heads or the body that carries them—we just want to steer them in the right direction—but this means the charioteer's work is never done.

We wake up with morning breath, smelly, tired. Every morning we accept the need to brush our teeth and shower. We don't judge ourselves for needing to wash up. When we get hungry, we don't say to ourselves, *Oh my God, I'm the worst. Why am I hungry* again? Bring the same patience and understanding when you're low on motivation, unfocused, anxious, or addled and the charioteer is weak. Waking him up is like taking a shower and feeding yourself, an everyday practice.

Matthieu Ricard, "the World's Happiest Man," told me that we should cultivate inner peace as a skill. "If you ruminate on sadness and negativity," he explained, "it will reinforce a sense of sadness and negativity. But if you cultivate compassion, joy, and inner freedom, then you build up a kind of resilience, and you can face life with confidence." When I asked him how we cultivate those skills, he said, "We train our brains. In the end, it is your mind that translates the outside world into happiness or misery."

The good news is that the more practice you have at tuning in to your mind, the less effort it takes. Like a muscle that you exercise regularly, the skill grows stronger and more reliable. If we work every day to cleanse our thoughts, gently redirecting the ones that don't serve us, then our minds are pure and calm, ready for growth. We can deal with new challenges before they multiply and become unmanageable.

As the Bhagavad Gita advises, "Cultivate buddhi or your discriminating intelligence to discern true knowledge, and practice wisdom so that you will know the difference between truth and untruth, reality and illusion, your false self and true self, the divine qualities and demonic qualities, knowledge and ignorance and how true knowledge illuminates and liberates while ignorance veils your wisdom and holds you in bondage."

Our ego is often what holds us back from true knowledge, steering the mind toward impulse and impression. Next we will examine how it influences the mind and how we can bring it back down to size.

EIGHT

EGO

Catch Me If You Can

They are forever free who renounce all
selfish desires and break away from the
ego cage of "I," "me," and "mine"
—Bhagavad Gita, 2:71

The Sanskrit word *vinayam* means "humility" or "modesty." When we are humble, we are open to learning because we understand how much we don't know. It follows that the biggest obstacle to learning is being a know-it-all. This false self-confidence is rooted in the ego.

The Bhagavad Gita draws a distinction between the ego and the false ego. The real ego is our very essence—the consciousness that makes us aware and awake to reality. The false ego is an identity crafted to preserve our sense of being the most significant, the most important, the one who knows everything. When you trust the false ego to protect you, it's like wearing armor that you thought was made of steel but is actually made of paper. You march onto the battlefield, confident that it will protect you but are easily wounded with a butter knife. The Sama Veda says, "Pride of wealth destroys wealth, pride of strength destroys strength and in the same manner pride of knowledge destroys knowledge."

THE EGO IS A MASK

An unchecked ego harms us. In our eagerness to present ourselves as the greatest and smartest, we hide our true natures. I've mentioned the persona that we present to the world. It is a complex stew of who we are, who we want to be, how we hope to be seen (as discussed in Chapter One), and what we are feeling in any given moment. We are a certain person at home, alone, but we present the world with another version of ourselves. Ideally, the only difference between the two is that our public persona is working harder to be considerate, attentive, and generous. But sometimes our egos intrude. Insecurities make us want to convince ourselves and everyone else that we're special, so we contrive a dishonest version of ourselves in order to appear more knowledgeable, more accomplished, more confident. We present this inflated self to others, and we do everything we can to protect it: the self we want others to perceive. Fourth-century monk Evagrius Ponticus (also called Evagrius the Solitary, because sometimes monks get cool nicknames) wrote that pride is "the cause of the most damaging fall for the soul."

Vanity and ego go hand in hand. We put enormous effort into polishing the appearance of the self we present to the world. When we dress and groom for ourselves, it is because we want to feel comfortable and appropriate (easily achieved through a daily "uniform") and even because we appreciate the color or style of certain clothes. But the ego wants more—it wants us to get attention for how we look, a big reaction, praise. It finds confidence and joy in impressing others. There is a meme that shows Warren Buffett and Bill Gates standing side by side. The caption reads, "$162 Billion in one photo and not a Gucci belt in sight." I have nothing against Gucci belts, but the point is that if you are satisfied with who you are, you don't need to prove your worth to anyone else.

To contemplate the difference between yourself and your persona, think about the choices you make when you're alone, when there's nobody to judge you and nobody you're trying to impress. Only you know whether you choose to meditate or watch Netflix, to take a nap or go for a run, to wear sweatpants or designer threads. Only you know whether you eat a salad or a column of Girl Scout cookies. Reflect on the you who emerges when nobody else is around, no one to impress, no one with something to offer you. That is a glimpse into who you truly are. As the aphorism goes, "You are who you are when no one is watching."

THE EGO MAKES US LIARS

Sometimes the ego works so hard to impress others that it does more than hype itself. It drives us to lie, and, counterproductively, all that effort only ends up making us look bad. For one of Jimmy Kimmel's "Lie Witness News" interviews with random people on the street, he sent a camera crew to Coachella to ask people walking into the venue what they thought of some completely fictitious bands. The interviewer says to two young women, "One of my favorite bands this year is Dr. Schlomo and the GI Clinic."

"Yeah they're always amazing," says one of the women.

"Yeah, I'm really excited to see them live," the other adds. "I think that's going to be one of the bands that's going to be really great live."

"Did you see them when they played at Lollapalooza?"

"No, I didn't. I'm so mad."

Then she asks a group of three, "Are you guys as excited as I am about the Obesity Epidemic?"

One of the guys responds enthusiastically, "I just like their whole style, like their whole genre is great. They're kind of like innovative and they're new."

The ego craves recognition, acknowledgment, praise; to be right, to be more, to put others down, to raise us up. The ego doesn't want to be better. It wants to be seen as better. When we bluff our way through life, pretending to be who we are not, we end up looking worse than we truly are.

The story of Frank Abagnale Jr., told in his memoir *Catch Me If You Can* and the movie of the same name, is a spot-on example of the false ego in play. Abagnale was a talented con man, forging and acting his way into jobs as an airplane pilot and a surgeon, jobs he hadn't earned and couldn't perform. Wrapped up in his ego, he used his natural abilities for low, selfish purposes, and lost himself. But after he was released from prison, he used the same skills and talents to lead an honest life as a security consultant. Real ego—a healthy self-image—comes from acting out your dharma for the highest purposes. Presumably his stint in prison gave him time for reflection and humility, and he found his way to a higher purpose.

THE EGO CREATES FALSE HIERARCHIES

Building a facade of confidence and knowledge isn't the only strategy the false ego uses to convince itself and everyone else that it's great. It also goes to great lengths to put other people down—because if others are "less than" we are, then we must be special. Our egos accomplish this by ranking ourselves and other people based on physical attributes, education, net worth, race, religion, ethnicity, nationality, the cars we drive, the clothes we wear—we find countless ways to judge others unfavorably just because they're different.

Imagine if we segregated people based on what toothpaste they used. That divide is clearly ridiculous. Discriminating based on elements of our bodies or where we were born is an equally false divide. Why should skin color matter more than blood type? We all come from the same cells. The Dalai Lama says, "Under the bright sun, many of us are gathered together with different languages, different styles of dress, even different faiths. However, all of us are the same in being humans, and we all uniquely have the thought of 'I' and we're all the same in wanting happiness and in wanting to avoid suffering."

In Chapter Five we talked about misappropriation of the *varnas* in India's caste system. The idea that Brahmins, determined by birth, are superior to others and therefore should have senior positions in government is an ego-driven interpretation of the *varnas*. The humble sage values every creature equally. This is why monks don't eat animals. According to the Gita, "Perfect yogis are they who, by comparison to their own self, see the true equality of all beings, in both their happiness and their distress."

When success goes to our heads, we forget that everyone is equal. No matter who you are or what you've achieved, notice if you are expecting or demanding special treatment because of your presumed status. Nobody deserves a better seat in the theater of life. You might wait in line for hours the night before the tickets go on sale, pay more for a closer seat, or be given a better view out of gratitude for your support of the theater. Or you might simply hope for a better seat as most of us do. But if you feel like you are *entitled* to better, dig into that feeling. What makes you better than the other audience members? **The arrogant ego desires respect, whereas the humble worker *inspires* respect.**

I often wonder what it would take for all of us to see each other as citizens of the world. I shot a couple of videos for the Ad Council as part of a public service campaign called "Love Has No Labels." In Orlando I spoke to people about the aftermath of the Pulse nightclub shooting and heard stories from diverse members of the communities about how they came together in the aftermath of this tragedy. I met with Reverend Terri Steed Pierce, from a church near Pulse with many LGBTQ+ congregants, and Pastor Joel Hunter, whose congregation is mostly white and straight. In the aftermath of the tragedy, they worked together and became friends. "Somebody will find hope merely because we're having the conversation," Reverend Pierce said, and Dr. Hunter added, "And that is the bottom line of what will change the future." As Reverend Pierce put it, they are "two very like-minded people that want to make a difference in the world."

The question this beautiful friendship evokes is: **Why does it take a tragedy for us to come together?** Our ego sets us on a path where we put more value on ourselves and those whom we recognize as being "like us."

Why is it that we walk this path until a bulldozer plows through it? Presuming equality keeps the ego in check. Whenever you think someone's status or worth is less than yours, turn your gaze back toward yourself and look for why your ego feels threatened. It is core to monks to treat everyone with equal honor and respect.

JUDGMENT

Even without segregating, outwardly ranking ourselves, or excluding others, we attempt to elevate ourselves by judging others, including our colleagues, friends, and family. There's a Zen story about four monks who together decide to meditate in complete silence for seven days and nights. The first day goes well, but as evening approaches, the first monk grows impatient because the monk whose job it was to light the lamps is still sitting, motionless. Finally, the first monk erupts, "Friend! Light the lamps, already!"

The second monk turns to him. "You broke the silence!" he exclaims.

The third monk jumps in, "Fools! Now you have both broken the silence!"

The fourth looks at his companions, a proud smile creeping across his face. "Well, well, well," he boasts, "Looks like I'm the only one who has remained silent."

Every monk in this story reprimanded another monk for speaking and, in so doing, became guilty of that same sin himself. That is the nature of judgment: It almost always backfires on us in one way or another. In the act of criticizing others for failing to live up to higher standards, we ourselves are failing to live up to the highest standards.

In many cases, we're passing judgment to deflect others' attention or our own from shortcomings we see in ourselves. "Projection" is the psychological term for our tendency to project onto others emotions or feelings that we don't wish to deal with ourselves. And projection happens a lot! So, before judging others, pause for a moment and ask: *Am I finding fault in order to distract myself or others from my own insecurities? Am I projecting my own weakness onto them? And even if I'm doing neither of those things, am I any better than the person I'm criticizing?* I can't say what the answers to the first two questions will be in every case. But the answer to the third question is always "No!"

THE EGO IS AN OBSTACLE TO GROWTH

All of this artifice leaves us in ignorance. Like Frank Abagnale, who didn't make the effort to actually qualify as a pilot or a doctor, our efforts to construct an impressive facade distract us from learning and growing. Even those of us who aren't con artists miss out. When you're sitting in a group of people, waiting for someone to finish talking so you can tell your fabulous story or make a witty comment, you're not absorbing the essence of what's being said. Your ego is champing at the bit, ready to show how clever and interesting you are.

In our desire to show ourselves and others that we know it all, we jump to conclusions, fail to listen to our friends, and miss potentially valuable new perspectives. And once we've got a point of view, we're unlikely to change it. In her popular TED Talk, "Why You Think You're Right Even When You're Wrong," Julia Galef, host of the podcast *Rationally Speaking*, calls that rigidity "soldier mindset." A soldier's job is to protect and defend their side. Conversely, there's the "scout mindset." Galef says, "Scout mindset means seeing what's there as accurately as you can, even if it's not pleasant." Soldiers have already signed on to a cause, so they value continuity. Scouts are investigating their options, so they value truth. Soldier mindset is rooted in defensiveness and tribalism; scout mindset is rooted in curiosity and intrigue. Soldiers value being on the right side; scouts value being objective. Galef says whether we're a soldier or a scout has less to do with our level of intelligence or education and more to do with our attitude about life.

Are we ashamed or grateful when we discover we were wrong about something? Are we defensive or intrigued when we find information that contradicts something we believe? If we aren't open-minded, we deny ourselves opportunities to learn, grow, and change.

INSTITUTIONAL EGO

It isn't just individuals whose egos limit their perspectives. Governments, schools, and organizations—under close-minded leadership—fail to look beyond what they know and end up constructing an ego-driven culture. Elected officials fight for their constituents and/or donors, without concern for the world beyond their supporters and those who will come after we all have gone. Textbooks tell history from the perspective of the winners. Organizations get trapped in business-as-usual mindsets, without responding to changes around them. When Reed Hastings, the cofounder of Netflix, offered to sell a 49 percent stake in the company to Blockbuster in 2000, he was turned down. Ten years later Blockbuster went bankrupt, and today Netflix is worth at least $100 billion. There is danger in the words "We've always done it this way," or "I already know that."

The Blockbuster/Netflix story is well known in the tech world, so when I told it to around seventy marketing directors at a conference, I asked them, "How many of you, when I shared this, felt you already knew what I was going to say?" About half of them raised their hands, and I told them that the conviction that they already knew what they needed to know was exactly the problem that these companies had. When you presume knowledge, you put up a barrier that nothing can cross, and miss out on a potential learning opportunity. What if there was an extra piece of that story? (This point itself was the extra piece.) You can write off the familiar, or you can use it as a deeper reflection point. Even if you think you already know a story, try to live it as a new experience every time.

Nan-in, a Zen master, received a university professor who had come to inquire about Zen. When Nan-in served tea, he poured his visitor's cup full, and then kept on pouring. The professor watched the overflow until he no longer could restrain himself. "It is overfull. No more will go in!"

"Like this cup," Nan-in said, "you are full of your own opinions and speculations. How can I show you Zen unless you first empty your cup?" You can only be filled up with knowledge and rewarding experiences if you allow yourself to be empty.

THE EGO ISOLATES US

When a Roman general returned from victorious battles, it is said that it was customary to have a slave stand behind him whispering "Remember you are a man" in his ear. No matter how well he had done and how lauded he was for his leadership, he was still a man, like all other men. If you're at the top of your game, beware. Ego isolates you. Don't live in a world where you start thinking you're so special that one person is worth your time and another isn't.

In an interview, Robert Downey Jr., offered a modern version of the same wisdom. When he's at home, he isn't Iron Man. He said, "When I walk into my house people aren't like, 'Whoa!' Susan's like, 'Did you let Monty out? Did you let the cat out?' I'm like, 'I don't know.' She's like, 'I don't think he's in the house—go look for him.'" This is a reminder to him (and to us) that even a movie star is just a person in their own home. If you believe you're Iron Man, it should be because you can actually do what Iron Man does. If you inspire special treatment, it is because people appreciate you, but when you demand or feel entitled to it, you are looking for respect that you haven't earned.

THE DOUBLE-EDGED EGO

The false self that builds us up, just as easily tears us down. When our weaknesses are exposed, the ego that once told us we were brilliant and successful has no defense. Without our personas, our lies, our prejudices, we are nothing, as Frank Abagnale must have felt when he was arrested. Egotism often masks, then transforms into, low self-esteem. In both circumstances, we are too wrapped up in ourselves and how others perceive us.

You can only keep up the myth of your own importance for so long. **If you don't break your ego, life will break it for you.**

I've been at the ashram for three years, and I've been struggling with my health. I may not be this body, but I still need to live in it. I end up in the hospital, exhausted, emaciated, lost.

I'm here undergoing Ayurvedic treatment for two months. The monks visit and read to me, but I'm alone, and in my solitude two things come to me.

First, I am not physically cut out for the life I'm trying to live. Second, and more disturbingly, to live in the ashram may not be my calling. My drive to spread wisdom doesn't fit perfectly into the monk framework. I am compelled to share ideas and philosophy in ways that are more modern. This may be my dharma, but it is not the goal of being a monk. It is not the sacred practice.

I don't know if this path is for me.

This thought hits me, and it upsets me deeply. I can't see myself leaving. And I wonder if my doubts come from my physical state. Am I in the right frame of mind to make a decision?

When I leave the hospital, I go to London for further medical attention. Radhanath Swami and I go for a drive. I tell him what I've been thinking. He listens for a while, asks some questions, thinks. Then he says, "Some people who go to university become professors, and some go to university and become entrepreneurs. Which is better?"

"Neither," I say.

"You've done your training. I think it's best for you to move on now."

I am stunned. I didn't expect him to come down on one side so quickly and definitively. I can tell he doesn't see me as a failure, but I can't help projecting that onto myself. I have failed, and he is breaking up with me. Like he is saying, "It's not you, it's me, it's not working out."

Not only am I reeling with the idea of giving up my leaders, my plans, my dream, but this is a huge blow to my ego. I've invested so much of myself in this place, this world, and all my future plans are based on that decision. But I know it's not the right path, and my teachers know it's not the right path. I won't achieve what I set out to do. Furthermore, I'd taken the enormous step of declaring this path to my family, my friends, and everyone I knew. My ego was wrapped up in what they would think of me if I failed. Joining the ashram was the hardest decision I'd ever made. Leaving is harder.

I move back to my parents with nothing, purposeless, broken, consumed by my failure, with $25,000 of debt from college. It's kind of exciting to buy some chocolate, but it is only a circumstantial fix to my existential crisis. I'd *gone away thinking I was going to change the world. Back in London, nobody knows what I've done or understands its value. My parents aren't sure how to engage with me or what to tell their friends. My extended family is asking my parents if I've come to my senses. My college friends are wondering if I'm going to get a "real" job. They're kind of like, "You failed at being a monk? You failed at thinking about nothing?"*

My biggest dream has been destroyed, and I feel the blow to my ego deeply. It is one of the toughest, most humiliating, crushing experiences of my life. And one of the most important.

Though the monks couldn't have been more supportive of me and my decision, leaving the ashram upended everything that made me confident in who I was and what I was doing. When my world was rocked, my self-esteem plummeted. Low self-esteem is the flip side of an inflated ego. If we're not everything, we're nothing. If I was not this man of high intentions and deep spirituality, then I was a failure. If I'm not great, I'm terrible. The two extremes are equally problematic. Sometimes it takes the deflated ego to show you what the inflated ego thought of itself. I was humbled.

HUMILITY: THE ELIXIR OF THE EGO

The ego is two-faced. One moment it tells us we're great at everything, and the next moment it tells us we're the worst. Either way, we are blind to the reality of who we are. True humility is seeing what lies between the extremes. *I'm great at some things and not so good at others. I'm well intentioned but imperfect.* Instead of the ego's all or nothing, humility allows us to understand our weaknesses and want to improve.

In the tenth canto of the Srimad-Bhagavatam, Lord Brahma, the god of creation, prays to Krishna, the supreme god. He is apologizing to Krishna, because in the course of building the world, Brahma has been pretty impressed with himself. Then he encounters Krishna, and he confesses that he is like a firefly.

At night, when a firefly glows, it thinks, *How bright I am. How amazing! I'm lighting up the whole sky!* But in the light of day, no matter how brightly the firefly glows, its light is weak, if not invisible, and it realizes its insignificance. Brahma realizes that he thought he was lighting the world, but when Krishna brings the sun out, he realizes that he is no more than a firefly.

In the darkness of the ego we think we're special and powerful and significant, but when we look at ourselves in context of the great universe, we see that we only play a small part. To find true humility, like the firefly, we must look at ourselves when the sun is out and we can see clearly.

PRACTICE HUMILITY

At the ashram, the most straightforward path to humility was through simple work, menial tasks that didn't place any participant at the center of attention. We washed huge pots with hoses, pulled weeds in the vegetable garden, and washed down the squat toilets—the worst! The point wasn't just to complete the work that needed to be done. It was to keep us from getting big-headed. I've talked about how impatient I was with some of this work. Why was I wasting my expertise picking up trash? The monks said that I was missing the point. Some tasks build competence, and some build character. The brainless activities annoyed me, but eventually I learned that doing an activity that was mentally unchallenging freed space for reflection and introspection. It was worthwhile after all.

Performing mundane tasks at an ashram isn't exactly replicable in the modern world, but anyone can try this simple mental exercise we used to become more aware of our ego on a daily basis. We were taught that there are two things we should try to remember and two things we should try to forget.

The two things to **remember** are the bad we've done to others and the good others have done for us. By focusing on the bad we've done to others, our egos are forced to remember our imperfections and regrets. This keeps us grounded. When we remember the good others have done for us, we feel humbled by our need for others and our gratitude for the gifts we have received.

The two things that we were told to **forget** are the good we've done for others and the bad others have done to us. If we fixate on and are impressed by our own good deeds, our egos grow, so we put those deeds aside. And if others treat us badly, we have to let that go too. This doesn't mean we have to be best friends with someone hurtful, but harboring anger and grudges keeps us focused on ourselves instead of taking a broader perspective.

I heard another way of thinking about this from Radhanath Swami when he was giving a talk at the London temple about the qualities we need for self-realization. He told us to be like salt and pointed out that we only notice salt when there is too much of it in our food, or not enough. Nobody ever says, "Wow, this meal has the perfect amount of salt." When salt is used in the best way possible, it goes unrecognized. Salt is so humble that when something goes wrong, it takes the blame, and when everything goes right, it doesn't take credit.

In 1993, Mary Johnson's son, Laramiun Byrd, was just twenty years old when, after an argument at a party, he was shot in the head by sixteen-year-old Oshea Israel, who served more than fifteen years in prison for the killing. Johnson probably had the most valid reason any of us can imagine for hating someone, and hate Israel she did. Eventually, it struck her that she wasn't the only one hurting; Israel's family had lost their son too. Johnson decided to start a support group called From Death to Life for other mothers whose children had been killed, and she wanted to include mothers whose children had taken a life. Johnson didn't think she could deal with the mothers of murderers unless she truly forgave Israel, so she reached out and asked to speak to him. When they met, he asked if he could hug her. She says, "As I got up, I felt something rising from the soles of my feet and leaving me." After the initial meeting, the pair began to meet regularly, and when Israel was released from prison, Johnson spoke to her landlord and asked if Israel could move into her building. "Unforgiveness is like cancer. It will eat you from the inside out," says Johnson. She wears a necklace with a double-sided locket; on one side is a picture of her with her son, and on the other is a picture of Israel, who says he is still trying to forgive himself. The pair, who now live next door to each other, visit prisons and churches to talk about their story and the power of forgiveness.

Remembering your mistakes and forgetting your achievements restrains the ego and increases gratitude—a simple, effective recipe for humility.

KEEP AN EYE ON YOUR EGO

With increased awareness, we begin to notice specific moments or circumstances when our egos flare.

Once a group from the ashram backpacked across Scandinavia, hosting pop-up meditations in city centers. Most people we encountered were very warm, interested in health, and open to meditation. But at one of our stops in Denmark I went up to a gentleman and asked, "Have you heard of meditation? We'd love to teach you."

He said, "Couldn't you do anything better with your life?"

My ego flared. I wanted to say, "I'm not stupid. I'm smart! I graduated from a really good school! I could be making six figures. I didn't have to do this—I chose it!" I really wanted to set this guy straight.

Instead I said, "I hope you have a wonderful day. If you want to learn how to meditate, please come back."

I felt my ego respond. I noticed it but refused to indulge it. This is the reality of keeping our ego in check. It doesn't disappear, but we can observe it and limit its power over us.

True humility is one step beyond simply repressing the ego as I did. In a class at the London temple, some of my fellow monks were being rude—laughing at the exercise we were doing and talking when they should have been quiet. I looked to our teacher, Sutapa, who was the head monk in London. I expected Sutapa to reprimand them, but he stayed quiet. After class, I asked him why he tolerated their behavior.

"You're looking at how they're behaving today," he said. "I'm looking at how far they've come."

The monk was remembering the good they'd done and forgetting the bad. He didn't take their behavior as a reflection of himself, or of their respect for him. He took a longer view that had nothing to do with himself.

If someone is treating you badly, I'm not advising you to tolerate it like the monk. Some mistreatment is unacceptable. But it's useful to look beyond the moment, at the bigger picture of the person's experience—Are they exhausted? Frustrated? Making improvements from where they once were?—and to factor in what has led to this behavior, before letting your ego jump in. Everyone has a story, and sometimes our egos choose to ignore that. Don't take everything personally—it is usually not about you.

DETACH FROM YOUR EGO

The monk and I both used the same approach to quiet our egos. We detached from the reaction and became objective observers. We think we're everything we've achieved. We think we're our job. We think we are our home. We think we are our youth and beauty. Recognize that whatever you have—a skill, a lesson, a possession, or a principle—was given to you, and whoever gave it to you received it from someone else. This isn't directly from the Bhagavad Gita, but to summarize how it sees detachment, people often say, **"What belongs to you today, belonged to someone yesterday and will be someone else's tomorrow."** No matter what you believe in spiritually, when you recognize this, then you see that you're a vessel, an instrument, a caretaker, a channel for the greatest powers in the world. You can thank your teacher and use the gift for a higher purpose.

Detachment is liberating. When we aren't defined by our accomplishments, it takes the pressure off. We don't have to be the best. I don't have to be Denmark's most impressive visiting monk. My teacher doesn't have to see his students sit in stunned wonder at every moment.

Detaching inspires gratitude. When we let go of ownership, we realize that all we have done has been with the help of others: parents, teachers, coaches, bosses, books—even the knowledge and skills of someone who is "self-made" have their origins in the work of others. When we feel grateful for what we've accomplished, we remember not to let it go to our heads. Ideally, gratitude inspires us to become teachers and mentors in our own way, to pass on what we've been given in some form.

TRY THIS: TRANSFORMING EGO

Look out for these opportunities to detach from your ego and put forth a thoughtful, productive response.

1. *Receiving an insult.* Observe your ego, take a broader view of the person's negativity, and respond to the situation, not the insult.
2. *Receiving a compliment or accolades.* Take this opportunity to be grateful for the teacher who helped you further this quality.
3. *Arguing with a partner.* The desire to be right, to win, comes from your ego's unwillingness to admit weakness. Remember you can be right, or you can move forward. See the other person's side. Lose the battle. Wait a day and see how it feels.
4. *Topping people.* When we listen to others, we often one-up them with a story that shows how we have it better or worse. Instead, listen to understand and acknowledge. Be curious. Don't say anything about yourself.

STEP OUTSIDE OF FAILURE

When we feel insecure—we aren't where we want to be in our careers, our relationships, or in reference to other milestones we've set for ourselves—either the ego comes to our defense or our self-esteem plummets. Either way, it's all about *us*. In *Care of the Soul*, psychotherapist and former monk Thomas Moore writes, "Being literally undone by failure is akin to 'negative narcissism.' . . . By appreciating failure with imagination, we reconnect it to success. Without the connection, work falls into grand narcissistic fantasies of success and dismal feelings of failure." Humility comes from accepting *where* you are without seeing it as a reflection of *who* you are. Then you can use your imagination to find success.

Sara Blakely wanted to go to law school, but despite taking the exam twice, she didn't pull the LSAT scores she wanted. Instead of becoming an attorney, she spent seven years going door-to-door selling fax machines, but she never forgot what her father taught her. Every night at their dining room table, her dad would ask her and her brother not "What did you do at school today?" but "What did you fail at today?" Failing meant they were trying, and that was more important than the immediate result. When Sara got an idea to start her own company, she knew the only failure would be if she didn't try, so she took $5,000 of her own money and started the business that just fifteen years later would make her a billionaire—Spanx. So often we don't take chances because we fear failure, and that often boils down to a fear of our egos getting hurt. If we can get past the idea that we'll break if everything doesn't go our way immediately, our capabilities expand exponentially.

My own version of Blakely's revelation came in London, a week or so after I'd left the ashram.

I had believed that my dharma was to serve as a monk, spreading wisdom and aid. Now, back at my childhood home, I don't want to settle for a lower purpose. What can I do? Our family is not well off. I can't just relax and wait for answers to come to me. I am scared, nervous, anxious. All the things that I've been trained not to be rush back at me.

One night, washing the dishes after dinner, I look out the window above the sink. The garden is out there, but in the darkness, all I can see is my own reflection. I wonder, What would I be doing if I were in the ashram right now? *It's 7 p.m. I would probably be reading, studying, or on my way to give a talk. I spend a moment visualizing myself walking down a path in the ashram, on my way to the library for an evening class. Then I think,* It's the same time of day here as it is there. I have a choice right now. If I use this time wisely, I can make this evening meaningful and purposeful, just as I would in the ashram, or I can waste it in self-pity and regret.

It is then that I let go of my deflated ego to realize that as a monk I've been taught how to deal with anxiety, pain, and pressure. I am no longer in a place where it is natural and easy to achieve those goals, but I can put all I've learned to the test here in a louder, more complicated world. The ashram was like school; this is the exam. I have to earn money, and I won't have the same quantity of time to devote to my practice, but the quality is up to me. I can't study scripture for two hours, but I can read a verse every day and put it into practice. I can't clean temples to clean my heart, but I can find humility in cleaning my home. If I see my life as meaningless, it will be. If I find ways to live my dharma, I will be fulfilled.

I begin to get dressed every day, as if I have a job. I spend most of my time at the library, reading broadly about personal development, business, and technology. Humbled, I return to being a student of life. It is a powerful way to reenter the world.

Being a victim is the ego turned inside out. You believe that the worst things in the world happen to you. You get dealt the worst cards.

When you fail, instead of giving in to a sense of victimhood, think of the moment as a humility anchor, keeping you grounded. Then ask yourself, "What is going to restore my confidence?" It won't grow from an external factor that's beyond your control. I couldn't control whether someone gave me a job, but I focused on finding a way to be myself and do what I loved. I knew I could build confidence around that.

BUILD CONFIDENCE, NOT EGO

Here's the irony: If you've ever pretended you know something, you probably discovered that it often takes the same amount of energy to feign confidence and feed vanity as it takes to work, practice, and achieve true confidence.

Humility allows you to see your own strengths and weaknesses clearly, so you can work, learn, and grow. Confidence and high self-esteem help you accept yourself as you are, humble, imperfect, and striving. Let's not confuse an inflated ego with healthy self-esteem.

The ego wants everyone to like you. High self-esteem is just fine if they don't. The ego thinks it knows everything. Self-esteem thinks it can learn from anyone. The ego wants to prove itself. Self-esteem wants to express itself.

EGO	SELF-ESTEEM
FEARS WHAT PEOPLE WILL SAY	FILTERS WHAT PEOPLE SAY
COMPARES TO OTHERS	COMPARES TO THEMSELVES
WANTS TO PROVE THEMSELVES	WANTS TO BE THEMSELVES
KNOWS EVERYTHING	CAN LEARN FROM ANYONE
PRETENDS TO BE STRONG	IS OK BEING VULNERABLE
WANTS PEOPLE TO RESPECT THEM	RESPECTS SELF & OTHERS

The table above doesn't just show the difference between an inflated ego and a healthy self-worth. It can be used as a guide to grow your confidence. If you look closely, you will see that all of the self-awareness that we have been developing serves to build the interwoven qualities of humility and self-worth. Instead of worrying what people will say, we filter what people will say. Instead of comparing ourselves to others, we cleanse our minds and look to improve ourselves. Instead of wanting to prove ourselves, we want to *be* ourselves, meaning we aren't distracted by external wants. We live with intention in our dharma.

SMALL WINS

Accumulating small wins builds confidence. Olympic swimming gold medalist Jessica Hardy says, "My long-term goals are what I would consider to be my 'dreams,' and my short-term goals are obtainable on a daily or monthly basis. I like to make my short-term goals something that makes me feel better and sets me up to better prepare for the long-term goals."

TRY THIS: WRITE DOWN THE AREAS IN WHICH YOU REALLY WANT TO BE CONFIDENT

Health, career, relationship—pick one of these three.

Write down what is going to make you feel confident in this area, something that's realistic and achievable.

Break your area down into small wins. Things you can achieve today.

SOLICIT FEEDBACK

Confidence means deciding who you want to be without the reflection of what other people think, but it also means being inspired and led by others to become your best self. Spend time with healed, wise, service-driven people and you will feel humbled—and motivated toward healing, wisdom, and service.

When you ask for feedback, choose your advisors wisely. We commonly make one of two mistakes when we seek feedback: We either ask everyone for advice about one problem or we ask one person for advice about all of our problems. If you ask too broadly, you'll get fifty-seven different options and will be overwhelmed, confused, and lost. On the other hand, if you drop all your dilemmas on one person, then they'll be overwhelmed, unequipped, and at some point tired of carrying your baggage.

Instead, cultivate small groups of counsel around specific areas. Make sure you choose the right people for the right challenges. We'll go deeper into finding people who provide competence, character, care, and consistency in Chapter Ten, but for now, in order to recognize productive feedback, consider the source: Is this person an authority? Do they have the experience and wisdom to give you helpful advice? If you choose your advisors wisely, you'll get the right help when you need it without wearing out your welcome.

The monk approach is to look to your guru (your guide), *sadhu* (other teachers and saintly people), and *shastra* (scripture). We look for alignment among these three sources. In the modern world many of us don't have "guides," and if we do, we probably don't put them in a different category than teachers. Nor are all of us followers of religious writings. But what the monks are going for here is advice from trusted sources who all want the best for you, but who offer different perspectives. Choose from those who care most about your emotional health (often friends and family, serving as gurus), those who encourage your intellectual growth and experience (these could be mentors or teachers, serving as *sadhu*s), and those who share your values and intentions (religious guides and/or scientific facts, serving as *shastra*s).

Always be alert to feedback that doesn't come from the usual suspects. Some of the most useful feedback is unsolicited, even unintentional. Temper the ego by paying close attention to how people react to you nonverbally. Do their expressions show intrigue or boredom? Are they irritated, agitated, tired? Here, again, it's worth looking for alignment. Do many different people drift off when you're talking about a subject? It might be time to pull back on that one.

When people offer their reflections, we must pick and choose what we follow carefully and wisely. The ego wants to believe it knows best, so it is quick to write off feedback as criticism. On the flip side, sometimes the deflated ego sees criticism where it doesn't exist. If the response to your job application is a form letter saying, "Sorry, we have lots of applications," this is not useful feedback. It says nothing about you.

The way around these obstacles is to filter the feedback. Reflect instead of judging. Be curious. Don't pretend you understand. Ask clarifying questions. Ask questions that help you define practical steps toward improvement.

The easy check to confirm that someone is offering criticism in good faith is to see if the person is willing to invest in your growth. Are they just stating a problem or weakness, or do they want to help you make a change, if not by taking action themselves, then at least by suggesting ways to move forward?

When soliciting and receiving feedback, make sure you know *how* you want to grow. Feedback often doesn't tell you which direction to follow, it just propels you on your way. You need to make your own decisions and then take action. These three steps—soliciting, evaluating, and responding to feedback—will increase your confidence and self-awareness.

TRY THIS: **RECEIVE FEEDBACK PRODUCTIVELY**

Choose one area where you want to improve. It might be financial, mental and emotional, or physical.

Find someone who is an expert in that field and ask for guidance.

Ask questions for clarity, specificity, and how to practically apply the guidance to your individual situation.

Sample questions:

Do you think this is a realistic path for me?

Do you have any recommendations when it comes to timing?

Is this something you think others have noticed about me?

Is this something that needs retroactive repair (like apologies or revisions), or is this a recommendation for how to move forward?

What are some of the risks of what you're recommending?

DON'T BUY INTO YOUR OWN HYPE

If you are so lucky as to be successful, hear the same words those victorious Roman generals heard: Remember you are but a man, remember you will die. (Feel free to tweak the gender.) Instead of letting your achievements go to your head, detach from them. Feel gratitude for your teachers and what you have been given. Remind yourself who you are and why you are doing the work that brings you success.

Remember the bad and forget the good to keep your own greatness in perspective. In high school I was suspended from school three times for all sorts of stupidity. I'm ashamed of my past, but it grounds me. I can look back and I think, *No matter what anyone says about me today or how*

I think I've grown, I have anchors that humble me. They remind me of who I was and what I might have become if I hadn't met people who inspired me to change. Like everyone, I got where I am through a mix of choices, opportunities, and work.

You are not your success or your failure.

Sustain this humility after you've achieved something too. When you are complimented, commended, or rewarded, neither lap it up nor reject it. Be gracious in the moment, and afterward remind yourself of how hard you worked, and recognize the sacrifices you made. Then ask yourself who helped you develop that skill. Think of your parents, your teachers, your mentors. Someone had to invest their time, money, and energy to make you who you are today. Remember and give thanks to the people who gave you the skills you're getting recognition for. Sharing the success with them keeps you humble.

REAL GREATNESS

You shouldn't feel small compared to others, but you should feel small compared to your goals. My own approach to remaining humble in the face of success is to keep moving the goalposts. The measure of success isn't numbers, it's depth. Monks aren't impressed by how long you meditate. We ask how deep you went. Bruce Lee said, "I fear not the man who has practiced 10,000 kicks once, but I fear the man who has practiced one kick 10,000 times."

No matter what we achieve, we can aspire to greater scale and depth. I'm not concerned with vanity metrics. I often say that I want to take wisdom viral, but I want it to be meaningful. How can I reach a lot of people but without losing an intimate connection? Until the whole world is healed and happy, I haven't finished. Aiming higher and higher—beyond ourselves to our community, our country, our planet—and realizing the ultimate goal is unattainable is what keeps us humble.

Indeed, our goal of humility is ultimately unattainable.

The moment you feel like you have arrived, you're starting the journey again. This paradox is true for many things: If you feel safe, that's when you're most vulnerable; if you feel infallible, that's when you're at your weakest. André Gide said, "Believe those who search for the truth; doubt those who have found it." Too often when you do good, you feel good, you live well, and you start to say, "I got this," and that's when you fall. If I sat here and said I had no ego, that would be a complete lie. Overcoming your ego is a practice not an accomplishment.

Real greatness is when you use your own achievements to teach others, and they learn how to teach others, and the greatness that you've accomplished expands exponentially. Rather than seeing achievement as status, think of the role you play in other people's lives as the most valuable currency. When you expand your vision, you realize that even people who have it all derive the greatest satisfaction from service.

No matter how much you help others, feel no pride because there's so much more to be done. Kailash Satyarthi is a children's rights activist who is dedicated to saving kids from exploitation. His NGOs have rescued tens of thousands of children, but when asked what his first reaction was to winning the 2014 Nobel Peace Prize, he responded, "The first reaction? Well, I wondered if I had done enough to be getting this award." Satyarthi is humbled by the knowledge of how much more there is to do. The most powerful, admirable, captivating quality in any human is seen when they've achieved great things, but still embrace humility and their own insignificance.

We have been digging deep into who you are, how you can lead a meaningful life, and what you want to change. This is a lot of growth, and it won't happen overnight. To aid your efforts, I suggest that you incorporate visualization into your meditation practice. Visualization is the perfect way to heal the past and prepare for the future.

MEDITATION

VISUALIZE

During meditation, monks use visualization for the mind. When we close our eyes and walk our mind to another place and time, we have the opportunity to heal the past and prepare for the future. In the next three chapters we are going to embark on a journey to transform the way we see ourselves and our unique purpose in the world. While we do so, we'll use the power of visualization to assist us.

Using visualization, we can revisit the past, editing the narrative we tell ourselves about our history. Imagine you hated the last thing you said to a parent who passed away. Seeing yourself in your mind's eye telling your parent how much you loved them doesn't change the past, but, unlike nostalgia and regret, it starts the healing. And if you envision your hopes, dreams, and fears of the future, you can process feelings before they happen, strengthening yourself to take on new challenges. Before giving a speech, I often prepare by visualizing myself going on stage to deliver it. Think of it this way: Anything you see in the man-made world—this book, a table, a clock—whatever it is, it existed in someone's mind before it came to be. In order to create something we have to imagine it. This is why visualization is so important. Whatever we build internally can be built externally.

Everyone visualizes in daily life. Meditation is an opportunity to make this inclination deliberate and productive. Past or future, big or small, you can use visualization to extract the energy from a situation and bring it into your reality. For example, if you meditate on a place where you feel happy and relaxed, your breath and pulse shift, your energy changes, and you draw that feeling into your reality.

Visualization activates the same brain networks as actually doing the task. Scientists at the Cleveland Clinic showed that people who imagined contracting a muscle in their little finger over twelve weeks increased its strength by almost as much as people who did actual finger exercises over the same period of time. Our efforts are the same—visualization creates real changes in our bodies.

I've mentioned that we can meditate anywhere. Visualization can help you bring yourself into relaxation no matter what chaos surrounds you. Once I took a two-to-three-day train trip from Mumbai to South India on a crowded, filthy train. I found it tough to meditate and said to my teacher, "I'm not going to meditate right now. I'll do it when we stop or when it's calmer."

My teacher asked, "Why?"

I said, "Because that's what we do at the ashram." I was used to meditating in the serene ashram, surrounded by a lake and benches and trees.

He said, "Do you think the time of death will be calm? If you can't meditate now, how will you meditate then?"

I realized that we were being trained to meditate in peace so that we could meditate in chaos. Since then I've meditated in planes, in the middle of New York City, in Hollywood. There are distractions, of course, but meditation doesn't eliminate distractions, it manages them.

When I guide a meditation, I often begin by saying, "If your mind wanders, return to your regular breathing pattern. Don't get frustrated or annoyed, just gently and softly bring your attention back to your breathing, visualization, or mantra." Meditation is not broken when you're distracted.

It is broken when you let yourself pursue the distracting thought or lose your concentration and think, *Oh, I'm so bad at this.* Part of the practice of meditation is to observe the thought, let it be, then come back to what you were focusing on. If it isn't hard, you're not doing it right.

One important note: We want to choose positive visualizations. Negative visualizations trap us in painful thoughts and images. Yes, the "bad" in us emerges in meditation, but there's no benefit to imagining ourselves trapped in a gloomy maze. The whole point is to visualize a path out of the darkness.

There are two kinds of visualization—set and exploratory. In a set visualization, someone verbally guides you through a place. *You are at a beach. You feel the sand beneath your feet. You see a blue sky, and you hear seagulls and the crash of waves.* An exploratory visualization asks you to come up with your own details. If I ask meditation clients to imagine the place where they feel most at ease, one might see herself riding a bike on a seaside trail, while another might summon a tree house from his childhood.

TRY THIS: **VISUALIZATION**

Here are a few visualizations you can try. I also encourage you to go online to download an app, or to visit a meditation center—there are plenty of options out there to help your practice.

For the visualization exercises I describe below, begin your practice with the following steps.

1. Find a comfortable position—sitting in a chair, sitting upright with a cushion, or lying down.
2. Close your eyes.
3. Lower your gaze.
4. Make yourself comfortable in this position.
5. Bring your awareness to calm, balance, ease, stillness, and peace.

(continued on next page)

6. Whenever your mind wanders, just gently and softly bring it back to calm, balance, ease, stillness, and peace.

BODY SCAN

1. Bring your awareness to your natural breathing pattern. Breathe in and out.
2. Bring your awareness to your body. Become aware of where it touches the ground, a seat, and where it does not. You may find that your heels touch the ground but your arches don't. Or your lower back touches the bed or mat but your middle back is slightly raised. Become aware of all these subtle connections.
3. Now begin to scan your body.
4. Bring your awareness to your feet. Scan your toes, your arches, your ankles, your heels. Become aware of the different sensations you may feel. You may feel relaxed, or you may feel pain, pressure, tingling, or something totally different. Become aware of it and then visualize that you are breathing in positive, uplifting, healing energy and breathing out any negative toxic energy.
5. Now move upward to your legs, calves, shins, and knees. Again, just scan and observe the sensations.
6. Whenever your mind wanders, gently and softly bring it back to your body. No force or pressure. No judgment.
7. At some point you may come across pain you were not aware of before. Be present with that pain. Observe it. And again breathe into it three times and breathe out three times.
8. You can also express gratitude for different parts of your body as you scan them.
9. Do this all the way to the tip of your head. You can move as slowly or as quickly as you like, but don't rush.

CREATE A SACRED SPACE

1. Visualize yourself in a place that makes you feel calm and relaxed. It might be a beach, a nature walk, a garden, or the top of a mountain.
2. Feel the ground, sand, or water beneath your feet as you walk in this space.
3. Without opening your eyes, look left. What do you notice? Observe it and keep walking.
4. Look right. What do you notice? Observe it and keep walking
5. Become aware of the colors, the textures, and the distances around you.
6. What can you hear? The sounds of birds, water, or air?
7. Feel the air and wind on your face.
8. Find a calm, comfortable place to sit down.
9. Breathe in the calm, balance, ease, stillness, and peace.
10. Breathe out the stress, pressure, and negativity.
11. Go to this place whenever you feel you need to relax.

PRESENCE AND MENTAL PICTURE

Often the mental pictures we have form simply from the repetition of an activity rather than because we have chosen them. Visualization can be used to intentionally turn a moment into a memory. Use this visualization to create a memory or to capture joy, happiness, and purpose. It can also be used to deeply connect with an old memory, returning to a time and place when you felt joy, happiness, and purpose. If you are creating a memory, keep your eyes open. If you are reconnecting, then close them.

I use an anti-anxiety technique called 5-4-3-2-1. We are going to find five things you can see, four things you can touch, three things you can hear, two things you can smell, and one thing you can taste.

(continued on next page)

1. First, find five things you can see. Once you've found all five, give your attention to one at a time, moving your focus from one to the next.
2. Now find four things you can touch. Imagine you are touching them, feeling them. Notice the different textures. Move your focus from one to the next.
3. Find three things you can hear. Move your focus from one to the next.
4. Find two things you can smell. Is it flowers? Is it water? Is it nothing? Move your focus from one to the next.
5. Find one thing you can taste.
6. Now that you have attended to every sense, breathe in the joy and happiness. Take it inside your body. Let yourself smile naturally in response to how it makes you feel.
7. You have now captured this moment forever and can return to it anytime through visualization.

PART THREE

GIVE

NINE

GRATITUDE

The World's Most Powerful Drug

Appreciate everything, even the ordinary.
Especially the ordinary.
—Pema Chödrön

Once we have trained the mind to look inward, we are ready to look outward at how we interact with others in the world. Today it is common to talk about amplifying gratitude in our lives (we are all #blessed), but attaching a hashtag to a moment is different from digging to the root of all we've been given and bringing true, intentional gratitude to our lives every day.

Benedictine monk Brother David Steindl-Rast defines gratitude as the feeling of appreciation that comes when "you recognize that something is valuable to you, which has nothing to do with its monetary worth."

Words from a friend, a kind gesture, an opportunity, a lesson, a new pillow, a loved one's return to health, the memory of a blissful moment, a box of vegan chocolates (hint, hint). When you start your day with gratitude, you'll be open to opportunities, not obstacles. You'll be drawn to creativity, not complaint. You will find fresh ways to grow, rather than succumbing to negative thoughts that only shrink your options.

In this chapter we're going to expand our awareness of gratitude and why it's good for you. Then we'll practice finding reasons to be grateful every day; we'll learn when and how to express gratitude for both small gifts and those that have mattered most.

GRATITUDE IS GOOD FOR YOU

It's hard to believe that thankfulness could actually have measurable benefits, but the science is there. Gratitude has been linked to better mental health, self-awareness, better relationships, and a sense of fulfillment.

One way scientists have measured the benefits of gratitude was to ask two groups of people to keep journals during the day. The first group was asked to record things for which they felt grateful, and the second was asked to record times they'd felt hassled or irritated. The gratitude group reported lower stress levels at the end of the day. In another study, college students who complained that their minds were filled with racing thoughts and worries were told to spend fifteen minutes before bed listing things for which they were grateful. Gratitude journaling reduced intrusive thoughts and helped participants sleep better.

TRY THIS: **KEEP A GRATITUDE JOURNAL**

Every night, spend five minutes writing down things you are grateful for.

If you want to conduct your own experiment, spend the week before you start writing down how much sleep you get. The following week, keep a gratitude journal and in the morning write down how much sleep you got. Any improvement?

GRATITUDE AND THE MIND

When the monkey mind, which amplifies negativity, tries to convince us that we're useless and worthless, the more reasonable monk mind counters by pointing out that others have given us their time, energy, and love. They have made efforts on our behalf. Gratitude for their kindness is entwined with self-esteem, because if we are worthless, then that would make their generosity toward us worthless too.

Gratitude also helps us overcome the bitterness and pain that we all carry with us. Try feeling jealous and grateful simultaneously. Hard to imagine, right? **When you're present in gratitude, you can't be anywhere else.** According to UCLA neuroscientist Alex Korb, we truly can't focus on positive and negative feelings at the same time. When we feel grateful, our brains release dopamine (the reward chemical), which makes us want to feel that way again, and we begin to make gratitude a habit. Says Korb, "Once you start seeing things to be grateful for, your brain starts looking for more things to be grateful for." It's a "virtuous cycle."

For years, researchers have shown that gratitude plays a major role in overcoming real trauma. A study published in 2006 found that Vietnam War veterans with high levels of gratitude experienced lower rates of post-traumatic stress disorder (PTSD). If you've been through a breakup, if you've lost a loved one—if anything has hit you hard emotionally—gratitude is the answer.

Gratitude has benefits not just for the mind but for the physical body. The toxic emotions that gratitude blocks contribute to widespread inflammation, which is a precursor to loads of chronic illnesses, including heart disease.

Studies show that grateful people not only feel healthier, they're also more likely to take part in healthy activities and seek care when they're ill.

The health benefits of gratitude are so extensive that Dr. P. Murali Doraiswamy, head of the Division of Biologic Psychology at Duke University Medical Center, told ABC News, "If [thankfulness] were a drug, it would be the world's best-selling product with a health maintenance indication for every major organ system."

EVERYDAY GRATITUDE

If gratitude is good for you, then more gratitude must be better for you. So let's talk about how to increase the gratitude in our daily lives. Monks try to be grateful for everything, all the time. As the Sutta Pitaka, part of the Buddhist canon, advises, "Monks. You should train yourselves thus: 'We will be grateful and thankful and we will not overlook even the least favor done to us.'"

One of my most memorable lessons in gratitude came days after I arrived at the ashram.

A senior monk asks us new arrivals to write about an experience that we believe we didn't deserve. There is silence as we scribble in our notebooks. I pick an episode from my teenage years when one of my best friends betrayed me.

After about fifteen minutes, we share what we've written. One novice describes the painful premature death of his sister, others have written about accidents or injuries, some discuss lost loves. When we're done, our teacher tells us that the experiences we have picked are all valid, but he points out the fact that all of us have selected negative scenarios. Not one of us has written about a wonderful thing that came to us by good fortune or kindness rather than through our own efforts. A wonderful thing that we didn't deserve.

We're in the habit of thinking that we don't deserve misfortune, but that we do deserve whatever blessings have come our way. Now the class takes the time to consider our good fortune: the luck of being born into a family with the resources to care for us; people who have invested more in us than we have invested in ourselves; opportunities that have made a difference in our lives. We so easily miss the chance to recognize what has been given to us, to feel and express gratitude.

This exercise transported me to the first time I felt grateful for the life I had till then taken for granted.

I first visited India with my parents when I was around nine years old. In a taxi on our way back to the hotel, we stopped at a red light. Out the window, I saw the legs of a girl, probably the same age as me. The rest of her was bent over deep into a trash can. It looked like she was trying to find something, most likely food. When she stood up, I realized with shock that she didn't have hands. I really wanted to help her somehow, but I looked on helplessly as our car pulled away. She noticed my gaze and smiled, so I smiled back—that was all I could do.

Back at the hotel I was feeling pretty low about the girl I'd seen. I wished I'd taken action. I thought back to my community in London. So many of us had Christmas lists and birthday parties and hobbies, while there were kids out there just trying to survive. It was an awakening of sorts.

My family went to the hotel restaurant for lunch, and I overheard another child complaining that there was nothing he liked on the menu. I was appalled. Here we were with our choice of meals, and the girl I had seen had only a trash can for a menu.

I probably couldn't have articulated it then, but that day I gleaned how much had been given to me. The biggest difference between me and that girl was where and to whom we had been born. My father, in fact, had worked his way out of the slums in Pune, not far from Mumbai. I was the product of immense hard work and sacrifice.

In the ashram, I began my gratitude practice by returning to the awareness I'd started to feel at nine years old, and feeling grateful for what was already mine: my life and health, my ease and safety and the confidence that I would continue to be fed and sheltered and loved. All of it was a gift.

In order to take that appreciation for the gifts of the universe and turn it into a habit, monks begin every day by giving thanks. Literally. When we wake up on our mats, we flip over to our fronts and pay respect to the earth, taking a moment to give thanks for what it gives us, for the light to see, the ground to walk on, the air to breathe.

TRY THIS: EVERYDAY GRATITUDE PRACTICES

Morning gratitude. Let me guess. The first thing you do when you wake up in the morning is check your phone. Maybe it seems like an easy, low-impact way to get your brain moving, but as we've discussed, it doesn't start the day on the right note. Try this—it will only take a minute. (If you're so tired that you're in danger of falling back asleep, then make sure you've set a snooze alarm.) Take a moment right there in bed, flip over onto your belly, put your hands in prayer, and bow your head. Take this moment to think of whatever is good in your life: the air and light that uplift you, the people who love you, the coffee that awaits you.

Meal gratitude. One in every nine people on earth do not have enough food to eat every day. That's nearly 800 million people. Choose one meal of the day and commit to taking a moment before you dig in to give thanks for the food. Take inspiration from Native American prayers or make up your own. If you have a family, take turns offering thanks.

Ancient, timeless gratitude practices have arisen all around the world. Among Native Americans, traditions of thanksgiving abound. In one ritual observance, described by Buddhist scholar and environmental activist Joanna Macy, Onondaga children gather for a daily morning assembly to start their school day with an offering of gratitude. A teacher begins, "Let us gather our minds as one and give thanks to our eldest Brother, the Sun, who rises each day to bring light so we can see each other's faces and warmth for the seeds to grow." Similarly, the Mohawk people say a prayer, which offers gratitude for People, Earth Mother, the Waters, the Fish, the Plants, the Food Plants, the Medicine Herbs, the Animals, the Trees, the Birds, the Four Winds, Grandfather Thunder, Eldest Brother the Sun, Grandmother Moon, the Stars, the Enlightened Teachers, and the Creator. Imagine what the world might be like if we all started our day giving thanks for the most basic and essential gifts of life all around us.

TRY THIS: GRATITUDE MEDITATIONS

To access gratitude anytime, at will, I recommend the following meditations.

OM NAMO BHAGAVATE VASUDEVAYA

In the ashram we chanted this mantra, discussed on page 273, before reading spiritual texts as a reminder to feel grateful for those who helped those scriptures exist. We can use this chant in a similar way to feel grateful for the teachers and sages who have brought us insight and guidance.

I AM GRATEFUL FOR . . .

After sitting, relaxing, and doing breathwork, repeat "I am grateful for . . . ," completing the phrase with as many things as you can. This exercise immediately refocuses you. If possible, try to reframe negativities that spring to mind by finding elements of them for which you are grateful. You can also do this in a journal or as a voice note to keep as a reminder if these negative thoughts return.

JOY VISUALIZATION

During meditation, take yourself to a time and place where you experienced joy. Allow that feeling of joy to re-enter you. You will carry it with you when you finish the meditation.

THE PRACTICE OF GRATITUDE

Making gratitude part of your daily routine is the easy part, but here's my ask, and it's not small: I want you to be grateful in *all* times and circumstances. Even if your life isn't perfect, build your gratitude like a muscle. If you train it now, it will only strengthen over time.

Gratitude is how we transform what Zen master Roshi Joan Halifax calls "the mind of poverty." She explains that this mindset "has nothing to do with material poverty. When we are caught in the mind of poverty, we focus on what we are lacking; we feel we don't deserve love; and we ignore all that we have been given. The conscious practice of gratitude is the way out of the poverty mentality that erodes our gratitude and with it, our integrity."

Brian Acton exemplifies this conscious practice of gratitude. He had worked at Yahoo for eleven years when he applied for a job at Twitter, but even though he was quite good at what he did, he was rejected. When he received the news, he tweeted, "Got denied by Twitter HQ. That's ok. Would have been a long commute." He next applied for a job at Facebook. Soon after he tweeted, "Facebook turned me down. It was a great opportunity to connect with some fantastic people. Looking forward to life's next adventure." He didn't hesitate to post his failures on social media, and never expressed anything but gratitude for the opportunities. After these setbacks, he ended up working on an app in his personal time. Five years later Facebook bought WhatsApp, the app Brian Acton cofounded, for $19 billion.

The jobs at the companies that rejected Acton would have paid far less than he made off WhatsApp. Instead of fixating on the rejections and adopting a poverty mentality, he just waited gratefully to see what might be in store for him.

Don't judge the moment. As soon as you label something as bad, your mind starts to believe it. Instead, be grateful for setbacks. Allow the journey of life to progress at its own pace and in its own roundabout way. The universe may have other plans in store for you.

There's a story about a monk who carried water from a well in two buckets, one of which had holes in it. He did this every day, without repairing the bucket. One day, a passer-by asked him why he continued to carry the leaky bucket. The monk pointed out that the side of the path where he carried the full bucket was barren, but on the other side of the path, where the bucket had leaked, beautiful wildflowers had flourished. "My imperfection has brought beauty to those around me," he said.

Helen Keller, who became deaf and blind as a toddler after an unidentified illness, wrote, "When one door of happiness closes, another opens; but often we look so long at the closed door that we do not see the one which has been opened for us."

When something doesn't go your way, say to yourself, "There's more for me out there." That's all. You don't have to think, *I'm so grateful I lost my job!* When you say, "This is what I wanted. This was the only answer," all the energy goes to "this." When you say, "This didn't work out, but there's more out there," the energy shifts to a future full of possibility.

The more open you are to possible outcomes, the more you can make gratitude a go-to response. Brother David Steindl-Rast says, "People usually think that gratitude is saying thank you, as if this were the most important aspect of it. The most important aspect of the practice of grateful living is trust in life. . . . To live that way is what I call 'grateful living' because then you receive every moment as a gift. . . . This is when you stop long enough to ask yourself, 'What's the opportunity in this moment?' You look for it and then take advantage of that opportunity. It's as simple as that."

If your boss gives you feedback that you don't agree with, pause before reacting. Take a moment to think, *What can I learn from this moment?* Then look for gratitude: Maybe you can be grateful that your boss is trying to

TRY THIS: GRATITUDE IN HINDSIGHT

Think of one thing that you weren't grateful for when it first happened. Your education? Someone who taught you? A friendship? Is there a project that stressed you out? A responsibility for a family member that you resented? Or choose a negative outcome that is no longer painful: a breakup, a layoff, unwanted news.

Now take a moment to consider in what way this experience is worthy of your gratitude. Did it benefit you in an unexpected way? Did the project help you develop new skills or earn a colleague's respect? Was your relationship with the family member forever improved by your generosity?

Think of something unpleasant that is going on right now, or that you anticipate. Experiment with anticipating gratitude for an unlikely recipient.

help you improve—or grateful that your boss has given you another reason to leave this job. If you run to catch a bus and you succeed, you would ordinarily feel momentary relief, then go back to your day. Instead, stop. Take a moment to remember what it felt like when you thought you were going to miss it. Use this memory to appreciate your good fortune. And if you miss the bus, you will have a moment to reflect, so use it to put the situation in perspective. Another bus is coming. You weren't hit by a car. It could have been a lot worse. After celebrating the wins and mourning the losses, we deliberately look at either situation with perspective, accept it gratefully and humbly, and move forward.

EXPRESSING GRATITUDE

Now that we've broadened the gratitude we feel internally, let's turn that gratitude outward and express it to others.

A lot of the time, we feel deeply grateful, but we have no idea how to pass it on. There are many ways and depths of giving thanks and giving back.

The most basic way to show gratitude is to say thank you. But who wants to be basic? Make your thanks as specific as possible. Think about the thank-you notes you might receive after hosting a gathering. At least one will likely say, "Thanks for last night. It was awesome!" Another might say, "Thanks for last night—the food was wonderful, and I loved the funny, sweet toast you made to your friend." It's far better to express your gratitude in specific terms. The minute we are given even incrementally more detailed gratitude, the better we feel.

This is the key: Your friend felt joy at being part of the gathering that you put together, and the effort they took to compose that thank-you note brought joy back to you. For each of you, gratitude comes from realizing that someone else is invested in you. It's a feedback loop of love.

KINDNESS AND GRATITUDE ARE SYMBIOTIC

The feedback loop of love jibes with the Buddha teaching that kindness and gratitude must be developed together, working in harmony.

Kindness is as easy—and as hard—as this: genuinely wanting something good for someone else, thinking about what would benefit them, and putting effort into giving them that benefit.

If you have ever made a sacrifice for someone else's benefit, you can easily recognize the effort and energy someone else gives to you. That is to say, your own acts of kindness teach you what it takes to be kind, so your own kindness enables you to feel truly grateful. Kindness teaches gratitude. This is what is happening in the microcosm of the thoughtful thank-you note: The kindness of your dinner party inspired your friend's gratitude. That gratitude inspired her kindness to you.

Kindness—and the gratitude that follows—has a ripple effect. Pema Chödrön advises, "Be kinder to yourself. And then let your kindness flood the world." In our daily encounters, we want other people to be kind, compassionate, and giving toward us—who wouldn't?—but the best way to attract these qualities into our lives is to develop them ourselves. Studies have long shown that attitudes, behavior, and even health are contagious within our social networks, but what hadn't been clear was whether this is true simply because we tend to be friends with people who are like us. So two researchers from Harvard and the University of California, San Diego, set out to find out whether kindness is contagious among people who don't know each other. They set up a game where they arranged strangers into groups of four and gave each person twenty credits. Each player was instructed to decide, in private, how many credits to keep for themselves and how many to contribute to a common pot that at the end of the round would be divided evenly among the players. At the end of each round, the players were shuffled, so they never knew from game to game *who* was generous, but they knew *how* generous others had been to the group. As the game went on, players who had been the recipients of generosity from teammates tended to give more of their own credits in future rounds. Kindness begets kindness.

When you are part of a kindness-gratitude exchange, you will inevitably find yourself on the receiving end of gratitude. When we receive thanks, we must be mindful of our egos. It's easy to get lost in the fantasy of our own greatness. When monks are praised, we detach, remembering that whatever we were able to give was never ours to begin with. To receive gratitude with humility, start by thanking the person for noticing. Appreciate their attention and their intention. Look for a good quality in the other person and return the compliment.

Then take the gratitude you are given as an opportunity to be grateful to your teachers.

THE KINDNESS OF STRANGERS

Monks put our gratitude practice into action through all the small interactions of the day. I hopped into an Uber once, in a hurry and distracted. The car idled for an unusually long time, and when I finally noticed and asked the driver if everything was okay, he said, "Yes, I'm just waiting for you to say hi back to me." It was a wake-up call, and you can bet I'm more careful about acknowledging people now.

Being short and direct may be more efficient and professional, but spending our days on autopilot blocks us from sharing the emotions that bind us together and sustain us. A study encouraging some people on the Chicago commuter trains to start conversations with strangers on any subject, for any amount of time, found that those who got up the courage to chat reported a more positive commuting experience. Most of these commuters had anticipated the opposite outcome, and on further investigation, researchers found it wasn't that people thought strangers would be unpleasant, but they feared the awkwardness of starting a conversation and worried they might be rebuffed. That wasn't the case, and most of the strangers were happy to engage. When we make the effort to connect with those around us, we create opportunities for gratitude instead of languishing in anonymity.

Think about all the daily activities that involve other people: commuting, a project at work, grocery shopping, dropping kids off at school, small talk with our partner. These are the little events that fill our lives, and how much pleasure they give us is largely up to us. Specifically, it depends on how much kindness we bring to these interactions and how much gratitude we take from them.

TRY THIS: A GRATITUDE VISUALIZATION

Take a moment right now to think of three things others have given you:

1. A small kindness someone did you
2. A gift that mattered to you
3. Something that makes every day a little bit better

Close your eyes. Take yourself back to the place in time of one of these acts, and relive how it felt—the sights, scents, and sounds. Re-experience it with awe, and experience those feelings in a deeper way.

After this visualization, recognize that small things are happening for you. Don't overlook them or take them for granted. Next, take a moment to feel a sense of being cared for, thought of, loved. This should boost your self-esteem and self-confidence. Last, know that just feeling great is not the end goal. Let this reflection lead to you feeling like you want to reciprocate with love by giving back to those who have given to you, or by passing on the love and care to those who don't have it.

GRATITUDE THROUGH SERVICE

If we want to go beyond the incidental kindnesses of the day, we can actively inspire and increase our gratitude even more. We think of volunteering and serving others as ways of giving to those less fortunate, but they arguably do as much for the donor as they do for the recipient.

Service helps us transform negative emotions like anger, stress, envy, and disappointment into gratitude. It does this by giving us perspective.

"What brings you to me?" asked an old, wise woman of the young man who stood before her.

"I see joy and beauty around me, but from a distance," the young man said. "My own life is full of pain."

The wise woman was silent. She slowly poured a cup of water for the sad young man and handed it to him. Then she held out a bowl of salt.

"Put some in the water," she said.

The young man hesitated, then took a small pinch of salt.

"More. A handful," the old woman said.

Looking skeptical, the young man put a scoop of salt in his cup. The old woman gestured with her head, instructing the young man to drink. He took a sip of water, made a face, and spat it onto the dirt floor.

"How was it?" the old woman asked.

"Thanks, but no thanks," said the young man rather glumly.

The old woman smiled knowingly, then handed the young man the bowl of salt and led him to a nearby lake. The water was clear and cold. "Now put a handful of salt in the lake," she said.

The young man did as he was instructed, and the salt dissolved into the water. "Have a drink," the old woman said.

The young man knelt at the water's edge and slurped from his hands.

When he looked up, the old woman again asked, "How was it?"

"Refreshing," said the young man.

"Could you taste the salt?" asked the wise woman.

The young man smiled sheepishly. "Not at all," he said.

The old woman knelt next to the man, helped herself to some water, and said, "The salt is the pain of life. It is constant, but if you put it in a small glass, it tastes bitter. If you put it in a lake, you can't taste it. Expand your senses, expand your world, and the pain will diminish. Don't be the glass. Become the lake."

Taking a broader view helps us minimize our pain and appreciate what we have, and we directly access this broader view by giving. Research published in *BMC Public Health* points out that volunteering can result in lower feelings of depression and increased feelings of overall well-being. When I lived in New York a charity called Capes for Kids went into a school in Queens and helped the students make superhero capes for kids from tough backgrounds. The children who made the capes got to see the impact of their work and gifts, and it helped them realize how much they truly had. When we see the struggles of others in the clear light of day, when we use our talents to improve their world even a little bit, we immediately feel a surge of gratitude.

TRY THIS: EXPERIENCE GRATITUDE THROUGH VOLUNTEER WORK

Service broadens your perspective and alleviates negative emotions. Try volunteering—it can be once a month or once a week—but nothing will better help you develop gratitude more immediately and inspire you to show it.

PROFOUND GRATITUDE

Sometimes it's hardest to express gratitude to the people who mean the most to us—the family, friends, teachers, and mentors who made or still make a real difference in our lives.

TRY THIS: WRITE A GRATITUDE LETTER

Select one person to whom you feel deeply grateful—someone who makes it easy to feel grateful.

Write out a list of the broader qualities and values you appreciate in this person. Were they supportive? Were they loving? Did they have integrity? Then think of specific words and moments that you shared. Look ahead and write what you're going to do and say when you see them again. (If they have passed, you can lead with: "If I were to see you again, this is what I would say.")

Now write them a gratitude letter, pulling from the notes you've made.

Try to show love and appreciation in person if possible. Otherwise, giving a note, text, or phone call to specifically express what you appreciate about a person boosts that person's happiness and your own.

Sometimes, those you love will resist intimacy and brush you off. In this case, hold your ground. Receiving gratitude requires vulnerability and openness. We block these feelings because we're afraid of being hurt. If you encounter resistance, you might try shifting your approach. Take a moment to consider what form of gratitude the recipient would most appreciate. In some cases, expressing your gratitude in writing is the easiest way for both of you to have time and space to process these feelings.

When you write a gratitude letter to someone who means a lot to you, try to make them feel as cared for and loved as you felt when they helped you. A letter gives recognition to the value of their generosity with more permanence than a verbal thank-you. It deepens your bond. That recognition inspires both of you to be thoughtful and giving with each other, and this, as we have learned, ripples through your community.

GRATITUDE AFTER FORGIVENESS

Perhaps you're thinking, *My parents did a number on me. Why should I be grateful to them?* There are imperfect people in our lives—ones toward whom we feel unresolved or mixed emotions and therefore have trouble summoning gratitude. And yet, gratitude is not black-and-white. We can be grateful for some, but not all, of a person's behavior toward us. If your relationships are complicated, accept their complexity. Try to find forgiveness for their failures and gratitude for their efforts.

However, I'm absolutely not suggesting that you should feel grateful if someone has done you wrong. You don't have to be grateful for everyone in your life. Monks don't have an official stance on trauma, but the focus is always on healing the internal before dealing with the external. In your own pace, at your own time.

• • •

We tend to think of gratitude as appreciation for what we have been given. Monks feel the same way. And if you ask a monk what he has been given, the answer is everything. The rich complexity of life is full of gifts and lessons that we can't always see clearly for what they are, so why not choose to be grateful for what is, and what is possible? Embrace gratitude through daily practice, both internally—in how you look at your life and the world around you—and through action. Gratitude generates kindness, and this spirit will reverberate through our communities, bringing our highest intentions to those around us.

Gratitude is the mother of all qualities. As a mother gives birth, gratitude brings forth all other qualities—compassion, resilience, confidence, passion—positive traits that help us find meaning and connect with others. It naturally follows that in the next chapter we will talk about relationships—who we try to be with others, who we want to welcome into our lives, and how we can sustain meaningful relationships.

TEN

RELATIONSHIPS

People Watching

Every person is a world to explore.

—Thich Nhat Hanh

Monks are often imagined to be hermits, living in isolation, detached from humanity, and yet my experience as a monk has forever changed how I deal with other people. When I returned to London after deciding to leave the ashram, I found that I was much better at all kinds of relationships than I'd been before I took my vows. This improvement was even true for romance, which was a bit surprising given that monks are celibate and I'd had no romantic connections with women during my time in the ashram.

SETTING EXPECTATIONS

The village of the ashram fosters camaraderie, being there for each other, serving each other. Dan Buettner, the cofounder of Blue Zones—an organization that studies regions of the world where people live the longest and healthiest lives—saw the worldwide need for this kind of community. In addition to diet and lifestyle practices, Buettner found that longevity was tied to several aspects of community: close relationships with family (they'll take care of you when you need help), and a tribe with shared beliefs and healthy social behaviors. Essentially, it takes a village.

Like these blue zones, the ashram is an interdependent community, one that fosters a mood of collaboration and service to one another. Everyone is encouraged to look out not just for their own needs, but for those of other people. Remember the trees in Biosphere 2 that lacked roots deep enough to withstand wind? Redwood trees are another story. Famously tall, you'd think that they need deep roots to survive, but in fact their roots are shallow. What gives the trees resilience is that these roots spread widely. Redwoods best thrive in groves, interweaving their roots so the strong and weak together withstand the forces of nature.

THE CIRCLE OF LOVE

In a community where everyone looked out for each other, I initially expected my care and support for other monks to be returned directly by them, but the reality turned out to be more complex.

During my first year at the ashram, I become upset, and I approach one of my teachers for advice. "I'm upset," I say. "I feel like I'm giving out a lot of love, but I don't feel like it's being returned in kind. I'm loving, caring, and looking out for others, but they don't do the same for me. I don't get it."

The monk asks, "Why are you giving out love?"

I say, "Because it's who I am."

The monk says, "So then why expect it back? But also, listen carefully. Whenever you give out any energy—love, hate, anger, kindness—you will always get it back. One way or another. Love is like a circle. Whatever love you give out, it always comes back to you. The problem lies with your expectations. You assume the love you receive will come from the person you gave it to. But it

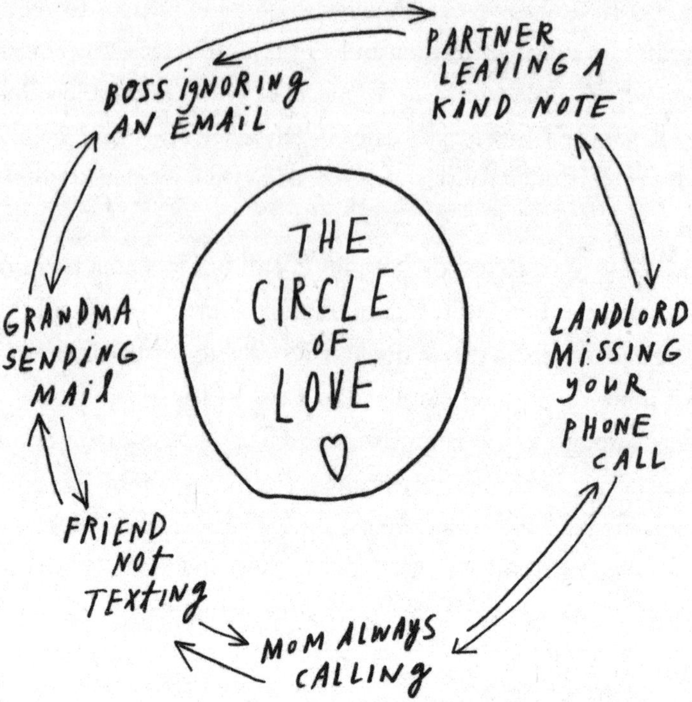

doesn't always come from that person. Similarly, there are people who love you who you don't give the same love in return."

He was right. **Too often we love people who don't love us, but we fail to return the love of others who do.**

I thought of my mother, who would always drop whatever she was doing to take my call. If she were to pick up the phone, the first person she'd reach out to would be me or my sister. In her heart she wanted to talk to me pretty much all the time. At the same time as I might be frustrated because someone wasn't responding to my texts, my mother was sitting there thinking, *I wish my son would call me!*

My teacher's description of the circle of love changed my life. Our lack of gratitude is what makes us feel unloved. When we think nobody cares, we need to check ourselves and realize that the love we give out comes back to us from a variety of sources, and, in a more general sense, whatever we put out will come back to us. This is an example of karma, the idea that your actions, good or bad, bring the same back to you. When we feel unloved, we need to ask ourselves: *Am I offering help as often as I ask for help? Who is giving to me without receiving anything in return?*

A NETWORK OF COMPASSION

It makes sense that monks look at the distribution of love and care as a network of compassion rather than a one-to-one exchange. Monks believe different people serve different purposes, with each role contributing to our growth in its own way. We have peers for friendship, students to teach, and mentors to learn from and serve. These roles are not wholly tied to age and experience. Every monk is always in every phase of that cycle. Monks believe that these roles aren't fixed. The person who is your teacher one day might be your student the next. Sometimes the senior monks would come to classes with young monks like us, sitting on the floor and listening to a new monk speak. They weren't there to check on us—they were there to learn for themselves.

TRY THIS: LEAD AND FOLLOW

Make a list of your students and teachers. Now write down what the students could teach you and what the teachers might learn from you.

THE FOUR TYPES OF TRUST

In the ashram, I was upset because I felt my care wasn't reciprocated. We often expect too much of others when we don't have a clear sense of their purpose in our lives. Let's consider four characteristics that we look for in the people we allow into our lives. You'll recognize these people—most of us know at least one person who falls into each of these categories.

Competence. Someone has to be competent if we are to trust their opinions and recommendations. This person has the right skills to solve

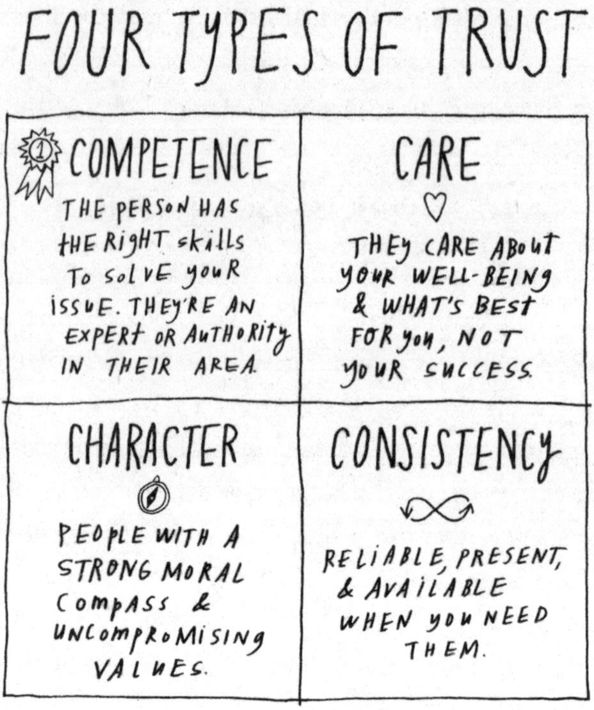

your issue. They are an expert or authority in their area. They have experience, references, and/or a high Yelp rating.

Care. We need to know a person cares if we are putting our emotions in their hands. Real care means they are thinking about what is best for you, not what is best for them. They care about your well-being, not your success. They have your best interests at heart. They believe in you. They would go beyond the call of duty to support you: helping you move, accompanying you to an important doctor's appointment, or helping you plan a birthday party or wedding.

Character. Some people have a strong moral compass and uncompromising values. We look to these people to help us see clearly when we aren't sure what we want or believe is right. Character is especially critical when we are in an interdependent partnership (a relationship, a business partnership, a team). These people practice what they preach. They have good reputations, strong opinions, and down-to-earth advice. They are trustworthy.

Consistency. People who are consistent may not be the top experts, have the highest character, or care most deeply for you, but they are reliable, present, and available when you need them. They've been with you through highs and lows.

Nobody carries a sign announcing what they have to offer us. Observe people's intentions and actions. Are they in alignment? Are they demonstrating what they say they value? Do their values correspond with yours? We learn more from behaviors than promises. Use the four types of trust to understand why you are attracted to a person and whether you are likely to connect as a friend, a colleague, or a romantic partner. Ask yourself, *What is my genuine intention for getting involved in this relationship?*

The four types of trust may seem like basic qualities that we instinctively look for and require, but notice that it's hard to think of someone who cares about you, is competent in every area, has the highest character, and is never too busy for you. Two of the most important people in my life are Swami (my monk teacher) and my mother. Swami is my go-to spiritual person. I have the utmost trust in his character. But when I told him I wanted to leave Accenture and go into media, he said, "I have no idea what you should do." He is one of my most valued advisors, but it was silly to expect him to have an opinion about my career, and he was wise enough not to pretend to have one. My mom would also not be the best person to ask about career moves. Like many mothers, she is most concerned with my well-being: how I'm feeling, whether I'm eating well, if I'm getting enough sleep. She is there with care and consistency, but she's not going to counsel me on managing my company. I needn't be angry at my mother for not caring about every aspect of my life. Instead I should save myself the time, energy, attention, and pain, and simply appreciate what she's offering.

We tend to expect every person to be a complete package, giving us everything we need. This is setting the bar impossibly high. It's as hard to find that person as it is to be that person. The four types of trust will help us keep in mind what we can and can't expect from them. Even your partner can't provide care, character, competence, and consistency in all ways at all times. Care and character, yes, but nobody is competent in all things, and though your partner should be reliable, nobody is consistently available in the way you need them. We expect our life partner to be our everything, to "complete us" (thanks, Jerry Maguire), but even within that deep and lifelong union, only you can be your everything.

Being at the ashram with people who weren't family or otherwise connected to us gave us a realistic perspective. There, it was clear that nobody could or should play every role. Interestingly, a *Psychology Today* article describes a field study of military leadership in Iraq done by Colonel J. Patrick Sweeney, a psychologist. Sweeney similarly found "3 Cs" of trust: competence, caring, and character. The difference is that he observed that all three qualities were necessary for soldiers to trust their leaders. Military and monk life both adhere to routine and principles, but monks aren't following their leaders and laying their lives on the line. To think like a monk about relationships, instead of looking for all four Cs, set realistic expectations based on what a person actually gives you, not what you want them to give you. When they don't have all four Cs, realize that you can still benefit from having them in your life.

And you should be at least as attentive to what you can offer them. With friends or colleagues, get into the habit of asking yourself, *What can I offer first? How can I serve? Am I a teacher, a peer, or a student? Which of the four Cs do I give to this person?* We form more meaningful relationships when we play to our strengths and, like Swami, don't offer expertise that we don't have.

Exercises like the one above aren't meant to attach labels to people; I'm against labels, as I've explained, because they reduce the many nuanced hues of life to black and white. The monk approach is to look for meaning and absorb what you need to move forward instead of getting

TRY THIS: REFLECT ON TRUST

Pick three diverse people in your life—perhaps a colleague, a family member, and a friend—and decide which of the four Cs they bring to your life. Be grateful for that. Thank them for it.

locked in judgment. However, when we apply filters like the four Cs, we can see if our network of compassion is broad enough to guide us through the complexity and chaos of life.

Even if we've got the four Cs covered, we benefit from multiple viewpoints within each of these categories. A mother's care isn't the same as a mentor's. One person with character might give great romantic advice, while another might help you through a family argument. And one consistent friend might be there for you during a breakup, while another is always available for a spirited hike.

MAKE YOUR OWN FAMILY

In order to find diversity, we have to be open to new connections. Part of growing up—at any age—is accepting that our family of origin may never be able to give us all that we need. It's okay to accept what you do and don't get from the people who raised you. And it's okay—necessary, in fact—to protect yourself from those in your family who aren't good for you. We should have the same standards for our family as we do for everyone else, and if the relationship is fraught, we can love them and respect them from a distance while gathering the family we need from the wider world. This doesn't mean we should neglect our families. But forgiveness and gratitude come more easily when we accept that we have friends and family, and we have friends that become family. Feeling connected at some level to all of humanity can be positively therapeutic for those whose own families have made their lives difficult.

THE HUMAN FAMILY

When you enter a new community—as I entered the ashram—you have a clean slate. You have none of the expectations that have already built up among family and friends. Most likely nobody shares your past. In situations like this, most of us rush to find "our people," but the ashram showed me another way. I didn't need to replicate a family, creating a small circle of comfort and trust. Everyone in the ashram was my family. And, as we traveled and connected with people across India and Europe, I began to recognize that everyone in the world was my family. As Gandhi said, "The golden way is to be friends with the world and to regard the whole human family as one."

The groups we establish for learning, growth, and shared experiences—like families, schools, and churches—help us categorize people. *These* are the people I live with. *These* are the people I learn with. *These* are the people I pray with. *These* are the people I hope to help. But I didn't want to discount someone's opinions or worth because they didn't fit neatly into one of these circles. Aside from the limits of practicality, there weren't certain people who deserved my attention or care or help more than others.

It's easier to look at everyone as a member of your family if you don't imagine that it's every human at every moment. A well-known poem by Jean Dominique Martin says, "People come into your life for a reason, a season or a lifetime." These three categories are based on how long that relationship should endure. One person might enter your life as a welcome change. Like a new season, they are an exciting and enthralling shift of energy. But the season ends at some point, as all seasons do. Another person might come in with a reason. They help you learn and grow, or they support you through a difficult time. It almost feels like they've been deliberately sent to you to assist or guide you through a particular experience, after which their central role in your life decreases. And then there are lifetime people. They stand by your side through the best and worst of times, loving you even when you are giving nothing to them. When you consider these categories, keep in mind the circle of love. Love is a gift without any strings attached. This means that with it comes the knowledge that not all relationships are meant to endure with equal strength indefinitely. Remember that you are also a season, a reason, and a lifetime friend to different people at different times, and the role you play in someone else's life won't always match the role they play in yours.

These days, there is a small, consistent group of people with whom I am closest, but that doesn't change the connection I feel to all humanity. And so I ask you to look beyond the people you recognize, beyond your comfort zone, to strangers and people you don't understand. You don't have to befriend them all, but see them all as equal, with equality of soul and the potential to add variety to your knowledge and experience. They are all in your circle of care.

TRY THIS: **BE REALISTIC ABOUT YOUR FRIENDSHIPS**

Make a list of the people you have seen socially over the past week or two. In a second column, identify whether the person is a Season, a Reason, or a Lifetime friend. This, of course, is labeling, which I have urged you not to do. We have to allow for fluidity in the roles people play. But roughly sketching the landscape of your current social life can give you an idea as to whether you are surrounded by a balanced group of people—one that provides excitement, support, and long-term love. Now, in a third column, consider what role you play for each of these people. Are you offering what you receive? Where and how could you give more?

TRUST IS EARNED

Once you have established reasonable expectations from a relationship, then it is easier to build and maintain trust. Trust is central to every relationship. Trust means we believe that the person is being honest with us, that they have our interests at heart, that they will uphold their promises and confidences, and that they will stay true to these intentions in the future. Notice that I didn't say they are right all the time or handle every challenge perfectly. Trust is about intentions, not abilities.

When an important person lets us down, the blow to our trust reverberates across all of our relationships. Even people with the best intentions change or don't follow the same path that we do. Other people give us plenty of signs that their intentions don't mesh with ours, but we ignore them. And sometimes, if we were more aware, there are people we would know not to trust in the first place. Other people's behavior is always out of our control—so how can we trust anyone?

STAGES OF TRUST

Trust can be extended to anyone from a taxi driver to a business partner to a lover, but obviously we don't have the same level of trust for everyone. It's important to be attentive to how deeply we trust someone and whether they've actually earned that level of trust.

Dr. John Gottman, one of the nation's top marriage experts, wanted to find out what makes couples get stuck in ongoing conflict instead of resolving it and moving on. He examined couples from all over the country, from varied socioeconomic and ethnic backgrounds, and in a variety of life situations, from newlyweds, to expecting parents, to families where one spouse was deployed in military service. Across the board, the most important issue to all of these couples was trust and betrayal. The language they used to describe their issues varied a bit, but the central question was always the same: Can I trust you to be faithful? Can I trust you to help with housework? Can I trust you to listen, to be there for me?

The couples had good reason to make trust a priority. According to studies by Dr. Bella DePaulo, people are dishonest in one-fifth of their interactions. Seventy-seven college students and seventy people from the community at large were asked to keep track of their social interactions for seven days. They were told to record all of their exchanges and to note how many lies they told. I know what you're thinking—what if they lied about lying? To encourage honesty, the researchers told the participants

that there was no judgment involved, and that their responses would help to answer fundamental questions about lying behavior. They also sold the experiment as a chance to get to know themselves better. In the end, the students reported some level of lying in one-third of their interactions and the community members in one out of every five interactions. No wonder so many of us have trust issues.

We know from our discussion of ego that we lie to impress, to present ourselves as "better" than we really are, but when these lies are discovered, the betrayal does far more damage to both people than honesty would have. If the seed of trust is not planted effectively in the beginning, we grow a weed of mistrust and betrayal.

We aren't careful with when and how we give our trust. We either trust other people too easily, or we withhold our trust from everyone. Neither of these extremes serve us well. Trusting everyone makes you vulnerable to deception and disappointment. Trusting no one leaves you suspicious and alone. Our level of trust should directly correspond to our experience with a person, growing through four stages of trust.

Neutral Trust. When you meet someone, it is normal not to trust them. You may find them funny, charming, a joy to be around. These positive qualities do not merit trust. They mean you think your new acquaintance is cool. We tend to conflate trustworthiness with likability. In studies examining jurors' perceptions of expert witnesses, those the jurors found to be likeable they also rated as more trustworthy. We also tend to trust people we find attractive. Rick Wilson, coauthor of *Judging a Book by Its Cover: Beauty and Expectations in the Trust Game*, says, "We found that attractive subjects gain a 'beauty premium' in that they are trusted at higher rates, but we also found a 'beauty penalty' when attractive people do not live up to expectations." When we equate likability or appeal with trust, we set ourselves up for huge disappointment. It is better to have neutral trust than to trust someone for the wrong reasons or to trust them blindly.

Contractual Trust. I derived this level of trust from *rajas*, the impulsive mode of life, where you are focused on getting the result that you want in the short-term. Contractual trust is the quid pro quo of relationships. It simply says: If I pay for dinner and you promise to pay me back, I have faith that you'll do it. If you make a plan, you can count on the person to show up—and there's no further expectation. Contractual trust is useful. Most of us share contractual trust with the majority of people who cross our paths, yet we expect them to trust us implicitly. The heart may want a deeper connection, but we have to be discerning. Expecting more from someone who is only showing you contractual trust is premature at best and dangerous at worst.

Mutual Trust. Contractual trust reaches a higher level when you help someone, expecting they would most likely do the same for you, in some way, at some unknown time in the future. Where contractual trust relies on a specific exchange both parties have agreed to in advance, mutual trust is far looser. This stage of trust is derived from *sattva*, the mode of goodness, where we act from a place of goodness, positivity, and peace. We all want to get to this level, and good friendships usually do.

Pure trust. The highest level of trust is pure goodness, when you know, no matter what happens, that another person has your back, and vice versa. College basketball coach Don Meyer used to give each of his teammates a blank piece of paper on which he'd ask them to draw a circle to represent their "foxhole." They wrote their names at the top of the circle, then drew lines at their left, right, and rear, and on each line they had to list the name of a teammate who they'd want in their foxhole with them. Those chosen most often by their teammates were the team's natural leaders. Choose your foxhole gang wisely.

If you were to graph the number of people you trust at each level, the result would probably look like a pyramid: a lot of people at neutral trust; fewer people at contractual trust; your close circle at mutual trust; and only a handful at the top level, pure trust.

No matter how dissatisfied you are with your pyramid, don't promote people without reason. They will only let you down. The biggest mistake we make is to assume that everyone else operates just like us. We believe that others value what we value. We believe that what we want in a relationship is what others want in a relationship. When someone says, "I love you," we think they mean exactly what we mean when we say "I love you." But if we think everyone is a reflection of ourselves, we fail to see things as they are. We see things as *we* are.

Mutual trust requires patience and commitment. It is built on a true understanding of the other person in spite of and because they are separate from us and view the world differently. The way to step back from making presumptions is to closely observe their words and behaviors. When people show you their level of trust, believe them.

I want you to feel grateful for the people you can trust and to feel honored by those who trust you. If you have neutral trust for someone, that's cool too. Accept people as they are, and you give them the chance to grow and prove to be more. We set ourselves up for long-term trust when we let it evolve naturally.

TRUST IS A DAILY PRACTICE

Relationships rarely get to a point where both participants can say, "I absolutely know this person and they absolutely know me." Like a curve that continually approaches but never reaches a line, you never get to the point of saying, "I trust them fully, and they trust me fully, forever and ever." Trust can be threatened in small and large ways and needs to be reinforced and rebuilt on a daily basis.

Build and reinforce trust every day by:

- Making and fulfilling promises (contractual trust)
- Giving those you care about sincere compliments and constructive criticism; going out of your way to offer support (mutual trust)
- Standing by someone even when they are in a bad place, have made a mistake, or need help that requires significant time (pure trust)

AN INTENTIONAL LOVE LIFE

Now that we have some tools to assess the roles people play in our lives, let's look at how we can deepen existing relationships and build strong new ones. Letting go of traditional family roles allowed us monks to broaden our connections with humanity. In the same way, celibacy freed the energy and attention that romantic love had consumed. Before you hurl this book across the room, I'm not recommending celibacy for non-monks. Celibacy is an extreme commitment and hardly an essential one for everyone, but it did lead me to revelations that I'd like to share. Let's say I did it so you don't have to.

To stop drinking? That was easy for me. To stop gambling? I'd never done much of that in the first place. And I'd stopped eating meat at sixteen. For me, giving up romantic relationships was the hardest sacrifice.

It sounded ridiculous, even impossible. But I knew the purpose behind it: to save the effort and energy that went into being validated in a romantic relationship and to use it to build a relationship with myself. Think of it the same way giving up sugar sounds like a drag—what sane person would want to forgo ice cream?—but we all know there's a good reason: to be healthy and live longer. When I looked at the monks, I could see that they were doing something right. Remember Matthieu Ricard, "the World's Happiest Man"? All the monks I met looked so young and seemed so happy. My romantic entanglements hadn't brought me fulfillment, so I was willing to try the experiment of self-control and discipline.

When I became a monk, one of my college friends asked, "What are we going to talk about? All we used to do was talk about girls." He was right. So much of my life had been absorbed in navigating romantic connections. There's a reason we watch countless sitcoms and movies about romance—it's endlessly entertaining—but as with any entertainment, it takes time away from serious matters. If I'd been dating or in a committed relationship for those three years instead of being at the ashram, I wouldn't be where I am today, with understanding of my strengths and who I am.

The Sanskrit for monk is *brahmacharya*, which can be translated to "the right use of energy." In the dating world, when you walk into a bar, you look around to see who is attractive. Or you swipe through potential mates online without giving a second thought to how much time you spend in the effort to hook up. But imagine if you could buy that time back for yourself, if you could recoup everything you've ever invested in relationships that didn't pan out. That attention and focus could be used for creativity, friendship, introspection, industry. Now, this doesn't mean every failed relationship is a waste of time. On the contrary, we learn from each mistake. But think of the time around the relationship, waiting for texts, wondering if they like you, trying to make someone change into the person you want them to be. If we are thoughtful about our needs and expectations, our time and energy go to far better use.

Sexual energy is not just about pleasure. It is sacred—it has the power to create a child. Imagine what it can create within us when it's harnessed. Certified sex educator Mala Madrone says, "Celibacy by conscious choice is a powerful way to work with your own energy and harness the potency of life energy. It can also help you strengthen your intuition, your boundaries, and your understanding of what consent truly means, including how to differentiate what kind of contact and interaction is truly welcome in your life and by your body." But your energy is squandered when it is spent tailoring yourself to someone else's ideal or shaping yourself into the person you think he wants or suspecting her of cheating on you. There is so much anxiety and negativity around dating and so much pressure to find "the one"—never mind whether we're ready or able to settle down with anyone.

Once the element of romantic pursuit was removed, I wasn't trying to promote myself as a boyfriend, to look good, to make women think anything of me, to indulge lust. I found my connections with female friends—with all my friends—growing deeper. I had more physical and mental space and energy for their souls. My time and attention were better spent.

Again, I'm not suggesting you give up sex (though you certainly could), but what if you give yourself permission to be single, by yourself, able to focus on your career, your friends, and your peace of mind? Minister and philosopher Paul Tillich said, "Our language has wisely sensed these two sides of man's being alone. It has created the word 'loneliness' to express the pain of being alone. And it has created the word 'solitude' to express the glory of being alone."

I spent three years as a monk, three years developing my self-awareness, at the end of which I was able to ask myself the right questions about a relationship. I may not have spent all of my waking hours in *sattva*—the mode of goodness—but I knew where I wanted to be and how it felt. I had the opportunity to become the person I would want to date. Instead of looking for others to make me happy, I was able to be that person for myself.

ATTRACTION VERSUS CONNECTION

Our increased intentionality gives us a clearer perspective with which to evaluate why we are initially attracted to people and whether those reasons support our values. There are five primary motivations for connection—and note that these don't exclusively apply to romantic prospects:

1. *Physical attraction.* You like what they look like—you are drawn to their appearance, style, or presence, or you like the idea of being seen with them.
2. *Material.* You like their accomplishments and the power and/or the possessions this affords them.
3. *Intellectual.* You like how they think—you're stimulated by their conversation and ideas.
4. *Emotional.* You connect well. They understand your feelings and increase your sense of well-being.
5. *Spiritual.* They share your deepest goals and values.

When you identify what's attracting you, it's clear if you're attracted to the whole person or just a part. In my experience, ask most people what attracts them to another person and they'll mention some combination of the top three qualities: looks, success, and intellect, but those qualities alone don't correlate with long-term, fortifying relationships.

Monks believe that someone's looks aren't who they are—the body is only a vessel for the soul. Similarly, someone's possessions aren't theirs—they certainly don't tell you about the person's character! And even if you're attracted to someone's intellect, there's no guarantee it will lead to a meaningful bond. These three qualities don't correlate with long-term, fortifying relationships, but they do show your chemistry with another person. The last two—emotional and spiritual—point to a more profound, lasting connection—they show your compatibility.

QUALITY, NOT QUANTITY

When it comes to the energy we expend and receive in relationships, the focus is quality, not quantity. I often hear from guilty parents (usually moms) that they feel bad having to work long hours and lose out on time with their kids. According to the first-ever large-scale study of the impact of mothers' time, it's the *quality* of time spent with kids, not the quantity, that counts. (That means put away your phone during family time.) I'm not a parent, but I know that as a child, I always felt my mom's energy. I never measured how much time she spent with me. My mother worked, and as a young child I went to daycare. I don't have a single memory from daycare—no painful memories of her absence—but I do remember her coming to pick me up. She'd always smile and ask about my day.

This is true in all relationships. Nobody wants to sit with you at dinner while you're on the phone. This is where we confuse time and energy. You can spend a whole hour with someone, but only give them ten minutes of energy. I'm not able to spend much time with my family, but when I'm with them I'm 100 percent there. I'd rather spend two hours with them, focused and engaged, than give them partial, distracted energy for a whole weekend.

A monk shows love through presence and attention. In the ashram, time invested was never seen as a reliable measure of care or engagement. As I've mentioned, after a meditation, nobody asked how long you'd meditated, they asked how deep you'd gone. If you have dinner together every night, great, but what is the quality of the conversation? Think like monks do, in terms of energy management not time management. Are you bringing your full presence and attention to someone?

TRY THIS: HANDCUFF ATTENTION THIEVES

These days, most of us are losing a battle for our attention. The victors are our screens. The only way to give another person your complete attention for a period of time is to turn off your screens. To give someone in your life the focus they deserve, sit down with them to agree on rules surrounding the phone, the laptop, and the TV. Choose specific activities that will be your quality time, without distraction. Agree to turn off your phones, put them in another room, or leave them at home. This may be a challenge at first. Perhaps conversation will lag, or friends and colleagues will be frustrated because they can't reach you. Setting these boundaries will establish new expectations on both fronts: Lapses in conversation will lose their awkwardness; friends and colleagues will accept that you are not available 24/7.

SIX LOVING EXCHANGES

Most couples don't sit down together, draw up a list of values, and see whether they share them. But once we have clarity about ourselves, we can connect with others in a more intentional way. The Upadesamrta talks about six loving exchanges to encourage bonding and growing together. (There are three types of exchanges; each involves giving *and* receiving, thus adding up to six.) They help us build a relationship based on generosity, gratitude, and service.

Gifts. Giving charity and receiving whatever is offered in return. This seems obvious, or maybe even materialistic—we don't want to buy each other's affection. But think about what it means to give to another person with intention. Do you get flowers for your partner on Valentine's Day? This is a very conventional gesture, so consider whether it is the one that brings your partner the most joy. If flowers it is, did you walk them past a flower shop six months ago to suss out their preferences in preparation for this day, or did you text a secret query to their closest friend? (Both actions entail a lot more intention than just ordering some roses online, though, of course, that's better than completely forgetting the day!) Is Valentine's Day the best moment to express your love, or would an unexpected gesture be even more meaningful? Have you taken the time to contemplate what an ill friend would really like? Maybe it isn't an object but an action, a service, our time. Cleaning their car, organizing activities, helping them with obligations, or bringing them someplace beautiful.

You can bring the same thoughtfulness to receiving a gift. Are you grateful for the effort that went into the gift? Do you understand why and what it means for the giver?

Conversation. Listening is one of the most thoughtful gifts we can give. There is no better way to show that we care about another person's experience. Listening intentionally means looking for the emotions behind the words, asking questions to further understand, incorporating what you've learned into your knowledge of the other person, doing your best to remember what they said, and following up where relevant. Listening also involves creating an atmosphere of trust, where the person feels welcome and safe.

It is also important to share your own thoughts and dreams, hopes and worries. The vulnerability of exposing yourself is a way of giving trust and showing respect for another person's opinion. It enables the other person to understand the previous experiences and beliefs you bring to whatever you do together.

SIX LOVING EXCHANGES

① GIVING with INTENTION
② RECEIVING with GRATITUDE

③ LISTENING WITHOUT JUDGMENT
④ SPEAKING WITH VULNERABILITY

⑤ PREPARING without AGENDA
⑥ RECEIVING with PRESENCE

TRY THIS: MAKE YOUR CONVERSATION INTO A GIFT

Ideally, you try to do this in conversations regularly, but this time, do it with focus and intention. Pick a moment you have coming up with someone important to you—a friend, a relative, your partner. Maybe it's a meal or walk you'll be taking together. During this time, shut off your phone. Give all your focus to the other person. Instead of having an agenda, be curious. If a topic doesn't emerge, ask them open-ended questions to land on a subject that's important to them: What's on your mind lately? How's your relationship with X? Listen carefully, ask follow-up questions. Share your own experiences without turning the conversation to yourself. A few days later, email or text the friend to follow up.

Food. The world was a very different place when the Upadesamrta was written, of course, and I interpret this exchange of food broadly to mean the exchange of experiences: any tangible expression of care and service that nourishes body or spirit, like giving a massage, creating a relaxing space for the other person in the home, or putting on music you know they enjoy. On a grander scale, my wife left her beloved family and moved to New York so she could live with me—an expression of care and generosity that nourished me more than I can say. Once we were in New York, I introduced her to other women to help her find a community. The experiences we exchanged didn't have to be perfectly matched—we look for what the other person needs most.

These six exchanges can be thoughtless and empty, or they can have true depth and meaning. But don't judge people's efforts without giving them a chance to succeed. Nobody can read minds. If your roommate or partner doesn't guess that you want them to organize your birthday party, it's not their fault. Instead, be clear and honest with them about what you need.

TRY THIS: ASK FOR WHAT YOU WANT

Tell the important people in your life how you like to receive love. When we don't tell people what we want, we expect them to read our minds and often judge them for failing to do so. This week, be more genuine in asking people for help rather than waiting for them to predict what you want.

1. Think of a complaint you have about a loved one's behavior. (But don't look too hard for faults! If nothing springs to mind, that's a great sign and you should skip this exercise.)
2. Dig to the root of the problem. Where is the real dissatisfaction? You might find that your need corresponds to the loving exchanges. Do you want more time to share and connect? (conversation) Do you feel unappreciated? (gifts) Do you want more support? (food or other acts of service)
3. Articulate it without criticism. Say, "This is what would make me feel more loved and appreciated" instead of "You do this wrong."

In this way you give a companion a path to connection, which is easier for them and more likely to fulfill you.

READY FOR LOVE

The six loving exchanges lay a foundation for any close relationship, but most of us are looking for "the one." The Harvard Grant Study followed 268 Harvard undergraduates for seventy-five years, collecting piles of data about them along the way. When researchers combed through the data, they found a single factor that reliably predicted the quality of participants' lives: love. Participants could have every other external marker for success—money, a thriving career, good physical health—but if they didn't have loving relationships, they weren't happy.

We all come to relationships with different levels of self-awareness.

With the encouragement of online quizzes and dating apps, we list the characteristics we want in a partner—sense of humor, caring, good-looking—but we don't look at what we really need. How do we want to be cared for? What makes us feel loved?

In *How to Love*, Thich Nhat Hanh writes, "Often, we get crushes on others not because we truly love and understand them, but to distract ourselves from our suffering. When we learn to love and understand ourselves and have true compassion for ourselves, then we can truly love and understand another person." After the ashram, when I was ready for a relationship (which was not, as some friends assumed, the moment I left), my sense of what I wanted in a partner was steered by self-knowledge. I knew what would complement me and what wouldn't. I knew what I needed in my life and what I had to offer. My ability to find the right relationship evolved because I had evolved.

As it happened, Radhi Devlukia, the woman who would become my wife, already had this self-knowledge too. Without the need for the same journey I'd made, she knew she wanted to be with someone spiritually connected, with high morals and values. I believe she would have done just fine without me. But I know my life would have been different, full of pain, if I hadn't taken the time to work on myself before diving into a serious relationship.

According to Massive Attack, love is a verb. *Dan in Real Life* says love is an ability. The Dalai Lama says, "Love is the absence of judgment." Love is also patient. It's kind. And apparently, love is all you need. With so many definitions of love in our culture, it's all a bit confusing. And I was confused, despite all my monk experience—my self-exploration and intentionality and compassion—when I ventured out on my first date back in London.

I already know I like her. The Think Out Loud group I started in college continued for some years after I left, and I stayed in touch, visiting and lecturing when I came to London. Radhi was part of that community, had come to some of my lectures, and had become friends with my sister. Now people from that community, including me and Radhi, have joined together to organize a charity event against racism and bullying for young kids in England. Seeing Radhi in that context has told me more about her than I would have learned on a dating profile, or even after a few dates. I've seen how respectful she is with everyone on the team. She has interesting opinions and cool ideas. I've had a chance to get a real look at who she is—anyone can be their online profile for a one-hour date. It may be their best self, but it doesn't give the full picture.

I still haven't gotten a full-time job, but I've been tutoring to make a bit of money. I've saved up a month's earnings, and I take Radhi to the theater to see Wicked. *Then I bring her to Locanda Locatelli, a fancy restaurant that's way above my pay grade.*

She's polite, but unimpressed. Afterward, she says, "You didn't have to do this," and confesses that her ideal date would be going to a supermarket, walking the aisles, and buying some bread. I'm mystified. Who would want to do that?

I hadn't had any relationships since becoming a monk, and I had yet to reconcile who I was spiritually with how I used to date. I felt like I had one foot in each world. In spite of my monk training, I snapped right back into my old relationship mode—the one where I tried to give the other person what media, movies, and music told me they wanted instead of developing my awareness of who they were. I myself love gifts and extravagant demonstrations of love, and for a while I cluelessly continued to shower Radhi with grand gestures. I got it completely wrong. She wasn't impressed by any of that. She's not very fancy. Even after my years in the ashram, I could still be swayed by external influences or my own preferences rather than careful observation of what she liked, but after my initial missteps, I was aware enough to figure it out, and, thank God, she married me.

If you don't know what you want, you'll send out the wrong signals and attract the wrong people. If you aren't self-aware, you'll look for the wrong qualities and choose the wrong people. This work is what we've talked about throughout this book. Until you understand yourself, you won't be ready for love.

Sometimes we find ourselves making the same mistake over and over again, attracting the same sort of incompatible partners or picking them in spite of ourselves. If this happens, it isn't bad luck—it's a clue that we have work to do. The monk perspective is that you carry pain. You try to find people to ease that pain, but only you can do that. If you don't work through it, it stays with you and interferes with your decisions. The problematic people who emerge reflect your unresolved issues, and they will keep reappearing until you learn the lesson you need to learn. As Iyanla Vanzant said to Oprah, ". . . until you heal the wounds of your past, you will continue to bleed. You can bandage the bleeding with food, with alcohol, with drugs, with work, with cigarettes, with sex; but eventually, it will all ooze through and stain your life. You must find the strength to open the wounds, stick your hands inside, pull out the core of the pain that is holding you in your past, the memories, and make peace with them."

Once you've unpacked your own bags and you've healed yourself (mostly), then you'll come to relationships ready to give. You won't be looking to them to solve your problems or fill a hole. Nobody completes you. You're not half. You don't have to be perfect, but you have to come to a place of giving. Instead of draining anyone else, you're nourishing them.

KEEPING LOVE ALIVE

Remember when we talked about the mind, we said that happiness comes when we are learning, progressing, and achieving. And yet as a relationship lengthens, we tend to long for the honeymoon phase, when we were first falling in love. How many times have you been in a relationship, and said to yourself, "I wish I could feel like that again," or "I wish we could go back to that time." But going to the same place for dinner or to the place you had your first kiss won't bring back all the magic. Many of us are so addicted to re-creating the same experiences that we don't make space for new ones. What you were actually doing at the start of your relationship was creating *new* memories with energy and openness. Love is kept alive by creating more new memories—by continuing to learn and grow together. Fresh experiences bring excitement into your life and build a stronger bond. I have many recommendations for activities couples can do together, but here are a couple of my favorites, drawn from monk principles.

1. *Find new in the old.* Remember when, as monks, we looked for a special stone on the same walk we took together every day? You too can open your eyes to the world you already live in. Have a candlelit dinner in the middle of the week. Read a book to each other before bed instead of staring at your phones. Take a walk together in the neighborhood and challenge each other to find a certain kind of mailbox or to be the first to spot a bird.

2. *Find new ways to spend time together.* A study by psychologist Arthur Aron found that couples strengthen their bonds when they do new and exciting activities together. My wife and I started to do escape rooms together. An escape room is a game where you're both locked in a room and have to find a way out. The staff gives you a few clues, and you have to work together to solve many steps of the puzzle. It may sound a little creepy, but it's actually a lot of fun. You get to learn together. You get to make mistakes together. It's an even playing field when neither of you has more experience or expertise than the other. When you experiment together as a couple, you feel yourselves growing together in all areas of your life. You could even try something really scary together—like skydiving or something else that's outside your comfort zone. Remember all the benefits that we found in getting close to our fears? Playing with fear together is a way to practice going into your deeper fears, sharing them with your partner, feeling their support, and together transforming fear.

3. *Serve together.* Just as serving gives meaning to your life, serving with your partner adds meaning to your connection, whether it's organizing charity events, feeding the homeless, or teaching something together.

My most bonding experiences in monk life came about when I took part in collective projects. The horrid two-day train journey that I've mentioned. Planting trees together. Building a school. Instead of focusing on the challenges of the relationship, we develop a shared perspective on real-life issues. Connecting for a higher purpose, we feel gratitude and bring that back into our relationship. I know many couples who have met through volunteering, so if you're looking for a well-suited partner, find a cause that is close to your heart. If you meet through an activity such as volunteering, from the start you already have something very deep in common, and you're more likely to form a deeper bond.

4. *Meditate and chant together.* (See page 270.) When a couple who has just had an argument comes into a room, you can feel the negative energy vibrating between them. The opposite is true when you and your partner chant together. You are bringing your energy to the same place and feel, literally, in tune with each other.

5. *Finally, envision together what you both want from the relationship.* When you are aware of what is important to each other, then you can figure out how much you're willing to adapt. Ideally, each of you is striving to live in your own dharma. In the best of relationships, you get there together.

OVERCOMING HEARTBREAK

It can be hard to see clearly when your heart is at stake, but there is one point I want to make abundantly clear: There is a difference between being grateful for what you have and settling for less than you deserve. If we are still listening to our child minds, we're attracted to people who aren't good for us but make us feel better in the moment. Don't wrap your self-esteem around someone else. Nobody deserves verbal, emotional, or physical abuse. It is better to be alone. Nor should you allow an abusive, manipulative, or toxic relationship to transition into friendship. The dynamic won't change, trust me.

In every relationship you have the opportunity to set the level of joy

you expect and the level of pain you'll accept. No relationship is perfect, but if joy never reaches a certain height, or holds to a low average, that won't change unless you both put in a lot of work. The same is true for how much disappointment you're willing to bear. Your connection may get a slow start—it can take a while to know each other—but if it never reaches a satisfying level, you need to decide whether to accept it or move on.

I know it's not easy. When you've spent quality time with someone, when you've invested in someone, when you've given yourself to someone, it's so hard to let go. Tibetan Buddhist nun Jetsunma Tenzin Palmo points out that we often mistake attachment for love. She says, "We imagine that the grasping and clinging that we have in our relationships shows that we love. Whereas actually, it is just attachment, which causes pain. Because the more we grasp, the more we are afraid to lose, then if we do lose, then of course we are going to suffer." Ultimately, holding on to the wrong person causes us more pain than letting them go.

The strategies I recommend to overcome heartbreak tie directly to monk ideas of the self, and how we find our way toward peace and purpose. No matter what thought we have, we don't run away from it. We give ourselves space to assess and make changes. **SPOT, STOP, SWAP.**

Feel every emotion. It's possible to distract yourself from heartbreak, but the fix is only temporary. And if you deny your feelings, you end up suffering in other ways. Researchers followed incoming college freshmen to see how well they adapted to their transition and found that those with a tendency to suppress their emotions had fewer close relationships and felt less social support. Instead, think about how the other person has made you feel in this situation. You might want to articulate your feelings by writing them down or recording them. Read what you've written and listen back objectively. Do you hear any recurring patterns?

You can also do a question meditation, asking yourself about the loss. We like to replay emotions: how perfect it was, how it could have been, how we thought it was going to go. Instead of reflecting on how romantic the relationship was before it crashed and burned, focus on the reality.

What were your hopes for the relationship? What did you lose? Is your disappointment tied to who the person was, or who they weren't? Explore your emotions until you uncover the root of the pain and disruption.

Learn from the situation. Movies, music, and other media send us limited, often inaccurate messages about what love should look like. Use the reality of the breakup to set realistic expectations about what you deserve and need from a new relationship and remember that yours can be different from the person you broke up with and/or the next person to come along. What was the biggest expectation you had that wasn't met? What was important to you? What was good in the relationship, what was bad? What was your role in its demise? Instead of exploring your pain here, you want to investigate the workings of the relationship in order to identify what you want from your next relationship, and what you might have to work on in yourself.

Believe in your worth. You may undervalue yourself in the moment of a breakup, but your value doesn't depend on someone's ability to fully appreciate you. If you wrap your identity around the relationship, the pain you feel is that you've had to sacrifice that part of your identity. If you expected one person to fulfill all of your needs, then of course there is a vacuum when they're gone. Now that you're single, use this time to build a community of people with shared interests whom you want to be in your life forever. Make yourself whole. You need to be someone who makes you happy.

Wait before dating again. Remember, if you haven't healed past pain, you might miss your next opportunity for an incredible connection with an incredible person. Don't rebound or revenge-date. This only causes more hurt and regret that spread further, a virus of pain. Instead, take some time to get to know yourself better. Build your self-esteem. Invest in your growth. **If you've lost yourself in the relationship, find yourself in the heartbreak.**

The monk way is to build awareness, address, and amend. Either within a relationship or before we enter one, we take a step back to evaluate and make sure we understand our own intentions. Then we can venture into the dating world or return to the relationship with self-awareness and love. **SPOT, STOP, SWAP.**

We have turned our attention outward to address the intimate relationships in our lives. Now we come to our relationship with the larger world. I mentioned that at the ashram I felt a bond beyond my ties to my family, a far greater force uniting and connecting us all. The astrophysicist Neil deGrasse Tyson said, "We are all connected; to each other, biologically. To the Earth, chemically. And to the rest of the universe, atomically." Knowing this, we must look to the universe to find true meaning in our lives.

ELEVEN

SERVICE

Plant Trees Under Whose Shade You Do Not Plan to Sit

The ignorant work for their own profit . . .
the wise work for the welfare of the world . . .
—Bhagavad Gita, 3:25

I am a novice at the ashram, and we've been dropped off in a village with no money and no food, with the mission to find our own way for thirty days.

The weather is decent, and we've been given a warehouse for shelter. We leave our mats there and venture into the village. There are simple huts from which people sell food, spices, and sundries. Laundry is strung between the huts. Most people travel by bike or on foot—some of the children are barefoot.

Untethered, without a plan, the first thing we feel is fear, which provokes us to do whatever it takes to survive. We ask for handouts—people in India are generous and often give bread, fruit, or coins to people in spiritual dress. We visit the temple where pilgrims are given free food called prasad*—this is sanctified food that is offered to God, then handed out. Anxious about our survival, we resort to selfishness and hoarding.*

By the second week, we're in better shape. We've figured out that we can earn our provisions by offering help to people in the village. We start assisting people with heavy loads or peddlers who could use a hand with their carts. We soon learn that opening our hearts and souls encourages others to do the same. The donations we receive aren't dramatically different from the ones we got when we first arrived, but the exchange gives us a warm sense of communal compassion and generosity, and I feel like I've absorbed the lesson of our journey. We thought we had nothing, and indeed we had barely any material possessions. But we were still able to give people our effort.

However, by the final week, we're well-fed and secure enough to notice something deeper. Though we had come with nothing, we still had a certain kind of wealth: we are stronger and more capable than a lot of the people in the village. There are seniors, children, and disabled people on the street, all of them in greater need than we are.

"I feel bad," one monk says. "This is short-term for us. For them it's forever."

"I think we're missing something," I add. "We can do more in this village than survive." We recall Helen Keller's refrain: "I cried because I had no shoes until I met a man who had no feet." This is, unfortunately, no exaggeration. In India, you often see people with missing limbs.

I realize that now that we have found our way, we can share the food and money we have received with those who aren't as able as we are. Just when I think I've learned the lesson of our journey, I come upon a revelation that affects me profoundly: Everyone, even those of us who have already dedicated our lives to service, can always give more.

These three stages of transformation felt like a microcosm of the entire monk experience: First, we let go of the external and the ego; second, we recognize our value and learn that we don't need to own anything in order to serve; and third, we continually seek a higher level of service. On that trip I recognized that there is always room to rise, there is always more to give. Sister Christine Vladimiroff, a Benedictine nun, as quoted in *The Monastic Way*, wrote, "Monastic spirituality teaches us that we are on a journey. The journey is inward to seek God in prayer and silence. Taken alone, we can romanticize this aspect of our life. . . . But to be monastic there is a parallel journey—the journey outward. We live in community to grow in sensitivity to the needs of others. . . . The monastery is then a center to come out of and to invite others into. The key is always to maintain both journeys—inward and outward."

THE HIGHEST PURPOSE

In his lecture at my college, Gauranga Das had inspired me when he said, "Plant trees under whose shade you do not plan to sit." That sentence captivated me and launched me on a trajectory I had never imagined. And now I have to make a confession. I've been holding out on you. We have talked about how to let go of the influences of external noise, fear, envy, and false goals. We have explored how to grow by harnessing our minds, our egos, and our daily practices to live in our dharma. All of this is toward the goal of leading fulfilling, meaningful lives—a worthy path. But here, and on social media, and in my classes, and in every medium in which I teach, I haven't yet revealed the most important lesson I learned as a monk and one that I carry with me every day of my life. Drumroll, please.

The highest purpose is to live in service.

It's not that I've been keeping service a secret; I mention it often. But I've waited until now to talk about the central role I believe it should play in all of our lives because, frankly, I think most of us are somewhat resistant to the idea. Sure, we want to help those in need, and maybe we already find ways to do so, but we are limited by the pressure and needs of our own work and lives. We want to solve our own issues first. "Jay, I'm the one who needs help! I have so much to figure out before I can devote myself to helping others." It's true. It's hard to think about selflessness when we are struggling. And yet that is exactly what I learned as a monk. Selflessness is the surest route to inner peace and a meaningful life. **Selflessness heals the self.**

Monks live in service, and to think like a monk ultimately means to serve. *The Monastic Way* quotes Benedictine monk Dom Aelred

Graham as saying, "The monk may think he has come [to the monastery] to gain something for himself: peace, security, quiet, a life of prayer, or study, or teaching; but if his vocation is genuine, he finds that he has come not to take but to give." **We seek to leave a place cleaner than we found it, people happier than we found them, the world better than we found it.**

We are nature, and if we look at and observe nature carefully, nature is always serving. The sun provides heat and light. Trees give oxygen and shade. Water quenches our thirst. We can—and monks do—view everything in nature as serving. The Srimad-Bhagavatam says, "Look at these fortunate trees. They live solely for the benefit of others. They tolerate wind, rain, heat, and snow, but still provide shelter for our benefit." The only way to be one with nature is to serve. It follows that the only way to align properly with the universe is to serve because that's what the universe does.

The sixteenth-century guru Rupa Goswami talks about *yukta-vairāgya*, which means to do everything for a higher purpose. That's real detachment, utter renunciation, perfection. Some monk sects strictly apply this standard to their practices, stripping themselves of material possessions altogether, but in reality the rest of us need to work for a living. We're all going to end up owning stuff. But we can look at how we use what we have. We can use our homes to foster community. We can use our money and resources to support causes we believe in. We can volunteer our talents for those in need. It's not wrong to have things if we use them for good.

The Bhagavad Gita sees the whole world as a kind of school, an education system structured to make us realize one truth: We are compelled to serve, and only in service can we be happy. Like fire is hot, as the sun is light and warm, service is the essence of human consciousness. Know the reality of the world in which you live. Know it to be impermanent, unreal, and the source of your suffering and delusion. Seeing the purpose of life to be sense gratification—making ourselves feel good—leads to pain and dissatisfaction. Seeing it as service leads to fulfillment.

SERVICE IS GOOD FOR THE BODY AND SOUL

Service fulfills us on many levels, beginning with my simple belief that we're born wired to care for others so service does us good. This instinct is most obvious in children, who aren't yet distracted by other demands on their time and attention. An image that went viral shows a little girl, probably about two years old, watching a politician crying on Japanese TV. She takes a tissue, goes up to the TV, and tries to wipe away the politician's tears. Such things go viral because we recognize—and perhaps miss—the little girl's compassion for another person, even a stranger.

In *Long Walk to Freedom*, Nelson Mandela writes, "No one is born hating another person because of the color of his skin, or his background, or his religion. People must learn to hate, and if they can learn to hate, then they can be taught to love, for love comes more naturally to the human heart than its opposite." Just as Mandela believed people were born to love but taught to hate, monks believe that we are born to serve, but the distractions of the external world make us forget our purpose. We need to reconnect with that instinct in order to feel like life has meaning.

I have already touched on Joseph Campbell's concept of the mythic hero's journey. It is a formula describing the steps that a hero goes through when he embarks on an adventure, encounters trials and obstacles, and returns victorious. One of the key elements of the hero's journey is one we often overlook—the last stage, which Campbell called "return with elixir." The hero's journey isn't fulfilled until he makes it home safely and shares what he has gained (the elixir) with others. The idea of service is woven into classic story structure as a key part of a happy ending.

Seane Corn is living out the hero's journey. She made her name as a teacher of yoga asana. She was (and still is) a marquee teacher at yoga conferences and festivals around the world, but at one point in her career as a yoga teacher, she realized that with her platform, she could make an even more meaningful impact in the world, so she shifted her focus to serving at-risk communities. Corn decided to try bringing breath and meditation techniques to those in need, starting with kids who'd been sexually exploited. Then she grew her practice into working with other people society deems as outcasts, such as prostitutes and drug addicts. From that vantage point, she reached back into the yoga community to cofound Off the Mat, Into the World, a nonprofit that links yoga with activism. As dedicated as she is to service, Corn maintains that she gets more than she gives. "Find me someone who has gone to the darkest parts of their own character where they were so close to their own self-destruction and found a way to get up and out of it, and I will bow on my knees to you. . . . You're my teacher."

As Corn found, service gives back to us.

Studies show that when we pursue "compassionate goals"—those aimed at helping others or otherwise helping to make the world a better place—we're less likely to have symptoms of anxiety and depression than when we focus on improving or protecting our own status or reputation. The act of giving to others activates the pleasure center of our brain. It's win-win-win. This may be why those who help others tend to live longer, be healthier, and have a better overall sense of well-being.

Monks believe that the pillar of service makes our lives better in many ways.

Service connects us. When you serve, it's hard to be lonely. In most scenarios, you have to go out into the world to help other people.

Service amplifies gratitude. Service gives you a broad view of all that you have.

Service increases compassion. When you serve, you see that the world needs what you have to offer.

Service builds self-esteem. Helping others tells you that you're making a difference in the world. You have a sense of meaning and purpose.

The ashram is designed around the intention to serve, and it's easier to live with that as your highest intention when everyone around you is on board. A life of service is far more challenging in the modern world, and we can't all follow the monks' 24/7 model, but the monk practice shows us why and how we should adopt a service mindset.

THE SERVICE MINDSET

The word *seva* is Sanskrit for selfless service. The Bhagavad Gita says that "giving simply because it is right to give, without thought of return, at a proper time, in proper circumstances, and to a worthy person, is sattvic giving"—giving in the mode of goodness. Monks are solely motivated by selfless service: to give others opportunities that we had and didn't have; to better others' lives and the human condition. We took this mission to heart in small and large ways. Within the ashram, we tried to serve each other every day. Monks don't make grand gestures. Love is in the small things. If someone was having trouble waking up on time, we'd help them. If someone was working late, we'd save food for them. We are consistent and intentional. We remember that we never know what someone is going through, so we treat them with the gentleness you would give someone who is in pain, with the generosity you would give someone who is hungry, with the compassion you would give someone who is misunderstood.

This attitude radiated beyond the ashram. When we traveled, we always carried extra food with us so that we had some to give away. We weren't ending world hunger, but to help any hungry person is to water the seeds of compassion.

On a larger scale, we participated in a program called Annamrita, which provides more than a million meals a day to the underprivileged children of India. We often went to Mumbai to cook in the kitchens or to serve food in the schools. The students were given *kitchari*, a rice and lentil porridge made with ghee that's considered a staple in Ayurvedic cooking, and afterward they would receive dessert, a sweet rice pudding called *kheer*. The first time I handed a child *kheer*, her gratitude was so apparent that I was humbled. It was the same with every child, every time, each face radiating joy. I hate cooking—the hot kitchen full of people, the massive pots to be tended. But the kids' faces—and the sad truth they told about how rare and special the food was to them—made it easy to feel grateful for the opportunity to serve.

At the ashram, instead of saying "How was work?" we might ask,

"Have you served today?" If you were wondering what monk water-cooler talk sounds like—there you have it. Set aside the obstacles for a moment and imagine if everyone had a service mindset. We would ask ourselves new questions: *How does this serve a broader purpose? How am I serving the people around me—at work, at home, in my community? How can I use my talents to serve others and make a difference?* Remember Emma Slade, who uses her financial skills to serve her charity work, and ask yourself, "What do I know that is of any use?"

We have seen that happiness and gratitude spread through communities. The same is true for service. When you serve, you mention it to your friends. You might bring someone else with you. Someone joins you, and they tell two friends. When you participate in service, you do your part to spread the value of service in our culture.

Most people think about just one person: themselves. Maybe their radius of care is a bit bigger, including their immediate family. That's, maybe, five to ten people worrying about one another. But if you expand your radius of care, I believe that people feel it. If others extend their

TRY THIS: EXTEND YOUR RADIUS OF CARE

Think of four to six people you would drop everything to help. How often do you think about these people? Do you ever actually have a chance to show your care for them? Can you start?

Now think of twenty people you would help if they asked. Before you give up, let me make that easier for you. Think of a *group* containing at least twenty people whom you would help. It might be a segment of your community or a group that a charity already serves. Let's bring these people into a closer circle of care.

If you don't know them, research the names of twenty people in this group or find another way to compile a list of at least twenty names. Tape the list to the mirror where you brush your teeth. Now you'll think of them at least twice a day (I hope!). Observe how this changes your motivation to serve them.

radius of care to include you, I believe that you would feel it. And what if we dare to imagine that everyone were thinking like this? You would have some 7.8 billion people thinking about you, and vice versa. I don't see why we shouldn't dream big.

WHEN WILL YOU BE READY TO SERVE?

Out in the modern world, no matter how much we want to help others, we are distracted from the service mindset by the desire to be financially and emotionally stable and secure. If you're lost and disconnected, your service will be cumbersome and less fulfilling. But when is the time right? Will it ever be right? Internal exploration has no endpoint. It's an ongoing practice. Your problems will never be completely solved.

Take care of yourself—yes. But don't wait until you have enough time and money to serve. You will never have enough. There are three simple modes to describe our relationship with money and material wealth. The first is selfish—I want more—as much as I can get—and I want it all for myself. The second is sufficiency—I have just enough to get by. I'm not suffering, but I have nothing to give. The third is service—I want to give what I have, and I want more in order to give more.

Moving from the sufficiency mindset to the service mindset means changing our relationship with ownership—the more detached we are, the easier it is to let go of our time and money.

Some of our trips as monks were pilgrimages to bathe in the sacred rivers. I went to the Ganges, the Yamuna, and the Kaveri. We didn't swim or play in the holy waters. Instead, we performed rituals; one involved scooping as much water as we could into our hands, then putting it back in the river. We took from water to give back to water as a reminder that we didn't own anything. Charity isn't giving of yourself. You're taking something that was already on earth and giving it back to earth. **You don't have to have to give.**

Sindhutai Sapkal was married at twelve to a thirty-year-old man. When she was twenty years old, with three sons, nine months pregnant, she was beaten and thrown into a cow shed. She gave birth there, cutting her own umbilical cord with a sharp rock. Shunned by her maternal village, she lived on the streets with her newborn, begging and singing for money. She was struck by the number of orphans she saw and took them under her wing. She began begging on their behalf as well as her own. Her efforts grew, and she became known as the "Mother of Orphans." Her organizations have now housed and helped more than fourteen hundred children in India. Sindhutai didn't serve because she had something to give. She served because she saw pain.

In a series of experiments, researchers at University of California, Berkeley, found that people with less money actually tend to give more. In one situation, people were given $10 and told they could choose an amount to share with an anonymous stranger. People who were lower in socioeconomic status were more generous than wealthier participants. These findings are backed up by a survey of charitable giving in 2011, which showed that Americans in the bottom percentage of income gave, on average, 3 percent of their earnings to charity where people in the top 20 percent gave half that—1 percent. (Just to be fair, the wealthy are still responsible for over 70 percent of charitable contributions.)

Why those with less give more may have to do with their exposure to hardship. UC Berkeley professor of psychology Dacher Keltner says that people with fewer resources tend to need to lean on others—family members, friends, those in their community—for help. Those with more money, conversely, can "buy" help and are therefore more distanced from this kind of day-to-day struggle. The poor may have greater empathy for others in need. Some philanthropists, such as Oprah Winfrey, have mentioned their own prior experience of poverty as a motivation for giving.

The question to contemplate is: Who is wealthier, the one with money or the one who serves?

SERVE WITH INTENTION

I had come to the ashram to serve, and when I was saying my goodbyes, one monk who had been a like a big brother to me took me aside. He said something like, "If your health and being a monk isn't right for you, that doesn't mean you can't serve. If you feel you can serve better by being married or becoming a chef or darning socks for the needy, that takes priority. Service to humanity is the higher goal." His words reassured me that just because I was leaving didn't mean my intention had to change.

One can serve with a mix of intentions, broad and narrow. We might do it to be liked, to feel good about ourselves, to look good, to connect with other people, to receive some kind of reward. But if you're out there helping your friends move, cooking for them, celebrating them, and then you wonder, *Why doesn't anyone come help me?* or *Why did everyone forget my birthday?*—you've missed the point. You're seeing yourself as the giver and them as the receiver and imagining that when service is done, a debt is created. True service doesn't expect or even want anything in return. Nonetheless, the service itself often yields happiness, as both the Bhagavad Gita and the science show. When I do something to serve you, and you're happy, I'm happy.

But is service selfish if it brings you joy? Is it selfish if it teaches your children a lesson? Of course not! If a certain kind of giving makes you happy or benefits you in some way, that's a great place to start. After I left the ashram, I led retreats from London to Mumbai, giving people from the UK and other parts of Europe a chance to serve "midday meals" with Annamrita. One man who came on a retreat with me brought his kids, aged thirteen and fourteen. They returned from that trip having witnessed and felt the gratitude of people who didn't have much in their lives. The father was thrilled at how transformed his kids were. His trip was not completely selfless—he wanted his children to learn and grow—but it was still the right thing to do. In fact, the learning opportunity he saw for his children is an example of the mutual benefits of service.

The problems that some of us face are mental—anxiety, depression, loneliness—whereas for many of the people in need of service the greatest challenges are more basic—food, clothing, shelter. We can heal our mental challenges by helping them with their physical needs. Service, therefore, is a reciprocal exchange. You're not saving anyone by helping them—you need help as much as they do.

When we're in service, we're an instrument of grace and compassion. We feel this, and sometimes it goes to our heads. But remember that whatever you are giving was given to you. When you pass it on, you can't take credit for it.

SERVE WITHIN YOUR DHARMA

Because service is a natural part of being human, it's easier than you think. **Just serve.** We can always, every day—right now!—find ways to serve through what we're already doing. If you're a musician, serve. If you're a coder, serve. If you're an entrepreneur, serve. You don't have to change your occupation. You don't have to change your schedule. You can serve from any situation.

If you look around, you will see opportunities for service everywhere: in schools, at religious institutions, with individuals on the street, charities. There are neighborhood food drives and used costume drives at school. You can run a race to raise money for charity or have a lemonade stand. You can help a friend gather toiletries to send to disaster victims. You can visit a sick or aging relative. If you live in a city, you can often carry your leftovers out of a restaurant and offer them to a homeless person. Those closest to us, and those who have nobody—there are infinite ways to serve. You don't have to do charity work every day or give away all your money. Simply realize you're in service and look for how you can connect what you already do to a higher purpose. Just as you bring your dharma to work, bring service to your dharma. It's about the spirit in which you do the same work. You can either see the world through the lens of love and duty, or through the lens of necessity and force. Love and duty are more likely to lead to happiness.

TRY THIS: WAYS TO SERVE

Over the course of a week, write down every place where you spend time. Open your eyes to the service opportunities by looking for one in every circumstance. Sometimes it is a need that you spot, sometimes it is an existing project you can join, sometimes it is attaching a fundraiser to an activity you already do, sometimes it is a friend's service effort. At the end of the week, pick the three opportunities that interest you most and reach out to one of them.

Here are some sample places where you can look for opportunities:

Work
School
Social event with friend(s)
Online community
Religious or other community group
Gym
Requests for help from a cause you've supported in the past

ALL SUFFERING BELONGS TO ALL OF US

When the monks and I were fending for ourselves in the village, the ultimate lesson for me was that there was always another level of service. This lesson emerged from looking past our own needs to see and feel and respond to the needs of those around us.

I think of compassion as *active* empathy—not only the willingness to see, feel, and ease the pain of others, but also the willingness to take on some of that pain. There is a Zen story about a young man who is world-weary and dejected. With no plan or prospects, he goes to a monastery, tells the master that he is hoping to find a better path, but he admits that he lacks patience. "Can I find enlightenment without all that meditation and fasting?" he asks. "I don't think I can handle it. Is there another way?"

"Perhaps," says the master, "But you will need the ability to focus. Are there any skills you've developed?"

The young man looks down. He hasn't been inspired by his studies or any particular interests. Finally, he shrugs. "Well, I'm not bad at chess."

The master calls over one of the monk elders and says, "I'd like you and this young man to play a game of chess. Play carefully, because I will cut off the head of the one who loses."

The young man breaks into a sweat. He's playing for his life! He plays weakly at first, but it soon becomes clear that his opponent's chess skills are fair at best. If he puts his mind to it, he will surely win. He soon loses himself in concentration and begins to beat the old monk. The master begins to sharpen his sword.

Now the young man looks across the table, sees the wise, calm face of the old monk, who in his obedience and detachment has no fear of the death that certainly awaits him. The disillusioned man thinks, *I can't be responsible for this man's death. His life is worth more than mine.* Then the young man's play changes—he deliberately begins to lose.

Without warning, the master flips the table over, scattering the pieces. "Today there will be no winner, and no loser," he states. The losing monk's calm demeanor doesn't change, but the astonished young man feels a great sense of relief. The elder says to him, "You have the ability to concentrate, and you are willing to give your life for another. That is compassion. Join us and proceed in that spirit. You are ready to be a monk."

There are approximately 152 million child laborers in the world, and Kailash Satyarthi has taken on an enormous amount of pain in his effort to end child labor. In 2016 the Nobel Peace Laureate launched the 100 Million, a campaign to enlist 100 million young people to speak out and act against child labor. In the course of his work he has been threatened and beaten many times. He says, "The world is capable to end child labor. We have the technology. We have the resources. We have laws and international treaties. We have everything. The only thing is that we have to feel compassion for others. My struggle is for the globalization of compassion."

Like Satyarthi, we are motivated to serve when we think of the whole world as one family. You wouldn't want your child to be enslaved or your parent to be homeless. Why would you want those hardships for anyone else's child or parent? If you stay shut in your world and never see how other people live, you'll never be focused on service. When we bear witness to other people's pain, we feel our shared humanity and are motivated to take action.

For heroes like Satyarthi and for monks—and ideally for all of us—there is no us and them.

FOLLOW THE PAIN IN YOUR HEART

An infinite number of people and causes need our help now. We need everyone in the world to do everything. The benefits to them and us are immediate.

While we should never avoid helping others when we see their need, we can and should develop a sense of what sorts of service we're best at and focus our attention on them. Choose where to serve based on your own compassion. Buddhist scholar and environmental activist Joanna Macy writes, "You don't need to do everything. Do what calls your heart; effective action comes from love. It is unstoppable, and it is enough."

TRY THIS: SERVE THE PAIN THAT YOU KNOW BEST

One route to service is through healing the pain that we know best. Write down three moments in your life when you felt lost or in need. Maybe you were depressed and could have used support. Maybe you wanted an education you couldn't afford. Maybe you needed guidance but didn't have the right teacher. Match a charity or cause to each area of pain. A teen hotline. A scholarship fund. A mentoring program. A politician. Now see if any of these options have opportunities to serve that suit your dharma.

Serving through your dharma, healing the pain that you connect with—this approach is very much in line with the philosophy of the Bhagavad Gita, which likes to meet you wherever you are and encourage you to reach higher. When I was a monk, I prepared food for children with Annamrita, cleaned temples, always carried food to hand out to strangers, and otherwise served in the ways that made sense for me at the time. Now, with a different platform, I've been able to help a YouTube campaign raise nearly $150,000 for the Kailash Satyarthi Children's Foundation of America. On Facebook my community raised over $60,000 for Pencils of Promise. ($75 provides a year of education for one child.) The sense of meaning and gratitude I feel has been constant as my path of giving evolves.

Here's the life hack: Service is always the answer. It fixes a bad day. It tempers the burdens we bear. Service helps other people and helps us. We don't expect anything in return, but what we get is the joy of service. It's an exchange of love.

When you're living in service, you don't have time to complain and criticize.

When you're living in service, your fears go away.

When you're living in service, you feel grateful. Your material attachments diminish.

Service is the direct path to a meaningful life.

MEDITATION

CHANT

We have explored how to connect to people around us through gratitude, relationships, and service. As we do this it is fitting to incorporate sound meditation into our practice to connect with the energy of the universe.

Sound transports us. A song can take us back to a high school memory, make us want to dance, get us fired up. Words themselves have power—they can change how we see the world and how we grow. When we chant, we ourselves are generating this energy. Sound meditations allow us to connect with our souls and the universe through words and song.

Ancient spiritual texts including the Agni Purana and the Vayu Purana discuss the why and how of chanting, suggesting that the repetition of sound purifies us. The sound is immersive, like giving our souls a regular bath. You can't put one drop of water on your body and be clean—you have to go underneath the water.

Recognizing the value of sound has carried through to modern times. Legendary inventor Nikola Tesla said, "If you want to find the secrets of the universe, think in terms of energy, frequency, and vibration." Tesla experimented extensively with machines that created healing fields using vibrations. That may strike you as a bit woo-woo, but modern science is actually resurrecting Tesla's research on vibrational healing. Modern brain research is also starting to uncover scientific explanations for the healing power of ancient healing rituals, like how repetitive drumming and singing can open pathways to the subconscious.

Monks harness the power of sound by repeating affirmations or mantras during meditation. An affirmation is a word or phrase you want to set as an intention. Virtually anything that inspires you can work. One of my clients says her favorite is: "At your own pace, in your own time." A friend of mine read a book called *Brave, Not Perfect* by Reshma Saujani and made the title her mantra for a while. I also like: "This too shall pass." Or a phrase from a poet, such as "Live everything" (by Rilke); a sports quote, like "This moment is yours" (from Olympic ice hockey coach Herb Brooks); a song lyric, like "Brush your shoulders off" (by Jay-Z), something from a movie, like "Woosah" (courtesy of *Bad Boys II*). Anything that connects you to the energy or idea you want to cultivate in your life can be effective. I recommend adding a mantra to your morning and/or evening meditation practice. It is beautiful to wake up or go to sleep listening to the sound of your own voice chanting.

Where affirmations change the way you speak to yourself, mantras change the way you speak to the universe. *Mantra* in a deep sense means "to transcend the mind," and a mantra is a spiritual sound expressing thought and meaning that summons a power greater than ourselves. Mantras can be chanted or sung in unison. We meditate to listen and find clarity. We pray to share and find connection with a higher power. Chanting is both—a dialogue with the universe.

The oldest, most common, and most sacred mantra is Om. In Vedic texts the sound is given many shades of meaning, from infinite knowledge to the essence of everything that exists to the whole Veda. Om also is called *pranava*, whose meaning can be described as "the sound by which the Lord is praised." In chanting, om comprises three syllables—A-U-M. In Vedic tradition, this is important because each sound embodies a different state (wakefulness, dreaming, and deep sleep) or period of time itself (past, present, and future). You could say that the word *om* represents everything.

The vibrations from om have been shown to stimulate the vagus nerve, which decreases inflammation. Vagus nerve stimulation is also used as a treatment for depression, and researchers are looking at whether chanting om may have a direct effect on mood. (It's already been shown to calm one of the brain's emotional centers.)

When a mantra is put to music it's called *kirtan*, a type of call-and-response chanting, which we often used at the ashram. A similar experience is fans chanting in a stadium—minus the alcohol and foul language. But the atmosphere that can be created has the same feeling of united energy.

Though sound itself is of value, when I temporarily lost my voice for medical reasons, I reached out to a monk teacher. I said, "I can't chant mantras. How can I meditate?"

He said, "Chanting was never from your mouth. It was always from your heart." He meant that, as with all acts, what mattered was whether the intention was full of devotion and love. The heart transcends instructions and perfection.

TRY THIS: **SEEING THROUGH SOUND**

For the sound exercises I describe below, begin your practice with the following steps.

1. Find a comfortable position—sitting in a chair, sitting upright with a cushion, or lying down.
2. Close your eyes.
3. Lower your gaze.
4. Make yourself comfortable in this position.

5. Bring your awareness to calm, balance, ease, stillness, and peace.
6. Whenever your mind wanders, just gently and softly bring it back to calm, balance, ease, stillness, and peace.
7. Chant each of these mantras three times each. When you chant them, bring your attention to each syllable. Pronounce it properly so that you can hear the vibration clearly. Really feel the mantra, repeating it genuinely and sincerely, and visualizing a more insightful, blessed, and service-filled life.

1. OM NAMO BHAGAVATE VASUDEVAYA

"I offer praise unto the all-pervading divinity present within every heart; who is the embodiment of beauty, intelligence, strength, wealth, fame, and detachment."

This mantra has been chanted for millennia by yogis and sages. It is cleansing and empowering, and connects one with the divinity in everything. It can be recited especially when you are seeking insight and guidance.

2. OM TAT SAT

"The absolute truth is eternal."

This mantra appears in the Bhagavad Gita. It represents divine energy and invokes powerful blessings. All work is performed as an offering of love and service. This mantra is recited especially before beginning any important work, to help perfect and refine our intentions and bring about balance and wholeness.

3. LOKAH SAMASTAH SUKHINO BHAVANTU

"May all beings everywhere be happy and free, and may the thoughts, words, and actions of my own life contribute in some way to that happiness and to that freedom for all."

This mantra, popularized by Jivamukti yoga, is a beautiful reminder to look beyond ourselves and to remember our place in the universe.

Conclusion

I hope this book has inspired you, and perhaps you will come away from it planning a fresh start. Maybe you're thinking about how to change your routines, to listen to your mind in new ways, to bring more gratitude into your life, and more. But when you wake up tomorrow, things will go wrong. You might sleep through your alarm. Something will break. An important appointment will cancel. The universe isn't going to suddenly give you green lights all the way to work. It's a mistake to think that when we read a book, attend a class, and implement changes that we'll fix everything. The externals will never be perfect, and the goal isn't perfection. Life is not going to go your way. You have to go your way and take life with you. Understanding this will help you be prepared for whatever may come.

There is no universal plan for peace and purpose. The way we get there is by training our minds to focus on how to react, respond, and commit to what we want in life, in our own pace, at our own time. Then, when life swerves, we return to that focus. If you've decided to be kind, and someone is rude to you, you know what you want to come back to. If you wake up resolved to focus on your dharma at work, and then your boss gives you an assignment that's not aligned with your strengths, it's up to you to find a way to put your dharma to use. When you fail, don't judge the process and don't judge yourself. Give yourself latitude to recover and return to a flexible focus on what you want. The world isn't with you or against you. You create your own reality in every moment.

Throughout this book, we have encountered paradoxes. We talk about getting close to fear to move away from it, finding the new in our routines, having confidence and humility, being selfish to be selfless. We live in a binary world, but the beauty of paradox is that two opposing ideas can coexist. Life isn't a computer program—it's a dance.

In *The Karate Kid*, Mr. Miyagi says, "Never trust [a] spiritual leader who cannot dance." When we dance, there are no rules. We must be open to whatever song comes on. We have strengths and weaknesses. We might fall, or hesitate over our next move, or have a moment of overenthusiasm, but we keep flowing, allowing ourselves to be messy and beautiful. Like a dancer, the monk mind is flexible and controlled, always present in the moment.

THE MONK METHOD

I can think of no better tool to help you find flexibility and control than meditation. Meditation helps you figure out what move to make in the dance. In meditation, we find clarity on who we need to be right now, in order to be our best in the moment. Our breath connects with our minds, our souls are uplifted in song, and in that place of energy and unity, we find answers.

I have introduced you to three different types of meditation, and now I'm going to give you a daily practice that includes all of them: breathwork, visualization, and chanting. I practice some form of this meditation every day. I recommend that you make it the first thing you do in the morning after brushing your teeth and showering, and last thing you do before bed. Start with twenty-one minutes once a day, using a timer to give yourself seven minutes each for breathwork, visualization, and mantra. When you are ready for more, expand to twenty-one minutes twice a day, ideally first thing in the morning and last thing at night. Make sure you always begin with breathwork. Like a warm-up before you exercise, it should not be skipped!

1. Find a comfortable position—sitting in a chair, sitting upright with a cushion, or lying down.
2. Close your eyes and lower your gaze. Bring your awareness to calm, balance, ease, stillness, and peace. It is natural for the chatter and clutter to be busy in your mind. Whenever your mind wanders, just gently and softly bring it back to calm, balance, ease, stillness, and peace.
3. Make yourself comfortable in this position. Roll back your shoulders, stretch your neck and body, and find a physical space of calm, balance, ease, stillness, and peace.
4. Now become aware of your natural breathing pattern. Breathe in through your nose and out through your mouth.
5. Take a deep breath. Breathe in for a count of 1 - 2 - 3 - 4. Breathe out for a count of 1 - 2 - 3 - 4.
6. Align your body and your breath by breathing in for the same amount of time as you breathe out.
7. Do this for what feels like five minutes. At first you might want to set a timer with a pleasant tone to signal that the five minutes have passed.
8. Ask yourself, "What am I grateful for today?" Breathe in gratitude and breathe out negative, toxic energy.
9. Now visualize a joy-, happiness-, and gratitude-filled memory. Think of five things you can see, four things you can touch, three things you can hear, two things you can smell, and one thing you can taste. Absorb the love, joy, and happiness. Take the love from that moment and visualize it flowing through your entire body. From your feet, to your legs, to your hips, to your stomach, to your chest, arms, back, neck, and head. Give love, joy, and gratitude to each part of your body. Do this for five minutes.
10. Ask yourself, "What is my intention for today?" Is it to be kind, to be confident, to be focused? Set that intention now.

11. Repeat the following to yourself 3 times each: "I am happy about who I am becoming. I am open to all opportunities and possibilities. I am worthy of real love. I am ready to serve with all I have."
12. To finish your practice, repeat this mantra 3 times: *Lokah Samastah Sukhino Bhavantu.* (See page 273.)

HOW TO KNOW IF IT'S WORKING

A novice monk went to his teacher and said, "I'm terrible at meditating. My feet fall asleep, and I'm distracted by the outside noises. When I'm not uncomfortable, it's because I can barely stay awake."

"It will pass," the teacher said simply, and by her expression the novice knew that the conversation was over.

A month passed, and the novice took his teacher aside, smiling proudly. "I think I've figured it out! I feel so serene—more focused and centered than I've ever been. My meditation is beautiful."

"It will pass," the teacher replied.

There is no measure of success, no goal, and no end to a meditation practice. Don't look for results. Just keep doing it. Practice consistently for four to twelve weeks, and you'll start to notice the effects.

The first sign that you're doing it right is that you'll miss it if you take a break. You only miss a person when you don't see them. When you eat every day, you don't think much about nourishment and fuel, but if you don't eat for a day, you quickly notice the power of food. The same is true for meditation—you have to develop a practice before you know what you're missing.

The second effect you'll notice is an increased awareness of what's going on in your mind. If you meditate and feel tired, you'll understand that meditation is telling you to get more sleep. Meditation is a signal or a mirror. If you meditate and can't focus, you'll see that you're living a distracted life and need to feel order, balance, and simplicity. If you can't sit with your thoughts for fifteen minutes, it's a clear indicator of the work to be done.

The third and most important benefit of meditation is that, though you won't emerge feeling calm and perfect every time, you'll gradually acquire a long-term mastery of self. When you drink a green juice, it doesn't always taste great. A nice glass of fresh orange juice looks better and tastes better. But, long-term, the less delightful green juice will better serve you. When you are adept at meditation, you'll feel a shift in your general attitude. Your intuition will be sharper. You'll be able to observe your life more objectively, without being self-centered. Your expanded perception will give you a sense of peace and purpose.

NOW AND FOREVER

Life begins with breath, breath carries you through all your days, and life and breath end together. Monks try to be present in the moment, but we are always conscious of now and forever. We measure our lives not by how big or small our impact is, but by how we make people feel. We use our time to establish how we will live on, through giving love and care, through supporting, communicating, creating—through the impact we have on humanity.

How will we be remembered? What will we leave behind?

Ultimately death can be seen as the greatest reflection point—by imagining the last moment you can reflect on everything that leads up to it.

Among the most common regrets dying people express are:

I wish I'd expressed my love to the people I care about.
I wish I hadn't worked so much.
I wish I'd taken more pleasure in life.
I wish I'd done more for other people.

Notice that most of these regrets address something the person *didn't* do. Monks believe we should prepare for death. We don't want to arrive at the end of our days knowing we haven't lived a purposeful, service-based, meaningful life.

Think of the topics we've considered in this book. In death, you should be fully cleansed, free of what you think you're supposed to do, free of comparison and criticism, having faced the root of your fear, free from material desires, living in your dharma, having used your time well, having not given in to the mind's demands, free from ego, having given more than you have taken, but then having given away all that you've taken, free from entitlement, free from false connections and expectations. Imagine how rewarding it will be to look back on a life where you have been a teacher while remaining a student.

Reflecting on the knowledge that we will die someday compels us to value the time we have and to spend our energy thoughtfully. Life's too short to live without purpose, to lose our chance to serve, to let our dreams and aspirations die with us. Above all, I ask you to leave people and places better and happier than you found them.

Working on ourselves is an unending practice. Have patience. A student went to her teacher and said, "I am committed to my dharma. How long will it take me to attain enlightenment?"

Without missing a beat, the teacher replied, "Ten years."

Impatient, the student persisted, "But what if I work very hard? I will practice, ten or more hours every day if I have to. Then how long will it take?"

This time the teacher took a moment to consider. "Twenty years."

The very idea that the student was looking to rush his work was evidence that he had ten extra years to study.

As I've mentioned, the Sanskrit word for monk, *brahmacharya*, means "student," but it also means "right use of energy." It's not like once you have the monk mindset, you've figured everything out. Instead, the monk mindset acknowledges that the right use of energy is to remain a student. You can never cease learning. You don't cut your hair or mow your lawn once. You have to keep at it. In the same way, *sustaining* the monk mindset requires self-awareness, discipline, diligence, focus, and constant practice. It is hard work, but the tools are already in your head, heart, and hands.

You have all you need to think like a monk.

TRY THIS: TWO DEATH MEDITATIONS

To imagine your own death gives you a bird's-eye view of your life. Try a death meditation whenever you are questioning whether or not to do something—to make a significant change, learn a new skill, take a trip. I recommend that you always do a death meditation at the beginning of a new year, to inspire new paths in the upcoming year.

1. Visualizing the inevitable will give you every lesson you need to live a fulfilling life. Fast-forward to yourself at age eighty or ninety, however long you want to live, and imagine yourself on your deathbed. Ask your future self questions such as:

   What do I wish I'd done?
   What experiences do I wish I'd had?
   What do I regret not giving more attention?
   What skills do I wish I'd worked on?
   What do I wish I'd detached from?

   Use these answers to motivate yourself—instead of having regrets on your deathbed, put those wishes into action today.

2. Imagine how you'd like to be remembered at your own funeral. Don't focus on what people thought of you, who loved you, and how sad they will be to lose you. Instead think about the impact you've had. Then imagine how you would be remembered if you died today. What's the gap between these two images? This too should galvanize you to build your legacy.

To find our way through the universe, we must start by genuinely asking questions. You might travel to a new place or go someplace where no one knows you. Disable your autopilot to see yourself and the world around you with new eyes. **Spot, Stop, Swap.** Train your mind to observe the forces that influence you, detach from illusion and false beliefs, and continually look for what motivates you and what feels meaningful.

What would a monk do in this moment?

When you're making a decision, when you're having an argument, when you're planning your weekend, when you're scared or upset or angry or lost, ask this question. You'll find the answer 99 percent of the time.

And eventually, when you've uncovered your real self, you won't even need to ask yourself what a monk would do. You can simply ask, "What will I do?"

Appendix

The Vedic Personality Test

Answer these questions as who you believe you are at the core. Beyond what friends, family, or society have made you choose.

1. Which of the following sounds *most* like what you're about?
a. Values and wisdom
b. Integrity and perfection
c. Work hard play hard
d. Stability and balance

2. What *role* do you play in your friends circle / family?
a. I am comfortable dealing with conflict and helping people find middle ground. My role is the mediator.
b. I make sure everything and everyone is taken care of. My role is the protector.
c. I help my family understand work ethic, hustle, and the value of having resources. My role is material support.
d. I focus on nurturing and wanting a healthy and content family. My role is emotional support.

3. What is most important to you in a partner?
a. Honest and smart
b. Strong presence and power
c. Fun and dynamic
d. Reliable and respectful

4. What do you watch most often on TV?
a. Documentaries, biographies, human observations
b. Entertainment, politics, current affairs
c. Comedy, sport, drama, motivational stories
d. Soap operas, reality TV, family, gossip, daytime shows

5. Which best describes how you behave when under stress?
a. Calm, composed, balanced
b. Irritated, frustrated, angry
c. Moody, loud, restless
d. Lazy, depressed, worried

6. What causes you the most pain?
a. Feeling like I don't live up to my own expectations
b. The state of the world
c. A sense of rejection
d. Feeling disconnected from friends and family

7. What is your favorite way of working?
a. Alone, but with mentors and guides
b. In a team as a leader
c. Independently, but with a strong network
d. In a team as a member

8. How would your *ideal* self spend spare time?
a. Reading, in deep discussion, and reflecting
b. Learning about issues and/or attending political events

c. There's no such thing as spare time! networking, connecting, working
d. Enjoying time with family and friends

9. How would you describe yourself in three words?
a. Idealistic, introverted, insightful
b. Driven, dedicated, determined
c. Passionate, motivated, friendly
d. Caring, loving, loyal

10. In what type of environment do you work best?
a. Remote, silent and still, natural
b. A meeting room or gathering space
c. Anywhere and everywhere (during my commute, in a coffee shop, in my bedroom)
d. A space specific to my type of work: home, office, laboratory

11. What's your work style?
a. Slow and reflective
b. Focused and organized
c. Fast and rushed
d. Specific and deliberate

12. How would you like to make a difference in the world?
a. Through spreading knowledge
b. Through politics and activism
c. Through business and/or leadership
d. Through local community

13. How do you prepare for a vacation?
a. By picking my reading material
b. By having a focused plan of key sites to visit
c. With a list of the best bars, clubs, and restaurants
d. With an easygoing attitude

14. How do you deal with tough conversations?
   a. Look for a compromise
   b. Fight for the most objective truth
   c. Fight to prove I'm right
   d. Avoid confrontation

15. If someone in your life is having a bad week, what do you do?
   a. Give them advice and guidance
   b. Become protective and encourage them to improve
   c. Urge them to have a drink or take a walk with me
   d. Go to them and keep them company

16. How do you see rejection?
   a. It's part of life
   b. It's a challenge I can rise to meet
   c. It's frustrating but I'll move on
   d. It's a real setback

17. At an event/party how do you spend your time?
   a. I have a meaningful discussion with one or two people
   b. I usually talk with a group of people
   c. I somehow end up the center of attention
   d. I help with whatever needs to be done

18. How do you feel if you make a mistake?
   a. I feel guilty and ashamed
   b. I have to tell everyone
   c. I want to hide it
   d. I reach out to someone supportive

19. What do you do when you have to make a big decision?
   a. I reflect privately
   b. I ask my mentors and guides

c. I weigh the pros and cons
d. I talk to family and friends

20. Which best describes your daily routine?
   a. It changes moment to moment
   b. It's very focused and organized
   c. I follow the best opportunity that comes up
   d. It's simple and scheduled

ANSWER KEY

Tally your answers now. The most selected letter likely reflects your *varna*.

A. Guide
B. Leader
C. Creator
D. Maker

Acknowledgments

I feel truly humbled and grateful to share this timeless and transformative wisdom with you, but I could not have done it alone. The Bhagavad Gita was compiled, preserved, shared, and resurrected by team efforts, and this book was no different. I'd like to thank Dan Schawbel, for introducing me to my amazing agent, James Levine, over three years ago. Jim is truly a wonderful human and deeply believes in every project that he works on. His direction, strategy, and friendship have made this book an extremely joyful journey. Thank you to Trudy Green, for her unlimited kindness, sleepless nights, and eternal dedication to this cause. To Eamon Dolan, for his already monk mind and unrelenting push for perfection. To Jon Karp, for believing in me and being present throughout the process. To Hilary Liftin, for the collaborative conversations and dynamic discussions. To Kelly Madrone, for her undying enthusiasm and can-do attitude. To Rula Zaabri, for making sure I never missed a deadline. To Ben Kalin, for his relentless commitment to checking the facts. Thank you, Christie Young, for bringing these timeless concepts to life through the beautiful illustrations. To the Oxford Center for Hindu Studies and specifically Shaunaka Rishi Das for assisting in verifying our sources and credits. Thank you to Laurie Santos for her kindness in connecting me with research on monks by some of the world's leading scientists. To the whole team at Simon & Schuster, who left no gaps in bringing my vision to life. To Oliver Malcolm and his team at HarperCollins UK, for their enthusiasm, dedication, and hard work from the start.

Thank you to Thomas Power, who pushed me to recognize my potential when I didn't believe in myself. To Ellyn Shook, for believing in my passion and introducing my work to Arianna Huffington. To Danny Shea and Dan Katz, who helped me launch my career at *HuffPost.* To Karah Preiss, who was the first person I told about the idea for this book, in 2016, and who became my ideation partner and greatest supporter in the US. To Savannah, Hoda, Craig, Al, and Carson, for giving me their collective attention on the *Today* show. To Ellen, for believing in me and giving me her platform to reach her audience. To Jada Pinkett Smith, Willow Smith, and Adrienne Banfield-Norris, for bringing me to the Red Table.

I've truly had an amazing few years, but everything you've seen online has only been possible due to the people that invested in me offline. Thank you to His Holiness Radhanath Swami, for always reminding me of the true meaning of life. To Gauranga Das, who has seen it all and been there for me since Day One. To my mentor Srutidharma Das, who always, no matter what, displays all the qualities in this book to the highest level. To Sutapa Das, who always encouraged me to write when I told him I just wanted to speak. To the guides I long to meet and thank, His Holiness the Dalai Lama and Thich Nhat Hanh. To all who have allowed me to mentor you, in that process you have taught me so much more than I could ever have imagined.

This book would not have existed without the Vedas, the Bhagavad Gita, and the teachers who tirelessly spread it across the world. Thank you to Srila Prabhupada and Ekanath Easwaran, who have created the most widely distributed Gitas today. To all my teachers in the ashram and across the world, many of whom have no idea how much they've given me.

To my mother, who is the embodiment of selfless service. To my father, who let me become who I wanted to be. To my sister, for always supporting my crazy decisions and loving me no matter what.

And, of course, to each and every one of you who has read this book. You were already thinking like monks, now you know it.

Author's Note

In this book I have drawn from the wisdom of many religions, cultures, inspirational leaders, and scientists. In every case I have done my very best to attribute quotes and ideas to their original sources, and these efforts are reflected here. In some cases I have come across wonderful quotes or ideas that I have found attributed to multiple different sources, widely attributed with no specified source, or attributed to ancient texts where I could not locate the original verse. In these cases I have, with the help of a researcher, tried to give the reader as much useful information as I could regarding the source of the material.

Notes

INTRODUCTION

ix **plant trees under whose shade:** Paraphrase of Nelson Henderson from Wes Henderson, *Under Whose Shade: A Story of a Pioneer in the Swan River Valley of Manitoba* (Ontario, Canada: W. Henderson & Associates, 1986).

x **In 2002, a Tibetan monk named Yongey Mingyur Rinpoche:** Daniel Goleman and Richard J. Davidson, *Altered Traits: Science Reveals How Meditation Changes Your Mind, Brain, and Body* (New York: Penguin Random House, 2017); Antoine Lutz, Lawrence L. Greischar, Nancy B. Rawlings, Matthieu Ricard, and Richard J. Davidson, "Long-Term Meditators Self-Induce High-Amplitude Gamma Synchronicity During Mental Practice," *Proceedings of the National Academy of Sciences* 101, no. 46 (November 16, 2004): 16369–16373, https://doi.org/10.1073/pnas.0407401101.

xi **scans of the forty-one-year-old monk's brain showed fewer signs of aging than his peers':** Goleman and Davidson, *Altered Traits.*

xi **Researchers who scanned Buddhist monk Matthieu Ricard's brain:** Frankie Taggart, "This Buddhist Monk Is the World's Happiest Man," *Business Insider*, November 5, 2012. https://www.businessinsider.com/how-scientists-figured-out-who-the-worlds-happiest-man-is-2012-11; Daniel Goleman and Richard J. Davidson, *Altered Traits: Science Reveals How Meditation Changes Your Mind, Brain, and Body* (New York: Penguin Random House, 2017); Antoine Lutz, Lawrence L. Greischar, Nancy B. Rawlings, Matthieu Ricard, and Richard J. Davidson, "Long-Term Meditators Self-Induce High-Amplitude Gamma Synchronicity During Mental Practice,"

Proceedings of the National Academy of Sciences 101, no. 46 (November 16, 2004): 16369–16373, https://doi.org/10.1073/pnas.0407401101.

xi **Twenty-one other monks:** Taggart, "This Buddhist Monk" and Lutz et al., "Long-Term Meditators."

xi **even during sleep:** Fabio Ferrarelli, Richard Smith, Daniela Dentico, Brady A. Riedner, Corinna Zennig, Ruth M. Benca, Antoine Lutz, Richard J. Davidson, and Guilio Tononi, "Experienced Mindfulness Meditators Exhibit Higher Parietal-Occipital EEG Gamma Activity During NREM Sleep," *PLoS One* 8, no. 8 (August 28, 2013): e73417, https://doi.org/10.1371/journal.pone.0073417.

xii **Brother David Steindl-Rast, a Benedictine monk:** David Steindl-Rast, *i am through you so i: Reflections at Age 90* (New York: Paulist Press, 2017), 87.

xiv **"India's most important gift to the world":** And general background on Vedic times from *The Bhagavad Gita*, introduction and translation by Eknath Easwaran (Tomales, CA: Nilgiri Press, 2007), 13–18.

xiv **"I owed—my friend and I owed":** Ralph Waldo Emerson, *The Bhagavad-Gita: Krishna's Counsel in Time of War*, translation, introduction, and afterword by Barbara Stoler Miller (New York: Bantam Dell, 1986), 147.

ONE: IDENTITY

3 **"I am not what I think I am":** Charles Horton Cooley, *Human Nature and the Social Order* (New York: Charles Scribner's Sons, 1902), 152.

4 **six films since 1998:** Daniel Day-Lewis filmography, IMDb, accessed November 8, 2019, https://www.imdb.com/name/nm0000358/?ref_=fn_al_nm_1.

4 **"I will admit that I went mad, totally mad":** Chris Sullivan, "How Daniel Day-Lewis's Notorious Role Preparation Has Yielded Another Oscar Contender," *Independent*, February 1, 2008, https://www.independent.co.uk/arts-entertainment/films/features/how-daniel-day-lewis-notoriously-rigorous-role-preparation-has-yielded-another-oscar-contender-776563.html.

8 **the words of Chaitanya:** Śrī Caitanya-caritāmṛta, Antya, 20.21.

8 **The foundation of virtually all monastic traditions:** "Social and Institutional Purposes: Conquest of the Spiritual Forces of Evil," Encyclopaedia Britannica, accessed November 8, 2019, https://www.britannica.com/topic/monasticism/Social-and-institutional-purposes.

11 **Our inclination is to avoid silence:** Timothy D. Wilson, David A. Reinhard, Erin C. Westgate, Daniel T. Gilbert, Nicole Ellerbeck, Cheryl Hahn, Casey L. Brown, and Adi Shaked, "Just Think: The Challenges of the Disengaged Mind," *Science* 345, no. 6192 (July 4, 2014): 75–77, doi: 10.1126/science.1250830.

12 **spend thirty-three years in bed:** Gemma Curtis, "Your Life in Numbers," Creative Commons, accessed November 15, 2019, https://www.dreams.co.uk/sleep-matters-club/your-life-in-numbers-infographic/.

13 **looking at TV and social media:** Ibid.

15 **According to the Gita, these are the higher values and qualities:** Verses 16.1–5 from *The Bhagavad Gita*, introduction and translation by Eknath Easwaran (Tomales, CA: Nilgiri Press, 2007), 238–239.

18 **A twenty-year study of people living in a Massachusetts town:** James H. Fowler and Nicholas A. Christakis, "Dynamic Spread of Happiness in a Large Social Network: Longitudinal Analysis over 20 Years in the Framingham Heart Study," *BMJ* 337, no. a2338 (December 5, 2008), doi: https://doi.org/10.1136/bmj.a2338.

TWO: NEGATIVITY

21 **As the Buddha advised:** Verse 4.50 from *The Dhammapada*, introduction and translation by Eknath Easwaran (Tomales, CA: Nilgiri Press, 2007), 118.

23 **Stanford psychologists took 104 subjects:** Emily M. Zitek, Alexander H. Jordan, Benoît Monin, and Frederick R. Leach, "Victim Entitlement to Behave Selfishly," *Journal of Personality and Social Psychology* 98, no. 2 (2010): 245–255, doi: 10.1037/a0017168.

24 **In the 1950s Solomon Asch:** Eliot Aronson and Joshua Aronson, *The Social Animal*, 12th edition (New York: Worth Publishers, 2018).

24 **We're wired to conform:** Zhenyu Wei, Zhiying Zhao, and Yong Zheng, "Neural Mechanisms Underlying Social Conformity," *Frontiers in Human Neuroscience* 7 (2013): 896, doi: 10.3389/fnhum.2013.00896.

24 **even people who report feeling better after venting:** Brad J. Bushman, "Does Venting Anger Feed or Extinguish the Flame? Catharsis, Rumination, Distraction, Anger, and Aggressive Responding," *Personality and Social Psychology Bulletin* (June 1, 2002), doi: 10.1177/0146167202289002.

25 **Studies also show that long-term stress:** Robert M. Sapolsky, "Why Stress Is Bad for Your Brain," *Science* 273, no. 5276 (August 9, 1996): 749–750, doi: 10.1126/science.273.5276.749.

28 **Catholic monk Father Thomas Keating said:** Thomas Keating, *Invitation to Love 20th Anniversary Edition: The Way of Christian Contemplation* (London: Bloomsbury Continuum, 2012).

29 **"Letting go gives us freedom":** Thich Nhat Hanh, *The Heart of the Buddha's Teaching: Transforming Suffering into Peace, Joy, and Liberation* (New York: Harmony, 1999).

30 **"Don't count the teeth":** Arthur Jeon, *City Dharma: Keeping Your Cool in the Chaos* (New York: Crown Archetype, 2004), 120.

31 **Sister Christine Vladimiroff says:** Hannah Ward and Jennifer Wild, eds., *The Monastic Way: Ancient Wisdom for Contemporary Living: A Book of Daily Readings* (Grand Rapids, MI: Wm. B. Eerdmans, 2007), 183.

31 **Competition breeds envy:** William Buck, *Mahabharata* (Delhi: Motilal Banarsidass Publishers, 2004), 341.

35 **The Vaca Sutta, from early Buddhist scriptures:** Thanissaro Bhikku, trans., "Vaca Sutta: A Statement," AccesstoInsight.org, accessed November 11, 2019, https://www.accesstoinsight.org/tipitaka/an/an05/an05.198.than.html.

36 **writing in a journal about upsetting events:** Bridget Murray, "Writing to Heal: By Helping People Manage and Learn from Negative Experiences, Writing Strengthens Their Immune Systems as Well as Their Minds," *Monitor on Psychology* 33, no. 6 (June 2002): 54.

36 **the *Harvard Business Review* lists nine more specific words:** Susan David, "3 Ways to Better Understand Your Emotions," *Harvard Business Review*, November 10, 2016, https://hbr.org/2016/11/3-ways-to-better-understand-your-emotions.

37 **Radhanath Swami is my spiritual teacher:** Radanath Swami, interview by Jay Shetty, *#FollowTheReader with Jay Shetty*, *HuffPost*, November 7, 2016, https://www.youtube.com/watch?v=JW1Am81L0wc.

39 **The Bhagavad Gita describes three *gunas*:** Verse 14.5–9 from *The Bhagavad Gita*, introduction and translation by Eknath Easwaran (Tomales, CA: Nilgiri Press, 2007), 224–225.

40 **Research at Luther College:** Loren L. Toussaint, Amy D. Owen, and Alyssa Cheadle, "Forgive to Live: Forgiveness, Health, and Longevity," *Journal of Behavioral Medicine* 35, no. 4 (August 2012), 375–386. doi: 10.1007/s10865-011-9632-4.

41 **Transformational forgiveness is linked:** Kathleen A. Lawler, Jarred W. Younger, Rachel L. Piferi, Rebecca L. Jobe, Kimberly A. Edmondson, and Warren H. Jones, "The Unique Effects of Forgiveness on Health: An Exploration of Pathways," *Journal of Behavioral Medicine* 28, no. 2 (April 2005): 157–167, doi: 10.1007/s10865-005-3665-2.

41 **sixty-eight married couples agreed:** Peggy A. Hannon, Eli J. Finkel, Madoka Kumashiro, and Caryl E. Rusbult, "The Soothing Effects of Forgiveness on Victims' and Perpetrators' Blood Pressure," *Personal Relationships* 19, no. 2 (June 2012): 279–289, doi: 10.1111/j.1475-6811.2011.01356.x.

44 **"I became a Buddhist because I hated my husband":** Pema Chödrön, "Why I Became a Buddhist," *Sounds True*, February 14, 2008, https://www.youtube.com/watch?v=A4slnjvGjP4&t=117s; Pema Chödrön, "How to Let Go and Accept Change," interview by Oprah Winfrey, *Super Soul Sunday*,

Oprah Winfrey Network, October 15, 2014. https://www.youtube.com/watch?v=SgJ1xfhJneA.

44 **Ellen DeGeneres sees the line clearly:** Anne-Marie O'Neill, "Ellen DeGeneres: 'Making People Feel Good Is All I Ever Wanted to Do,'" *Parade*, October 27, 2011, https://parade.com/133518/annemarieoneill/ellen-degeneres-2/.

THREE: FEAR

46 **his commencement address at Yale University:** "Tom Hanks Addresses the Yale Class of 2011," Yale University, May 22, 2011, https://www.youtube.com/watch?v=baIlinqoExQ.

49 **one of the world's leading security experts:** Gavin de Becker, *The Gift of Fear* (New York: Dell, 1998).

50 **Biosphere 2:** Tara Brach, "Nourishing Heartwood: Two Pathways to Cultivating Intimacy," *Psychology Today*, August 6, 2018, https://www.psychologytoday.com/us/blog/finding-true-refuge/201808/nourishing-heartwood.

50 **Alex Honnold stunned the world:** *Free Solo*, directed by Jimmy Chin and Elizabeth Chai Vasarhelyi, Little Monster Films and Itinerant Films, 2018.

56 **In the words of Śāntideva:** Śāntideva, *A Guide to the Bodhisattva Way of Life*, trans. Vesna A. Wallace and B. Alan Wallace (New York: Snow Lion, 1997).

60 **deep breathing activates:** Christopher Bergland, "Diaphragmatic Breathing Exercises and Your Vagus Nerve," *Psychology Today*, May 16, 2017, https://www.psychologytoday.com/us/blog/the-athletes-way/201705/diaphragmatic-breathing-exercises-and-your-vagus-nerve.

62 **"What you run from":** Chuck Palahniuk, *Invisible Monsters Remix* (New York: W. W. Norton & Company, 2018).

63 **one of the largest producers:** "Basic Information About Landfill Gas," Landfill Methane Outreach Program, accessed November 12, 2019, https://www.epa.gov/lmop/basic-information-about-landfill-gas.

FOUR: INTENTION

65 **"When there is harmony":** Some sources attribute this to commentaries on the Rig Veda.

66 **four fundamental motivations:** Bhaktivinoda Thakura, "The Nectarean Instructions of Lord Caitanya," *Hari kírtan*, June 12, 2010, https://kirtan.estranky.cz/clanky/philosophy---english/sri-sri-caitanya--siksamrta--the-nectarean-instructions-of-lord--caitanya.html.

68 **American spiritual luminary Tara Brach:** Tara Brach, "Absolute Cooperation with the Inevitable: Aligning with what is here is a way of practicing

presence. It allows us to respond to our world with creativity and compassion," *HuffPost*, November 4, 2013, https://www.huffpost.com/entry/happiness-tips_b_4213151.

69 **derived from a poem by Kabir:** Kabir, "'Of the Musk Deer': 15th Century Hindi Poems," Zócalo Poets, accessed November 11, 2019, https://zocalopoets.com/2012/04/11/kabir-of-the-musk-deer-15th-century-hindi-poems/.

69 **money does not buy happiness:** Daniel Kahneman and Angus Deaton, "High Income Improves Evaluation of Life But Not Emotional Well-Being," *PNAS* 107, no. 38 (September 21, 2010): 16489–16493, doi:10.1073/pnas.1011492107.

70 **happiness rates have consistently declined:** Jean M. Twenge, "The Evidence for Generation Me and Against Generation We," *Emerging Adulthood* 1, no. 1 (March 2, 2013): 11–16, doi: 10.1177/2167696812466548/.

70 **generally American incomes have risen since 2005:** Brigid Schulte, "Why the U.S. Rating on the World Happiness Report Is Lower Than It Should Be—And How to Change It," *Washington Post*, May 11, 2015, https://www.washingtonpost.com/news/inspired-life/wp/2015/05/11/why-many-americans-are-unhappy-even-when-incomes-are-rising-and-how-we-can-change-that/.

71 **"Money and mansions":** Some sources attribute this to commentaries on the Atharva Veda.

71 **"we can better handle discomfort":** Kelly McGonigal, *The Upside of Stress* (New York: Avery, 2016).

76 **researchers asked seminary students:** John M. Darley and C. Daniel Batson, "From Jerusalem to Jericho: A Study of Situational and Dispositional Variables in Helping Behavior," *Journal of Personality and Social Psychology* 27, no. 1 (1973): 100–108, doi: 10.1037/h0034449.

77 **"*everything* you do is your spiritual life":** Laurence Freeman, *Aspects of Love: On Retreat with Laurence Freeman* (Singapore: Medio Media/Arthur James, 1997).

81 **"we want to be good without even trying":** Benedicta Ward, ed., *The Desert Fathers: Sayings of the Early Christian Monks* (New York: Penguin Classics, 2003).

MEDITATION: BREATHE

86 **"As a fish hooked and left on the sand":** Verse 3.34 from *The Dhammapada*, introduction and translation by Eknath Easwaran (Tomales, CA: Nilgiri Press, 2007), 115.

86 **"breath is the extension of our inmost life":** Rig Veda, 1.66.1, and for

discussion Abbot George Burke, "The Hindu Tradition of Breath Meditation," BreathMeditation.org, accessed November 8, 2019, https://breathmeditation.org/the-hindu-tradition-of-breath-meditation.

86 **the Buddha described *ānāpānasati*:** Thanissaro Bhikku, trans., "Anapanasati Sutta: Mindfulness of Breathing," AccesstoInsight.org, accessed November 8, 2019, https://www.accesstoinsight.org/tipitaka/mn/mn.118.than.html.

86 **improving cardiovascular health, lowering overall stress, and even improving academic test performance:** Tarun Sexana and Manjari Saxena, "The Effect of Various Breathing Exercises (Pranayama) in Patients with Bronchial Asthma of Mild to Moderate Severity," *International Journal of Yoga* 2, no. 1 (January–June 2009): 22–25, doi: 10.4103/0973-6131.53838; Roopa B. Ankad, Anita Herur, Shailaja Patil, G. V. Shashikala, and Surekharani Chinagudi, "Effect of Short-Term Pranayama and Meditation on Cardiovascular Functions in Healthy Individuals," *Heart Views* 12, no. 2 (April–June 2011): 58–62, doi: 10.4103/1995-705X.86016; Anant Narayan Sinha, Desh Deepak, and Vimal Singh Gusain, "Assessment of the Effects of Pranayama/Alternate Nostril Breathing on the Parasympathetic Nervous System in Young Adults," *Journal of Clinical & Diagnostic Research* 7, no. 5 (May 2013): 821–823, doi: 10.7860/JCDR/2013/4750.2948; and Shreyashi Vaksh, Mukesh Pandey, and Rakesh Kumar, "Study of the Effect of Pranayama on Academic Performance of School Students of IX and XI Standard," *Scholars Journal of Applied Medical Sciences* 4, no. 5D (2016): 1703–1705.

FIVE: PURPOSE

93 **"When you protect your dharma":** *The Manusmriti*, Verse 8.15.

96 **the psychology of communication:** Albert Mehrabian, *Nonverbal Communication* (London: Routledge, 1972).

96 **She first entered the wilds of Tanzania:** "About Jane," Jane Goodall Institute, accessed November 11, 2019, https://janegoodall.org/our-story/about-jane.

99 **don't hit our stride quite so early:** Rich Karlgaard, *Late Bloomers: The Power of Patience in a World Obsessed with Early Achievement* (New York: Currency, 2019).

99 **Andre Agassi dropped a bombshell:** Andre Agassi, *Open: An Autobiography* (New York: Vintage, 2010).

100 **"It is trust in the limits of the self":** Joan D. Chittister, *Scarred by Struggle, Transformed by Hope* (Grand Rapids, MI: Eerdmans, 2005).

105 **studied hospital cleaning crews:** Amy Wrzesniewski, Justin M. Berg, and

Jane E. Dutton, "Managing Yourself: Turn the Job You Have into the Job You Want," *Harvard Business Review*, June 2010, https://hbr.org/2010/06/managing-yourself-turn-the-job-you-have-into-the-job-you-want; "Amy Wrzesniewski on Creating Meaning in Your Own Work," re:Work with Google, November 10, 2014, https://www.youtube.com/watch?v=C_igfnctYjA.

109 **imposed their own rigid class system:** Sanjoy Chakravorty, *The Truth About Us: The Politics of Information from Manu to Modi* (Hachette India, 2019).

117 **Joseph Campbell had no model of a career:** Robert Segal, "Joseph Campbell: American Author," *Encyclopaedia Britannica*, accessed November 11, 2019, https://www.britannica.com/biography/Joseph-Campbell-American-author; "Joseph Campbell: His Life and Contributions," Center for Story and Symbol, accessed November 11, 2019, https://folkstory.com/campbell/psychology_online_joseph_campbell.html; Joseph Campbell with Bill Moyers, *The Power of Myth* (New York: Anchor, 1991).

120 **dharma protects those:** *The Mahabharata*, Manusmriti verse 8.15.

121 **Emma Slade, lived in Hong Kong:** Emma Slade, "My Path to Becoming a Buddhist," TEDx Talks, February 6, 2017, https://www.youtube.com/watch?v=QnJIjEAE41w; "Meet the British Banker Who Turned Buddhist Nun in Bhutan," *Economic Times*, August 28, 2017, https://economictimes.indiatimes.com/news/international/world-news/meet-the-british-banker-who-turned-buddhist-nun-in-bhutan/being-taken-hostage/slideshow/60254680.cms; "Charity Work," EmmaSlade.com, accessed November 11, 2019, https://www.emmaslade.com/charity-work.

122 **"Just like a red, blue, or white lotus":** *The Dona Sutta*, Anguttara Nikaya verse 4.36.

SIX: ROUTINE

125 **85 percent of us need an alarm clock:** Til Roenneberg, *Internal Time: Chronotypes, Social Jet Lag, and Why You're So Tired* (Cambridge, MA: Harvard University Press, 2012).

125 **"a profound failure of self-respect":** Maria Popova, "10 Learnings from 10 Years of Brain Pickings," *Brain Pickings*, accessed November 11, 2019, https://www.brainpickings.org/2016/10/23/10-years-of-brain-pickings/.

125 **checking messages within ten minutes:** RootMetrics, "Survey Insights: The Lifestyles of Mobile Consumers," October 24, 2018, http://rootmetrics.com/en-US/content/rootmetrics-survey-results-are-in-mobile-consumer-lifestyles.

125 **There are only six cars:** "Fastest Cars 0 to 60 Times," accessed November 11, 2019, https://www.zeroto60times.com/fastest-cars-0-60-mph-times/.

127 **Tim Cook starts his day:** Lev Grossman, "Runner-Up: Tim Cook, the Technologist," *TIME*, December 19, 2012, http://poy.time.com/2012/12/19/runner-up-tim-cook-the-technologist/; Michelle Obama, "Oprah Talks to Michelle Obama," interview by Oprah Winfrey, *O, The Oprah Magazine*, April 2000, https://www.oprah.com/omagazine/michelle-obamas-oprah-interview-o-magazine-cover-with-obama/all#ixzz5qYixltgS.

129 **earlier sleep time can put you in a better mood:** Jacob A. Nota and Meredith E. Coles, "Duration and Timing of Sleep Are Associated with Repetitive Negative Thinking," *Cognitive Therapy and Research* 39, no. 2 (April 2015): 253–261, doi: 10.1007/s10608-014-9651-7.

129 **As much as 75 percent of the HGH:** M. L. Moline, T. H. Monk, D. R. Wagner, C. P. Pollak, J. Kream, J. E. Fookson, E. D. Weitzman, and C. A. Czeisler, "Human Growth Hormone Release Is Decreased During Sleep in Temporal Isolation (Free-Running)," *Chronobiologia* 13, no. 1 (January–March 1986): 13–19.

129 **Kevin O'Leary said that before he goes to sleep:** Ali Montag, "These Are Kevin O'Leary's Top 3 Productivity Hacks—and Anyone Can Use Them," CNBC, July 23, 2018, https://www.cnbc.com/2018/07/19/kevin-olearys-top-productivity-tips-that-anyone-can-use.html.

130 **each decision is an opportunity to stray from their path:** Christopher Sommer, "How One Decision Can Change Everything," interview by Brian Rose, *London Real*, October 2, 2018, https://www.youtube.com/watch?v=jgJ3xHyOzsA.

132 **"People living in the cities and suburbs":** Hannah Ward and Jennifer Wild, eds., *The Monastic Way: Ancient Wisdom for Contemporary Living: A Book of Daily Readings* (Grand Rapids, MI: Wm. B. Eerdmans, 2007), 75–76.

132 **not the same as noticing it:** Alan D. Castel, Michael Vendetti, and Keith J. Holyoak, "Fire Drill: Inattentional Blindness and Amnesia for the Location of Fire Extinguishers," *Attention, Perception, & Psychophysics* 74 (2012): 1391–1396, doi: 10.3758/s13414-012-0355-3.

133 **Kobe Bryant was onto this:** Kobe Bryant, "Kobe Bryant: On How to Be Strategic & Obsessive to Find Your Purpose," interview by Jay Shetty, *On Purpose*, September 9, 2019, https://jayshetty.me/kobe-bryant-on-how-to-be-strategic-obsessive-to-find-your-purpose/.

135 **"doing dishes is unpleasant":** Thich Nhat Hanh, *At Home in the World: Stories and Essential Teachings from a Monk's Life* (Berkeley, CA: Parallax Press, 2019).

136 **"Yesterday is but a dream":** Kālidāsa, *The Works of Kālidāsa*, trans. Arthur W. Ryder (CreateSpace, 2015).

141 **2 percent of us can multitask:** Garth Sundem, "This Is Your Brain on Multitasking: Brains of Multitaskers Are Structurally Different Than Brains

of Monotaskers," *Psychology Today*, February 24, 2012, https://www.psychologytoday.com/us/blog/brain-trust/201202/is-your-brain-multitasking.

141 **erodes our ability to focus:** Cal Newport, *Deep Work: Rules for Focused Success in a Distracted World* (New York: Grand Central Publishing, 2016).

141 **took a group of students:** Eyal Ophir, Clifford Nass, and Anthony D. Wagner, "Cognitive Control in Media Multitaskers," *PNAS* 106, no. 37 (September 15, 2009): 15583–15587, doi: 10.1073/pnas.0903620106.

143 **We overstimulate the dopamine (reward) channel:** Robert H. Lustig, *The Hacking of the American Mind: The Science Behind the Corporate Takeover of Our Bodies and Brains* (New York: Avery, 2017).

SEVEN: THE MIND

146 **the mind is compared to a drunken monkey:** Nārāyana, *Hitopadeśa* (New York: Penguin Classics, 2007).

146 **roughly seventy thousand separate thoughts each day:** "How Many Thoughts Do We Have Per Minute?," Reference, accessed November 12, 2019, https://www.reference.com/world-view/many-thoughts-per-minute-cb7fcf22ebbf8466.

146 **about three seconds at a time:** Ernst Pöppel, "Trust as Basic for the Concept of Causality: A Biological Speculation," presentation, accessed November 12, 2019, http://www.paralimes.ntu.edu.sg/NewsnEvents/Causality%20-%20Reality/Documents/Ernst%20Poppel.pdf.

147 **"your brain is not reacting to events in the world":** Lisa Barrett, "Lisa Barrett on How Emotions Are Made," interview by Ginger Campbell, *Brain Science with Ginger Campbell, MD*, episode 135, July 31, 2017, https://brainsciencepodcast.com/bsp/2017/135-emotions-barrett.

147 **our minds as monkeys:** Piya Tan, "Samyutta Nikaya: The Connected Sayings of the Buddha, Translated with Notes in the Sutta Discovery Series," Buddhism Network, accessed January 22, 2020, http://buddhismnetwork.com/2016/12/28/samyutta-nikaya/.

147 **"As irrigators lead water":** Verse 6.80 from *The Dhammapada*, introduction and translation by Eknath Easwaran (Tomales, CA: Nilgiri Press, 2007), 126.

148 **"For him who has conquered the mind":** Verse 6.6 from A. C. Bhaktivedanta Swami Prabhupada, *Bhagavad Gita As It Is* (The Bhaktivedanta Book Trust International, Inc.). https://apps.apple.com/us/app/bhagavad-gita-as-it-is/id1080562426.

148 **An enemy, according to the Oxford English Dictionary, is:** *Paperback Oxford English Dictionary* (Oxford, UK: Oxford University Press, 2012).

148 **weight of a bad decision isn't just metaphorical:** Martin V. Day and D.

Ramona Bobocel, "The Weight of a Guilty Conscience: Subjective Body Weight as an Embodiment of Guilt,"*PLoS ONE* 8, no. 7 (July 2013), doi: 10.1371/journal.pone.0069546.

148 **what researchers call our "should-self":** Max. H. Bazerman, Ann E. Tenbrunsel, and Kimberly Wade-Benzoni, "Negotiating with Yourself and Losing: Making Decisions with Competing Internal Preferences," *Academy of Management Review* 23, no. 2 (April 1, 1998): 225–241, doi: 10.5465/amr.1998.533224.

149 **in our everyday swirl of thoughts:** *The Dhammapada*, introduction and translation by Eknath Easwaran (Tomales, CA: Nilgiri Press, 2007), 65–66.

151 **a chariot being driven by five horses:** Katha Upanishad, Third Valli, 3–6, from *The Upanishads*, trans. Vernon Katz and Thomas Egenes (New York: Tarcher Perigee, 2015), 55–57.

152 **Shaolin monks are a wonderful example:** Elliot Figueira, "How Shaolin Monks Develop Their Mental and Physical Mastery," BBN, accessed November 12, 2019, https://www.bbncommunity.com/how-shaolin-monks-develop-their-mental-and-physical-mastery/.

152 **secured a thermal stimulator to their wrists:** Daniel Goleman and Richard J. Davidson, *Altered Traits: Science Reveals How Meditation Changes Your Mind, Brain, and Body* (New York: Penguin Random House, 2017).

155 **decided to busk outside a DC subway station:** Gene Weingarten, "Pearls Before Breakfast: Can One of the Nation's Great Musicians Cut Through the Fog of a D.C. Rush Hour? Let's Find Out," *Washington Post*, April 8, 2007, https://www.washingtonpost.com/lifestyle/magazine/pearls-before-breakfast-can-one-of-the-nations-great-musicians-cut-through-the-fog-of-a-dc-rush-hour-lets-find-out/2014/09/23/8a6d46da-4331-11e4-b47c-f5889e061e5f_story.html.

157 **asked them to locate specific items:** Gary Lupyan and Daniel Swingley, "Self-Directed Speech Affects Visual Search Performance," *Quarterly Journal of Experimental Psychology* (June 1, 2012), doi: 10.1080/17470218.2011.647039.

157 **"helps you clarify your thoughts":** Linda Sapadin, "Talking to Yourself: A Sign of Sanity," *Psych Central*, October 2, 2018, https://psychcentral.com/blog/talking-to-yourself-a-sign-of-sanity/.

160 **writing their "deepest thoughts and feelings":** James W. Pennebaker and Janel D. Seagal, "Forming a Story: The Health Benefits of Narrative," *Journal of Clinical Psychology* 55, no. 10 (1999): 1243–1254.

160 **Krysta MacGray was terrified of flying:** www.krystamacgray.com and personal interview, July 10, 2019.

163 **"how to be present to the moment":** Richard Rohr, "Living in the Now:

Practicing Presence," Center for Action and Comtemplation, November 24, 2017, https://cac.org/practicing-presence-2017-11-24/.

163 "*be here now*": Ram Dass, *Be Here Now* (New York: Harmony, 1978).

164 **The Gita defines detachment:** Verses 2.48 and 12.12 from the Bhagavad Gita, introduction and translation by Eknath Easwaran (Tomales, CA: Nilgiri Press, 2007), 94, 208.

165 **"Detachment is not that you own nothing":** This quote is attributed to Alī Ibn Abi Talib, the cousin and son-in-law of Muhammad, the last prophet of Islam.

168 **fasted for 423 days:** Bhavika Jain, "Jain Monk Completes 423 Days of Fasting," *Times of India*, November 1, 2015, http://timesofindia.indiatimes.com/articleshow/49616061.cms?utm_source=contentofinterest&utm_medium=text&utm_campaign=cppst.

168 **Japanese style of self-mummification:** Krissy Howard, "The Japanese Monks Who Mummified Themselves While Still Alive," *All That's Interesting*, October 25, 2016, https://allthatsinteresting.com/sokushinbutsu.

168 **ran a mile in 3:59.4 minutes:** "Sir Roger Bannister: First Person to Run a Mile in Under Four Minutes Dies at 88," BBC, March 4, 2018, https://www.bbc.com/sport/athletics/43273249.

172 **"If you ruminate on sadness and negativity":** Matthieu Ricard, interview by Jay Shetty, *#FollowTheReader with Jay Shetty*, *HuffPost*, October 10, 2016, https://www.youtube.com/watch?v=_HZznrniwL8&feature=youtu.be.

172 **Cultivate buddhi:** Jayaram V, "The Seven Fundamental Teachings of the Bhagavad-Gita," Hinduwebsite.com, accessed January 22, 2020, https://www.hinduwebsite.com/seventeachings.asp.

EIGHT: EGO

173 **They are forever free:** Verse 2.71 from the Bhagavad Gita, introduction and translation by Eknath Easwaran (Tomales, CA: Nilgri Press, 2007), 97.

173 **distinction between the ego and the false ego:** Verses 7.4 and 16.18 from *The Bhagavad Gita*, introduction and translation by Eknath Easwaran (Tomales, CA: Nilgiri Press, 2007), 152, 240.

173 **"Pride of wealth destroys wealth":** Some sources attribute this to commentaries on the Sama Veda.

174 **"the most damaging fall for the soul":** Dennis Okholm, *Dangerous Passions, Deadly Sins: Learning from the Psychology of Ancient Monks* (Grand Rapids, MI: Brazos Press, 2014), 161.

177 **"Perfect yogis are they who":** Verse 6.32 from A. C. Bhaktivedanta Swami

Prabhupada, *Bhagavad Gita As It Is* (The Bhaktivedanta Book Trust International, Inc.), https://apps.apple.com/us/app/bhagavad-gita-as-it-is/id1080562426.

179 **In her popular TED Talk:** Julia Galef, "Why You Think You're Right Even If You're Wrong," TEDx PSU, February 2016, https://www.ted.com/talks/julia_galef_why_you_think_you_re_right_even_if_you_re_wrong/transcript#t-68800.

180 **cofounder of Netflix, offered to sell:** Ken Auletta, "Outside the Box: Netflix and the Future of Television," *New Yorker*, January 26, 2014, https://www.newyorker.com/magazine/2014/02/03/outside-the-box-2; Paul R. LaMonica, "Netflix Joins the Exclusive $100 Billion Club," CNN, July 23, 2018, https://money.cnn.com/2018/01/23/investing/netflix-100-billion-market-value/index.html.

180 **who had come to inquire about Zen:** Osho, *A Bird on the Wing: Zen Anecdotes for Everyday Life* (India: Osho Media International, 2013).

181 **"Remember you are a man":** Mary Beard, *The Roman Triumph* (Cambridge, MA: Harvard University Press, 2009).

181 **In an interview, Robert Downey Jr.:** Robert Downey Jr., interview, *Cambridge Union*, December 19, 2014, https://www.youtube.com/watch?v=Rmpysp5mWlg.

183 **he is like a firefly:** Srimad-Bhagavatam, The Summum Bonum, 14.9-10.

185 **Mary Johnson's son, Laramiun Byrd:** Steve Hartman, "Love Thy Neighbor: Son's Killer Moves in Next Door," CBS News, June 8, 2011, https://www.cbsnews.com/news/love-thy-neighbor-sons-killer-moves-next-door/; "Woman Shows Incredible Mercy as Her Son's Killer Moves In Next Door," *Daily Mail*, June 8, 2011, https://www.dailymail.co.uk/news/article-2000704/Woman-shows-incredible-mercy-sons-killer-moves-door.html; "Mary Johnson and Oshea Israel," The Forgiveness Project, accessed November 12, 2019, https://www.theforgivenessproject.com/stories/mary-johnson-oshea-israel/.

187 **"What belongs to you today":** Kamlesh J. Wadher, *Nature's Science and Secrets of Success* (India: Educreation Publishing, 2016); Verse 2.14 from the Bhagavad Gita, introduction and translation by Eknath Easwaran (Tomales, CA: Nilgiri Press, 2007), 90.

188 **"Being literally undone by failure":** Thomas Moore, *Care of the Soul: A Guide for Cultivating Depth and Sacredness in Everyday Life* (New York: Harper Perennial, 1992), 197.

189 **Sara Blakely wanted to go to law school:** Sarah Lewis, *The Rise: Creativity, the Gift of Failure, and the Search for Mastery* (New York: Simon & Schuster,

2014), 111; "Spanx Startup Story," Fundable, accessed November 12, 2019, https://www.fundable.com/learn/startup-stories/spanx.

191 **Olympic swimming gold medalist:** "Goal Setting Activities of Olympic Athletes (And What They Can Teach the Rest of Us)," Develop Good Habits, September 30, 2019, https://www.developgoodhabits.com/goal-setting-activities/.

196 **a children's rights activist:** Rajesh Viswanathan, "Children Should Become Their Own Voices," *ParentCircle*, accessed November 12, 2019, https://www.parentcircle.com/article/children-should-become-their-own-voices/.

MEDITATION: VISUALIZE

198 **people who imagined contracting a muscle:** Vinoth K. Ranganathan, Vlodek Siemionow, Jing Z. Liu, Vinod Sahgal, and Guang H. Yue, "From Mental Power to Muscle Power—Gaining Strength by Using the Mind," *Neuropsychologia* 42, no. 7 (2004): 944–956, doi: 10.1016/j.neuropsychologia.2003.11.018.

NINE: GRATITUDE

205 **defines gratitude as the feeling of appreciation:** "What Is Gratitude?" A Network for Grateful Living, accessed November 12, 2019, https://gratefulness.org/resource/what-is-gratitude/.

206 **keep journals during the day:** Robert A. Emmons and Michael E. McCullough, "Counting Blessings Versus Burdens: An Experimental Investigation of Gratitude and Subjective Well-Being in Daily Life," *Journal of Personality and Social Psychology* 84, no. 2 (2003): 377–389, doi: 10.1037/0022-3514.84.2.377.

207 **we truly can't focus on positive and negative:** Alex Korb, "The Grateful Brain: The Neuroscience of Giving Thanks," *Psychology Today*, November 20, 2012, https://www.psychologytoday.com/us/blog/prefrontal-nudity/201211/the-grateful-brain.

207 **veterans with high levels of gratitude:** Todd B. Kashdan, Gitendra Uswatte, and Terri Julian, "Gratitude and Hedonic and Eudaimonic Well-Being in Vietnam War Veterans," *Behaviour Research and Therapy* 44, no. 2 (February 2006): 177–199, doi: 10.1016/j.brat.2005.01.005.

207 **"If [thankfulness] were a drug":** Mikaela Conley, "Thankfulness Linked to Positive Changes in Brain and Body," ABC News, November 23, 2011, https://abcnews.go.com/Health/science-thankfulness/story?id=15008148.

208 **"Monks. You should train yourselves":** Samyutta Nikaya, Sutta Pitaka, 20.21.

210 **In one ritual observance:** Joanna Macy, *World as Lover, World as Self: Courage*

for Global Justice and Ecological Renewal (Berkeley, CA: Parallax Press, 2007), 78–83.

211 **"the mind of poverty":** Roshi Joan Halifax, "Practicing Gratefulness by Roshi Joan Halifax," Upaya Institute and Zen Center, October 18, 2017, https://www.upaya.org/2017/10/practicing-gratefulness-by-roshi-joan-halifax/.

212 **Brian Acton exemplifies:** Bill Murphy Jr., "Facebook and Twitter Turned Him Down. Now He's Worth $4 Billion," *Inc.*, accessed November 13, 2019, https://www.inc.com/bill-murphy-jr/facebook-and-twitter-turned-him-down-now-hes-worth-4-billion.html; Brian Acton (@brianacton), Twitter post, May 23, 2009, https://twitter.com/brianacton/status/1895942068; Brian Acton (@brianacton), Twitter post, August 3, 2009, https://twitter.com/brianacton/status/3109544383.

212 **"When one door of happiness closes":** "Helen Keller," Biography, accessed November 13, 2019, https://www.biography.com/activist/helen-keller; Helen Keller, *We Bereaved* (New York: L. Fulenwider, 1929).

213 **"People usually think that gratitude":** Rob Sidon, "The Gospel of Gratitude According to David Steindl-Rast," *Common Ground*, November 2017, 42–49, http://onlinedigitaleditions2.com/commonground/archive/web-11-2017/.

215 **"Be kinder to yourself":** Pema Chödrön, *Practicing Peace in Times of War* (Boston: Shambhala, 2007).

215 **whether kindness is contagious:** James H. Fowler and Nicholas A. Christakis, "Cooperative Behavior Cascades in Human Social Networks," *Proceedings of the National Academy of Sciences*, 107, no. 12 (March 23, 2010): 5334–5338, doi: 10.1073/pnas.0913149107.

216 **people on the Chicago commuter:** Nicholas Epley and Juliana Schroeder, "Mistakenly Seeking Solitude," *Journal of Experimental Psychology: General* 143, no. 5 (October 2014): 1980–1999, doi: 10.1037/a0037323.

219 **volunteering can result in lower feelings of depression:** Caroline E. Jenkinson, Andy P. Dickens, Kerry Jones, Jo Thompson-Coon, Rod S. Taylor, Morwenna Rogers, Clare L. Bambra, Iain Lang, and Suzanne H. Richards, "Is Volunteering a Public Health Intervention? A Systematic Review and Meta-Analysis of the Health and Survival of Volunteers," *BMG Public Health* 13, no. 773 (August 23, 2013), doi: 10.1186/1471-2458-13-773.

TEN: RELATIONSHIPS

222 **"Every person":** Thich Nhat Hanh, *How to Love* (Berkeley, CA: Parallax Press, 2014).

223 **longevity was tied to several aspects of community:** Dan Buettner, "Power

9: Reverse Engineering Longevity," Blue Zones, accessed November 13, 2019, https://www.bluezones.com/2016/11/power-9/.

228 **a field study of military leadership in Iraq:** Michael D. Matthews, "The 3 C's of Trust: The Core Elements of Trust Are Competence, Character, and Caring," *Psychology Today*, May 3, 2016, https://www.psychologytoday.com/us/blog/head-strong/201605/the-3-c-s-trust.

230 **"The golden way is to be friends with the world":** K. S. Baharati, *Encyclopaedia of Gandhian Thought* (India: Anmol Publications, 2006).

230 **"People come into your life":** Jean Dominique Martin, "People Come Into Your Life for a Reason, a Season, or a Lifetime," accessed November 14, 2019, http://youmeandspirit.blogspot.com/2009/08/ebb-and-flow.html.

232 **couples get stuck in ongoing conflict:** John Gottman, "John Gottman on Trust and Betrayal," *Greater Good Magazine*, October 29, 2011, https://greatergood.berkeley.edu/article/item/john_gottman_on_trust_and_betrayal.

232 **people are dishonest:** Bella M. DePaulo, Deborah A. Kashy, Susan E. Kirkendol, Melissa M. Wyer, and Jennifer A. Epstein, "Lying in Everyday Life," *Journal of Personality and Social Psychology* 70, no. 5 (June 1996): 979–995, doi: 10.1037/0022-3514.70.5.979.

233 **we lie to impress:** Bella DePaolo, *The Lies We Tell and the Clues We Miss: Professional Papers* (CreateSpace, 2009).

234 **trust people we find attractive:** Dawn Dorsey, "Rice Study Suggests People Are More Trusting of Attractive Strangers," Rice University, September 21, 2006, https://news.rice.edu/2006/09/21/rice-study-suggests-people-are-more-trusting-of-attractive-strangers/.

234 **"We found that attractive subjects gain a 'beauty premium'":** Dawn Dorsey, "Rice Study Suggests People Are More Trusting of Attractive Strangers," *Rice News*, September 21, 2006, http://news.rice.edu/2006/09/21/rice-study-suggests-people-are-more-trusting-of-attractive-strangers/.

235 **a blank piece of paper:** Don Meyer, "Fox-Hole Test," CoachMeyer.com, accessed November 13, 2019, https://www.coachmeyer.com/Information/Players_Corner/Fox%20Hole%20Test.pdf.

238 **"Celibacy by conscious choice":** www.malamadrone.com and personal interview, September 7, 2019.

238 **"two sides of man's being alone":** Paul Tillich, *The Eternal Now* (New York: Scribner, 1963).

240 **the impact of mothers' time:** Melissa A. Milke, Kei M. Nomaguchi, and Kathleen E. Denny, "Does the Amount of Time Mothers Spend with Children or Adolescents Matter?" *Journal of Marriage and Family* 77, no. 2 (April 2015): 355–372, doi: 10.1111/jomf.12170.

241 **six loving exchanges:** *Sri Upadesamrta: The Ambrosial Advice of Sri Rupa Gosvami* (India: Gaudiya Vedanta Publications, 2003), https://archive.org/details/upadesamrta/page/n1.

245 **Harvard Grant Study:** Joshua Wolf Shenk, "What Makes Us Happy? Is There a Formula—Some Mix of Love, Work, and Psychological Adaptation—for a Good Life?" *Atlantic*, June 2009, https://www.theatlantic.com/magazine/archive/2009/06/what-makes-us-happy/307439/.

246 **"we get crushes on others":** Thich Nhat Hanh, *How to Love* (Berkeley, CA: Parallax Press, 2014).

246 **According to Massive Attack:** Massive Attack, "Teardrop," *Mezzanine*, Circa/Virgin, April 27, 1998; *Dan in Real Life*, directed by Peter Hedges, Touchstone Pictures, Focus Features, and Jon Shestack Productions, 2007.

248 **"until you heal the wounds of your past":** IyanlaVanzant, "How to Heal the Wounds of Your Past," Oprah's Life Class, October 11, 2011, http://www.oprah.com/oprahs-lifeclass/iyanla-vanzant-how-to-heal-the-wounds-of-your-past.

249 **couples strengthen their bonds:** Arthur Aron, Christina C. Norman, Elaine N. Aron, Colin McKenna, and Richard E. Heyman, "Couples' Shared Participation in Novel and Arousing Activities and Experienced Relationship Quality," *Journal of Personality and Social Psychology* 78, no. 2 (2000): 273–84, doi: 10.1037//0022-3514.78.2.273.

251 **we often mistake attachment for love:** Jetsunma Tenzin Palmo, "The Difference Between Genuine Love and Attachment," accessed November 13, 2019, https://www.youtube.com/watch?v=6kUoTS3Yo4g.

251 **followed incoming college freshmen:** Sanjay Srivastava, Maya Tamir, Kelly M. McGonigal, Oliver P. John, and James J. Gross, "The Social Costs of Emotional Suppression: A Prospective Study of the Transition to College," *Journal of Personality and Social Psychology* 96, no. 4 (August 22, 2014): 883–897, doi: 10.1037/a0014755.

ELEVEN: SERVICE

254 **"The ignorant work for their own profit":** Verse 3.25 from *The Bhagavad Gita*, introduction and translation by Eknath Easwaran (Tomales, CA: Nilgiri Press, 2007), 107.

255 **"we are on a journey":** Hannah Ward and Jennifer Wild, eds., *The Monastic Way: Ancient Wisdom for Contemporary Living: A Book of Daily Readings* (Grand Rapids, MI: Wm. B. Eerdmans, 2007), 183.

257 **"The monk may think":** Hannah Ward and Jennifer Wild, eds., *The Monastic Way: Ancient Wisdom for Contemporary Living: A Book of Daily Readings* (Grand Rapids, MI: Wm. B. Eerdmans, 2007), 190.

257 **"Look at these fortunate trees":** Srimad-Bhagavatam, The Summum Bonum, 22.32.

257 **The sixteenth-century guru Rupa Goswami talks about *yukta-vairāgya*:** Verse 1.2.255 from Srila Rupa Goswami, *Bhakti Rasamrta Sindhu (In Two Volumes): With the Commentary of Srila Jiva Gosvami and Visvanatha Cakravarti Thakur* (The Bhaktivedanta Book Trust, Inc, 2009).

258 **"No one is born hating":** Nelson Mandela, *Long Walk to Freedom: The Autobiography of Nelson Mandela* (Boston: Back Bay Books, 1995).

258 **one we often overlook:** Joseph Campbell, *The Hero with a Thousand Faces* (Novato, CA: New World Library, 2008).

258 **Seane Corn is living out the hero's journey:** Seane Corn, "Yoga, Meditation in Action," interview by Krista Tippett, *On Being*, September 11, 2008, https://onbeing.org/programs/seane-corn-yoga-meditation-in-action/.

259 **when we pursue "compassionate goals":** M. Teresa Granillo, Jennifer Crocker, James L. Abelson, Hannah E. Reas, and Christina M. Quach, "Compassionate and Self-Image Goals as Interpersonal Maintenance Factors in Clinical Depression and Anxiety," *Journal of Clinical Psychology* 74, no. 4 (September 12, 2017): 608–625, doi: 10.1002/jclp.22524.

259 **tend to live longer:** Stephen G. Post, "Altruism, Happiness, and Health: It's Good to Be Good," *International Journal of Behavioral Medicine* 12, no. 2 (June 2005): 66–77, doi: 10.1207/s15327558ijbm1202_4.

260 **"giving simply because it is right to give":** Verse 17.20 from *The Bhagavad Gita*, introduction and translation by Eknath Easwaran (Tomales, CA: Nilgiri Press, 2007), 248.

262 **Sindhutai Sapkal was married at twelve:** "About Sindhutai Sapkal (Mai)/ Mother of Orphans," accessed November 13, 2019, https://www.sindhutaisapakal.org/about-Sindhutail-Sapkal.html.

263 **people were given $10:** Paul K. Piff, Michael W. Krauss, Stéphane Côté, Bonnie Hayden Cheng, and Dacher Keltner, "Having Less, Giving More: The Influence of Social Class on Prosocial Behavior," *Journal of Personality and Social Psychology* 99, no. 5 (November 2010): 771–784, doi: 10.1037/a0020092.

263 **survey of charitable giving:** Ken Stern, "Why the Rich Don't Give to Charity: The Wealthiest Americans Donate 1.3 Percent of Their Income; The Poorest, 3.2 Percent. What's Up with That?" *The Atlantic*, April 2013, https://www.theatlantic.com/magazine/archive/2013/04/why-the-rich-dont-give/309254/.

263 **over 70 percent of charitable contributions:** Kate Rogers, "Poor, Middle Class and Rich: Who Gives and Who Doesn't?" *FOXBusiness*, April 24,

2013, https://www.foxbusiness.com/features/poor-middle-class-and-rich-who-gives-and-who-doesnt.

263 **Why those with less give more:** Daniel Goleman, *Focus: The Hidden Driver of Excellence* (New York: HarperCollins, 2013), 123.

263 **Some philanthropists:** Kathleen Elkins, "From Poverty to a $3 Billion Fortune: The Incredible Rags-to-Riches Story of Oprah Winfrey," *Business Insider*, May 28, 2015, https://www.businessinsider.com/rags-to-riches-story-of-oprah-winfrey-2015-5.

267 **Kailash Satyarthi has taken on:** Ryan Prior, "Kailash Satyarthi Plans to End Child Labor In His Lifetime," CNN, March 13, 2019, https://www.cnn.com/2019/02/19/world/kailash-satyarthi-child-labor/index.html.

268 **"You don't need to do everything":** Joanna Macy, *World as Lover, World as Self: Courage for Global Justice and Ecological Renewal* (Berkeley, CA: Parallax Press, 2007), 77.

MEDITATION: CHANT

270 **the why and how of chanting:** Agni Purana 3.293 and Vayu Purana 59.141.

270 **Recognizing the value of sound:** "Tesla's Vibrational Medicine," Tesla's Medicine, accessed November 12, 2019, https://teslasmedicine.com/teslas-vibrational-medicine/; Jennifer Tarnacki, "This Is Your Brain on Drumming: The Neuroscience Behind the Beat," Medium, September 25, 2019, https://medium.com/indian-thoughts/this-is-your-brain-on-drumming-8ed6eaf314c4.

271 **anything that inspires you can work:** Rainer Maria Rilke, *Letters to a Young Poet* (New York: W. W. Norton & Company, 1993); "29 Inspiring Herb Brooks Quotes to Motivate You," Sponge Coach, September 13, 2017, http://www.spongecoach.com/inspiring-herb-brooks-quotes/; Jay-Z, "Dirt Off Your Shoulder," *The Black Album*, Roc-A-Fella and Def Jam, March 2, 2004; *Bad Boys II*, directed by Michael Bay, Don Simpson/Jerry Bruckheimer Films, 2003.

271 **most sacred mantra is Om:** "Why Do We Chant Om?" Temples in India Info, accessed November 12, 2019, https://templesinindiainfo.com/why-do-we-chant-om/; "Om," Encyclopedia Britannica, accessed November 12, 2019, https://www.britannica.com/topic/Om-Indian-religion.

272 **Vagus nerve stimulation:** Bangalore G. Kalyani, Ganesan Venkatasubramanian, Rashmi Arasappa, Naren P. Rao, Sunil V. Kalmady, Rishikesh V. Behere, Hariprasad Rao, Mandapati K. Vasudev, and Bangalore N. Gangadhar, "Neurohemodynamic Correlates of 'OM' Chanting: A Pilot Functional Magnetic Resonance Imaging Study," *International*

Journal of Yoga 4, no. 1 (January–June 2011): 3–6, doi: 10.4103/0973-6131.78171; C. R. Conway, A. Kumar, W. Xiong, M. Bunker, S. T. Aronson, and A. J. Rush, "Chronic Vagus Nerve Stimulation Significantly Improves Quality of Life in Treatment Resistant Major Depression," *Journal of Clinical Psychiatry* 79, no. 5 (August 21, 2018), doi: 10.4088/JCP.18m12178.

273 **Om Tat Sat:** Verse 17.23 from *The Bhagavad Gita*, introduction and translation by Eknath Easwaran (Tomales, CA: Nilgiri Press, 2007), 249.

CONCLUSION

279 **Among the most common regrets:** Grace Bluerock, "The 9 Most Common Regrets People Have at the End of Life," mindbodygreen, accessed on November 13, 2019, https://www.mindbodygreen.com/0-23024/the-9-most-common-regrets-people-have-at-the-end-of-life.html.

Next Steps

GENIUS COACHING COMMUNITY

If you've enjoyed this book, and you'd like to further explore how you can improve and optimize every area of your life, enroll in Jay Shetty's Genius Coaching Community.

With over 12,000 members in over 100 countries around the world, you'll be part of a transformational personal development community.

Join Jay live every week for a powerful guided meditation and structured coaching session where he will share the strategies, tools and frameworks to unlock your greatest potential and uncover your inner genius based on his first-hand experience as a monk and years of study.

As a member, you'll get access to these live sessions and hundreds of recorded sessions on every topic from relationships to career, spiritual development to health and well-being.

You can also join our monthly in-person meetups in over 140 locations around the world and connect with like-minded people.

For more information, please go to www.jayshetty.me/genius.

JAY SHETTY CERTIFICATION SCHOOL

If you want to guide others along their journeys of personal change, the Jay Shetty Certification School, backed by science, common sense, and ancient monk wisdom, is for you.

Join Jay on his quest to inspire and impact the world by becoming an accredited Certified Coach. The curriculum, consisting of guided study, supervised peer coaching, and interactive group sessions will provide you with the skills, techniques, and strategies for guiding anyone to new perspectives and personal change.

In addition, you will learn how to build a thriving professional coaching practice and be listed in our global database of approved Jay Shetty coaches.

You can study from anywhere in the world, online, at your pace, and on your own time. You can even choose to train live with Jay Shetty himself during our training events offered in different countries.

For more information, please visit www.jayshettycoaching.com.

Index